Betrayal at the Vel d'Hiv

Betrayal at the Vel d'Hiv

Claude Lévy and Paul Tillard

Preface by Joseph Kessel
of the Académie Française

Translated by Inea Bushnaq

 Hill and Wang *New York*

Contents

Illustrations are on pages 103–118.

In order not to slow down the reader—for we think that this book should be read without interruption—we have decided not to weigh down the text with elaborate notes at the foot of each page. The notes have been reduced to a minimum, though it must be stressed that not one line of this book was written without supporting evidence either from the testimony of eyewitnesses interviewed by us or from official documents or from books already published on the subject. Any reader wanting to check the sources will find them at the end of the book.

(1) There are two appendixes giving details on, first, the condition and circumstances of Jews in France before and during the first years of the German occupation and, second, the setting up of the administrative machinery for the application of the Final Solution in France.

(2) A bibliography and list of documents and archives.

(3) An alphabetical list of the names of persons mentioned in the book who played an important part in the operation in France in 1942, both French and German.

Preface

Since 1945, not one year has passed, one could say not one month, without the appearance of some work inspired by the concentration camps. Memoirs. Essays. Rough notes. Disciplined research and studies.

According to their emotional needs and spiritual make-up, some have felt the urge to shout aloud about what they have seen as soon as they have the freedom to do so, while others have let considerable time pass before making their report. But every journey into the memory of those days has brought back a load of forgotten pain, along with horrified and horrifying shadows.

The same is true for this book. In addition, it has the singular merit of shedding light on one terrible episode in the chronicle of martyrdom which has not so far been pieced together in detail. Here the great roundup of the Jewish population in Paris, which took place on July 16, 1942, is described step by step, exposing one atrocity after another.

On that day, that one day, acting on instructions from the German anti-Jewish service controlled by Eichmann, whose duty it was to send the victims of the cremation ovens to their fate, the Vichy government had 13,000 Jews arrested by the police. In one day, only one day!

But even 13,000 prisoners were only half the expected haul of 28,000 persons. Many escaped and many were secretly warned.

So on July 16, 1942, 13,000 people—men, women, children, old people, and invalids—were seized without warning, piled into buses, and taken to the Vélodrome d'Hiver. There, in horribly crowded conditions, with next to no sanitary facilities, this crowd of unhappy, innocent people was left to await the time for their departure to Auschwitz.

That was the first stage on a journey toward death which the authors of this book describe from beginning to end.

An undertaking of this sort, covering such a wide field, could only succeed after careful preparation, with every minute detail drawn up in strict order like the mobilization of an army. Document follows document, showing us the painstaking steps with which this monstrous trap was set. We watch as the operation is conceived, discussed, approved, perfected, and organized up to zero hour.

The day breaks. The manhunt begins. And the victims are crowded into the Vel d'Hiv, haggard, squeezed against each other, with no air under a burning sun, and choked by their own excrement.

In describing this, the two authors refrain from using literary effects. Their story is told in the tone of a report and with the ruthless economy of a documentary.

They have searched through archives with infinite patience. They have traced and collected every possible eyewitness account. Some survivors' evidence came from Canada and Australia to contribute to the sum of facts.

The discipline and respect for detail have had their results. In this book the crime of July 16, 1942—Black Thursday, as it was called by the victims—takes place before our eyes, from its murky origins to its terrifying end.

Every person involved is shown in his true place, whether chief or subordinate, organizer or employee, collaborator or accomplice, German or French. And there are some sinister surprises.

We go from one surprise to the next, the most sinister being Pierre Laval's important role in the decision to deport the

children. "The children too"—the text is there. All the
documents are there. Let us read them.

JOSEPH KESSEL
Académie Française

Introduction

The persecution of Jews in Europe during the Second World War has been described in many books. The worst of the tragedy took place in the East, and some people may consider what happened west of Germany as of relatively less importance.

But in the literature on the subject many facts have been glossed over and many responsibilities diminished. At least that is what Paul Tillard and I felt. It seemed to us, as it no doubt did to all deportees, that not only a veil of forgetfulness, but a covering of untruths consciously woven together has been thrown over the events. And the voices of firsthand witnesses, survivors, and those who escaped are too few to be heard.

Both of us had enough memories and motives for wanting to make our own contribution to the history of these events. We thought that the story of July 16, 1942, and the great roundup of Jews in Paris, the memory of which is very vivid to those who experienced it, was worth the telling. We must mention here that the feeling we had, that there had been a falsification of the history of the time, in no way influenced our research; unfortunately it was confirmed both by witnesses and by the documents.

As far as the victims were concerned, we found very few people to interview; the number of those who escaped that day is infinitesimal. We often started with one document or one piece of information and then had to trace it back, checking statements, looking for confirmation. Often we searched an entire street, going from concierge to concierge with a photo and illegibly signed name, knocking at every door in a building, consulting the police registers of furnished rooms and hotels page by page, and interviewing hundreds of people. Often we were embarrassed and moved by witnesses who could not keep from crying as they described the events.

In contrast, when we appealed to the administration of the gendarmerie and the municipal police who had carried out the arrests, doors were closed to us. We even felt that when, fifty years after the events, the official archives are opened to historians and researchers, many documents will have vanished. The Ministry for War Veterans possesses a list of those who fell victim to the raids of July 16 and 17, 1942. But in a letter dated September 20, 1966, we were told that "the information in these documents is only for administrative purposes and is not the historical documentation you are looking for."

Luckily, like the historians of the ghetto of Warsaw, who buried their daily reports each night so that they might one day be found, the members of the Resistance, like a new kind of war correspondent, were assigned the mission of preserving accounts of events during the occupation for future historians. Their abundant documentation was one of our main sources of information. But we also used a scribbled note thrown from a train by a deportee and the graffiti on the wall of a prison cell.

Throughout our work and researches, which took us as far as Canada and Australia to record the evidence of some survivors, I was impressed by the talent and enthusiasm of Paul Tillard. Having known life in a concentration camp and having already shown his deep understanding of those times and that whole world in his writings, he made it possible for us to undertake this project. I would have hesitated much longer before beginning the task, which I had thought about for some time, if he had not kindly promised to give me his valuable help.

But Paul Tillard has died, before his time, like many of the surviving deportees. I have lost a dear friend, but nevertheless we continued to work, as if he were with us, to complete this book.

C.L.

Introduction to the English-Language Edition

After the publication of this story, many witnesses have written to me confirming certain facts, providing further details on others, or giving me additional information. Some people have recognized themselves or their families from descriptions in the book and so have enabled me to identify some of the dramatis personae. It was extremely satisfying to receive confirmation of the truth of our story from these correspondents.

Some of the policemen who took the initiative and saved some Jews that day have made themselves known. One of them, Mr. André Pingenet, whom we mentioned without knowing his name, told us: "I make no boast, but I am sure if everyone had done as much within the limits of his possibilities, there would be far fewer of these unfortunate people missing."

A few others have denied the role we have attributed to them, but none of these protests withstands the test of documents and other evidence. In one case, however, we have amended the biographical notes, the policeman in question having subsequently helped persecuted Jews.

Mr. René de Chambrun, son-in-law of Pierre Laval, has also challenged the authenticity of one of the documents we cite.

I thank the editor for the few modifications or additions he has agreed to include in this edition.

C.L.

April, 1968

The shrug of a policeman's shoulders has remained more deeply engraved on my memory than the screams of the tortured.—ARTHUR KOESTLER, *The Spanish Testament*

Chapter 1

Operation Spring Wind

Paris—Wednesday July 15, 1942. The working day was almost over, though the sun was still high in the sky. By the clock it was only 4 P.M., but the rush hour crowds of Parisians poured out of offices and workshops into the afternoon light. Since the Germans had occupied France, Paris lived by Berlin time, one hour ahead of the sun. Traveling home after work was an uncomfortable obstacle race beginning with a stampede by the commuters for the few suburban trains that were still running. Buses too were rare and slow moving, like great tired monsters, disfigured by their protruding reserve gas tanks. The metro was erratic: speeding through many stations that had been shut down, it was faster than in peacetime, except that at the first warning of an air raid it was liable to be held up for as long as two hours. In spite of this, it was always jammed full—especially the last car of each train, the only one in which Jews were allowed to ride. For some time now the Jews had been distinguished from the rest of the population by being forced to wear prominently on their chests a yellow star of David.

In front of the grocery stores, housewives shopping for supper formed long lines. For that week they could buy half a pound of noodles or tapioca on their DN ration card, half a pound of string beans or greens on the 36 card, and half a pound of split peas on the DR ration card. Among all the thin and tired women you would not have found one Jewess; Jews were allowed to shop only between three and four in the afternoon, when most stores were closed anyway.

The evening was very warm, and people lingered on their
terraces sipping synthetic apéritifs and admiring the view of
the city, which looked beautiful in the evening light, its streets
empty of cars because of the gasoline shortage, and only bicycles
moving on the asphalt. The one blemish on the otherwise
peaceful-looking scene was the large white billboards edged in
black and covered with German lettering. From time to time
people would glance up at the summer sky, wondering when
the next air raid siren would shatter the silence.

In contrast to the seemingly quiet atmosphere outside, the
offices of the Chief of Police, the Prefecture, and the Ministry
of the Interior were filled with a bustle of feverish activity;
people hurrying to and fro and telephones ringing without a
stop. Paris was on the eve of the largest police operation and
the most thorough roundup the city had known since the arrest
of the Templars and the St. Bartholomew's Day massacre. Zero
hour had been set for three in the morning, and there were still
hundreds of details to be checked.

It was customary for the Germans to give an operation of this
nature some topical nickname. The giant roundup of all Jews
that had just been launched in occupied Europe, aiming at
their total extermination, had been dubbed "Operation ·
Reinhardt," in honor of SS General Reinhardt Heydrich, who
had been killed by Czech patriots in Prague the month before.
Then some Nazi officer, with an eye for detail and a morbidly
poetic bent, elaborated this further, subdividing Operation
Reinhardt into "Operation Sea Spray" for the persecution of
the Jews taking place in Eastern Europe and "Operation
Spring Wind" for the roundup of the Jews about to take place
in Western Europe and planned for Paris that evening.*

At the heart of the great web being woven to be spread over

---

* The decision to nickname the operation "Reinhardt" in honor of
Reinhardt Heydrich is reported in many well-known documents, while
the nicknames "Sea Spray" and "Spring Wind" are cited by Ray
Petitfrère, historian of the Nazi regime, in his book *La Mystique de la
croix gammée*. They are also mentioned in Ernst Jünger's book *Journal
de guerre et d'occupation*.

the whole city, there was a card index, a filing system established by the French police with a card for every Jew living in the Paris region—*der Gross Paris,* as the Germans called it. In preparation for Operation Spring Wind, 25,334 cards had been taken out for the city proper and 2,054 cards for the suburbs; in all, 27,388 cards were extracted bearing details of the Jews in the area who were not of French nationality.

This index was not new. It had been set up in the early days of the German occupation, when a census had been taken under the joint direction of General de La Laurencie on the French side and Hauptsturmfuehrer Théo Dannecker representing the Germans. The basic information for this census had been collected from the local police stations, and from that the information relative to the index was taken to the "administrative headquarters of General police affairs." The man responsible for organizing the card index was Tulard, working under the immediate supervision of Commissioner François, director of the camps of Drancy, Pithiviers, and Beaune-la-Rolande, for whom the imminent roundup was of consuming interest.

The index was a model of its kind. The master cards had been duplicated several times, one set being sent to the Gestapo on Avenue Foch and the rest used to classify the names into various categories: alphabetically by surname, address, zone, occupation, and nationality.

For Tulard and the index, this was a time of crisis. Preparations for Operation Spring Wind had disrupted normal routine in the police force. Inspectors had been recruited to help with the sorting and assessment of the 27,388 cards, and even so more hands were needed. Female helpers, women like those who handed out ration cards at the municipal offices each month, had to be brought in. There was one more day to go before the efficiency of the index would be put to the test, and Tulard was as anxious as Commissioner François.

Mr. Tulard's office was not the only one to be working overtime that night. At the offices of the Police for Jewish

Affairs, there was the same tension. The directors and staff of this unusual organization, created by the occupation forces, were preparing themselves for an exacting effort the next day. They looked as if they were preparing to launch a crusade— and for them it was a crusade, a large-scale anti-Jewish crusade, its headquarters in Berlin and its orders relayed directly through Vichy.

The network was easy to trace. At the Paris end there were two SS men, Hauptsturmfuehrers Dannecker and Roethke, whose responsibility it was to organize Operation Spring Wind. At the Gestapo in Paris they headed Section IV B4, also known as IV J and called the Section for Anti-Jewish Activity. These two had received their instructions personally from SS General Reinhardt Heydrich, who had come to Paris on May 5, not long before his death, as it turned out, for on May 28 Heydrich was mortally wounded in Prague by two Czech paratroopers who had come from London to accomplish this mission. In giving Dannecker and Roethke their orders, Heydrich was only carrying out the decision taken at what was known as the Wannsee conference, a meeting held in January, 1942, at the conclusion of which the motion had been carried that all European Jews be exterminated. At this meeting, held in Eichmann's office in Berlin at 56/58 Grossen Wannsee-Strasse, the Nazis worked out the Final Solution, which was to be the complete annihilation of all European Jewry. Presiding over the SS elite that day was General Reinhardt Heydrich. In a cozy, relaxed atmosphere, they discussed the murder of millions of people, and the conference ended with Heydrich, Eichmann, and SS Muller sitting and chatting by the fire. Operation Spring Wind, due to begin in France on July 16, was only one step toward the Final Solution.

Even though many people working on this operation were not informed what its object was and had never heard of Wannsee, everyone concerned, whether he was a German attached to the Gestapo on Avenue Foch or a Frenchman whose pay, promotion, and orders still came from the French Ministry of the Interior (then under Pierre Pucheu), everyone was getting ready as if for a war.

That same evening an important council of war was being
held at the home of Darquier de Pellepoix, Head of the
Commission for Jewish Affairs. Like the Police for Jewish
Affairs, the Commission was a product of the occupation. With
the increase of rules and new regulations laid down by the
Germans and applicable to Jews only, it had very soon become
necessary to create this agency to deal with infringements of
these rules. The Commission's first task had been to define what
constituted a Jew. According to the statute of April 26, 1941:

> Anyone having at least three grandparents of purely
> Jewish extraction shall be considered as a Jew.
> An ancestor who has at any time belonged to the Jewish
> faith shall without further question be considered as of
> purely Jewish extraction.
> Anyone having two grandparents of purely Jewish
> extraction and at the time of the publication of the
> Statute of April 26, 1941, belongs to the Jewish faith or
> who subsequently joined the Jewish faith, or who at the
> time of the German Statute of April 26, 1941, was married
> to a Jew or subsequently married a Jew, shall be con-
> sidered as Jewish.
> In deciding doubtful cases, anyone belonging to the
> Jewish faith or who has at any time belonged to the
> Jewish faith, shall be considered as Jewish.

Meanwhile Marshal Pétain's government had drawn up a
wider definition of Jew. Hauptsturmfuehrer Dannecker was
particularly pleased with it and on the eve of Operation Spring
Wind said: "Since the French definition of Jew is less
restrictive than the German, it shall be used for the
determination of doubtful cases."

The night of July 15 was an armed vigil for the high
ranking Paris police officials too. They had been informed of
the planned operation only one week before, on July 7, when
the Gestapo had summoned to Avenue Foch, Darquier de
Pellepoix as head of the Commission for Jewish Affairs;
Leguay, the Director General of the Police; Commissioner
François, in charge of internment camps; Hennequin, chief of
the municipal police, Tulard of the card index; Garnier as
representative of the Prefect of Police; Gallien, who was in

charge of Darquier de Pellepoix's office; and Guidot, a staff officer of the municipal police.

The session, chaired by two Germans, Hauptsturmfuehrer Théo Dannecker and SS Unterscharfuehrer Heinrichsohn, had been a true briefing. Darquier de Pellepoix had opened the meeting by announcing solemnly that "the occupation forces had declared their willingness to rid the French nation of its Jews and that the present meeting had been called in order to discuss the technical details involved in deporting the Jews." Then Dannecker had checked the extent of the powers of the eight representatives of the French government, and, speaking like a captain briefing his men on the target of an air raid and the timing, he had gone on to reveal the aim of the operation: the arrest of twenty-eight thousand Jews, and the dates set for it—Monday, July 13, through Wednesday, July 15. It was at this meeting that the Vel d'Hiv (short for Vélodrome d'Hiver, a covered cycle-racing track) was chosen as the most convenient gathering point for the deportees. Numerous questions about practical details were brought up, such as the capacity of the camps and the means of transport available for the deportations to Germany. The escort for the journey would be provided by the French gendarmerie under the supervision of a squad of German armed police composed of eight men and one lieutenant. Problems of food and provisions were also touched on.

Now, only one week after the meeting with the Gestapo in Paris, with only a few hours before the start of Operation Spring Wind, these French officials, who had staked their future on helping the enemy, were anxiously praying that the operation would succeed. The dates mentioned at the meeting were postponed at the last minute, the night of July 13–14 being considered risky, since July 14, Bastille Day, on which all France would be celebrating the anniversary of the French Revolution, might prove a difficult day for such an operation. People would be out on the streets in their tricolor ties, scarves, and shirts, some women even dressed in whole suits of red, white, and blue, and the mood might become ugly. The night of July 15–16 would be better. Even though the people to be arrested were Jews, foreign Jews at that, who according to the current prejudices were a kind of subspecies of the human race with whom it was hardly likely that the French populace would sympathize, one could never be certain.

Happily for those conducting Operation Spring Wind, a frantic propaganda drive had for some weeks been successfully instilling a sense of xenophobia in the Parisians and encouraging anti-Semitic feeling in every way possible. When a film called *The Jewish Peril* (scenario by a Dr. Taubert) was shown at the Cinema César, Lucien Rebatet, holder of the Renaudot prize for his book *Les Décombres,* wrote the following review in the *Petit Parisien* under the pseudonym of François Vinneuil:

> Obviously one cannot properly understand the Jews unless one has seen how they live in their large ghettos in Central Europe, around the Carpathian mountains, in Hungary, and especially in Rumania and Russia.
>
> The first half of this film was shot in the Polish ghettos by members of the Wehrmacht, shortly after the lightning campaign of 1939. It is a masterpiece in documentary reporting, like almost everything these cameramen in uniform record, whether behind the lines or at the front. . . .
>
> Of the Jews in Europe at this time, 80 per cent are second or at most third generation descendants of that European Jewry which has for centuries harbored and cultivated a hate for Christians—learning in their Talmud and in their rabbinical schools to cheat and exploit our race and prepare for a hegemony of Israel.
>
> The Jews we come across daily, here in France, have been able to adopt a light varnish of French custom and behavior. But beneath the superficial Western traits, they are aliens, though shorn of their beards and robes. We must learn from now on to recognize in them the eternal Jew—the exotic outsider who will never belong.

On July 3, in the *Cri du Peuple* under the headline "In the Light of the Yellow Star," was the following:

> One has only to spend one quarter of an hour on a Sunday, strolling between the Madeleine and the Place de

la République, in order to convince oneself of the reality of the Jewish peril. The proportion of passersby marked with a yellow star surpasses anything one might have imagined. Even the dumbest Gaullist cannot help admitting to himself that they are decidedly too many. Last Sunday on a walk between the Porte St. Denis and the Rue Montmartre, one of our reporters passed 268 people wearing yellow stars on his side of the street alone, and all in the space of ten minutes.

On July 4, under the headline "The Jews, A Leisure Class," the same paper published the following:

> Groups of young Jewish men and women, aged between eighteen and thirty, spend hours every morning sauntering along the elegant paths of the Bois de Boulogne. All that these favored young people do is repeat the words of the latest news broadcast from the BBC and spout criticism of the French government. Others among them prefer to paddle canoes on the lake or on the river Marne. The swimming pools of Paris are choked with arrogant young Jews joking with each other at the tops of their voices: "My dear, somehow in a swimsuit you seem quite ordinary. You really look much sharper with a yellow star on." Are we going to tolerate this gang of idlers? There is no shortage of work. Let us put the Jews to work.

For those who might not be impressed by this kind of journalism, the Commanding Officer in *Gross Paris* had dictated a grim warning, the barbarity of which seems hardly credible. From July 13 onwards, this warning, signed by General Oberg, *der Höhere SS und Polizeiführer im Bereich des Militärbefehlshabers in Frankreich,* was pasted on every wall and published in every paper in the city, so that the Parisians would be sure to see it. The notice described what measures would be taken by the German authorities against the family of anyone who dared to offer resistance:

1. All the male next of kin in the ascending line, as well as brothers-in-law and cousins over 18 years of age, will be shot.

2. All female next of kin similarly related will be condemned to hard labor.

3. All children of men or women against whom these measures are taken, up to the age of seventeen years, will be put into a house of correction controlled by the German authorities.

Knowing how much importance the Germans attached to the success of Operation Spring Wind, Fernand de Brinon, the representative of the Pétain Government in Paris, was also nervous about the events of the next day. Every possible person had been mobilized, lists of names were combed, last minute telephone calls were made to the headquarters of the *Parti Populaire Français,* a youth party founded and organized by Jacques Doriot. Both in Paris and in the suburbs, loyal members were alerted, and some three to four hundred French adolescents came the next day wearing dark blue shirts, leather belts and PPF armbands, to help the police in their work.

At the Prefecture of Police, the work of preparation seemed endless—lists of names and maps of the city zones had to be marked; everything had to be checked and double-checked. The arrests of the next day were to be effected by a force of nine thousand men, the equivalent of a small division; to maneuver such an army according to a precise schedule was no mean task. The gendarmerie, the mobile guard, the judiciary police, the mass media and public transport would all be involved in Operation Spring Wind, and every man taking part would be a Frenchman. Frenchmen, not Germans, would knock at the victims' doors in the middle of the night, surround city zones, and block the streets. Applications for leave of absence were canceled, and so were classes at the Police Training School; as a practical exercise, the students would take part in the roundup. There were 888 teams of three or four men each to go to the listed addresses and make the arrests, with reinforcements for the zones more densely inhabited by Jews. Of these, 156 teams were to be sent into the III Arrondissement, 139 to the IV, 152 into the X, 246 into the XI, 121 into the XVIII, 131 into the XII, and 255 into the XX. All were ready for the signal to start.

Hennequin's instructions, dictated on July 12, had been

mimeographed and distributed to each of the 888 arrest teams. To make sure that everyone understood them clearly, they were read aloud just before the operation started. At that very moment last-minute orders were being given all along the battle front. In England the RAF men were preparing to take off in their Hurricanes and Spitfires to fight the Nazis. In Russia, Africa, the Pacific; in the mountains of Greece and Albania and Yugoslavia; inside China, men were getting ready by the thousands to continue the worldwide battle against the enemy. The difference in Paris was that all the force and efficiency of the guards and the gendarmerie was being mobilized to arrest thirty thousand innocent and unarmed civilians. And yet the procedure was as strict as that on a battle front. Nothing was left to chance; the instructions covered every eventuality:

> 1. As soon as the identity of a listed Jew has been confirmed, inspectors and guards are to proceed with the arrest, taking no notice of any protest or argument the prisoner may offer.
> 2. Every Jew listed is to be brought to the preliminary collecting center, no notice being taken of the state of health of the prisoners or exceptions made for that reason.

Once the prisoners were brought to the preliminary collecting centers, which were police stations, schools, gymnasiums, or whatever local building was the most suitable for holding a large number of people, they were to be divided into two categories by the German authorities—the childless adults, which included men and women, single and married, and those with children. The first group was to be sent to the camp at Drancy, while families with children were to be taken to the Vel d'Hiv, which, though it had been chosen as a convenient collection point, had not in any way been prepared for the purpose.

The question of the arrest of children had been covered by Article 6 of the instructions:

> Children living with the person or persons arrested shall be taken away with them, and no member of the

family shall remain in the apartment. Nor are children
to be left with neighbors.

In principle, a French child born of a foreign mother was not
to be arrested. As opposed to the treatment of the children,
prisoners were advised to leave with the concierge any cats or
dogs that would otherwise be abandoned. Water and electricity
were to be turned off. Each prisoner was to take with him
enough food for two days.

Article 7 on the sheet of instructions summed up the general
tone of the operation:

> Guards and inspectors are responsible for the success
> of the operation, which must be carried out with the
> maximum speed and without useless conversation or
> argument.

In case of any disappointments there was the following
instruction:

> Where an individual named on the list has not been
> arrested, guards and inspectors are to give the reasons for
> the failure, keeping their report brief and to the point.

By midnight everything was ready. The TCRP (*Compagnie
des Transports en Commun de la Région Parisienne,* the
Parisian public transport company at that time) had lined up
the buses to be used for the transport of Jews in its depots. Six
buses were parked in the courtyard of the Prefecture of Police
(later to be renamed Courtyard of the 19th of August) as a
reserve. Nine thousand men were ready and waiting for zero
hour. As for the victims, they were safely in their homes—a
sitting target. The curfew in Paris started at 11 P.M., and no
one could go out on the streets after that without *le ausweis,* as
the Parisians learned to call the pass issued by the German
authorities. It was inconceivable that an alien Jew should
possess such a pass.

At Drancy the Jewish prisoners who had been forced to
prepare room in the prison knew that a large number of their
compatriots were expected, and that could only mean a large-
scale roundup. Finding space to put the victims had been one

of the problems of the operation. Eventually the camp at
Drancy, which was a kind of human reservoir where the
Germans kept all prisoners intended for eventual deportation,
had been chosen. It was conveniently situated about three
miles outside Paris on the St. Denis road. With its five tall
skyscrapers, the prison stood out from the surrounding
countryside and was easily distinguishable in the distance. The
prison proper, however, was not in the tall buildings but in a
large U-shaped construction, four floors high, which had
originally been designed as a low income housing project and
had never been completed.

It was part of the prison system to put every four rooms with
access onto a staircase in the care of one of the prisoners, who
was called a "head of staircase." On July 14, one of these heads
of staircase, Georges Wellers, was summoned to a meeting by
Captain Vieux, a gendarmerie officer in charge of the camp. On
arriving there, Georges Wellers found that twenty-two other
heads of staircase, as well as their assistants, had been called
like himself, altogether about eighty prisoners. The captain,
who was usually brutal and coarse with a tendency to use his
whip to emphasize a point, on this occasion appeared almost
polite. He had summoned the prisoners to announce the arrival
very soon of large numbers of new prisoners. Room had to be
made for them, and there was cleaning to be done. These
preparations were completed by Georges Wellers and the others
by Wednesday evening in an atmosphere of anxiety, at the
thought of the unsuspecting Jews about to be arrested, and a
certain excitement at the prospect of possibly meeting
acquaintances among the new arrivals and perhaps hearing
news of wives and children, from whom they had been
separated since their internment.

The camp at Drancy had been declared a "military
penitentiary" in August, 1941, and some of the prisoners had
been there since then. They worried about their wives living
alone in Paris, but none imagined that the coming round
would include women and children among its victims. One of
them, named Cymering, knew that his wife, whom he left with

their little son at their apartment in Rue Trousseau, was
depressed and pessimistic about the future, but he never
expected to see her in the dreary setting of Drancy prison. So
far there had never been women and children among the
prisoners at Drancy. Furthermore, there was a definite spirit of
hopefulness in the camp, thanks to the clever lies of the
authorities. A Mr. Falkenstein, who spent some months at
Drancy at that time, described the feelings of the prisoners as
follows:

> The first group of deportees to be sent off to Germany
> had been those under twenty-five. I just escaped being
> included, having had my twenty-fifth birthday two weeks
> before. The Germans had given that departure every
> semblance of reassuring normality, at the same time
> spreading a rumor that these young men were going to
> work somewhere in Germany until the end of the war.
> They would be joining other teams of foreign prisoners
> when they got to Germany. I must admit that this fable
> did seem convincing at the time, especially as that first
> group consisted of young men only, who would be good as
> workers, and they were given some kind of perfunctory
> medical examination before they went.

The system devised by Commissioner François, according to
Dannecker's instructions, provided for any surplus of prisoners,
once Drancy was filled to capacity, by sending them to two
camps in the Loiret—Pithiviers and Beaune-la-Rolande. Both
these camps had a terrible reputation. They were in the charge
of members of the judiciary police and guarded by French
gendarmes. The food rations were scandalously meager. One
young Red Cross worker, Yvonne Cocher, was so shocked that
she protested against the inhuman conditions in a report to the
Prefect of the Loiret, a man called Morane. But the only effect
of that report was to bring about her dismissal. A friend and
colleague of Miss Cocher, Annette Monod, tried a different
method of calling attention to the prison conditions. For three
weeks she lived on prison rations and then asked for an
interview with the prefect. When he expressed his surprise at
seeing her so thin and weak, she replied: "It should not

astonish you, sir; I am eating the same rations as your prisoners
at Pithiviers."

Just as at Drancy, the prison administrators at Pithiviers had
announced that new arrivals were being expected. Room had
been prepared for them on June 22 by deporting to Auschwitz
one thousand of the prisoners already held at the prison. On
June 25, another 999 prisoners were deported from Beaune-la-
Rolande, and a further 1,038 from Pithiviers on June 28. The
Germans had decided that each convoy should consist of at
least one thousand persons. So strict were they about this that
when the chief of security police at Orléans found there were
only 930 Jews at the local camp, he felt obliged to arrest some
more to make up the required number. In a report to his boss
in Paris, dated June 29, 1942, he explained how by arresting
107 Jews and a doctor called Crémieux on his own initiative, he
had been able to send off a convoy of 1,038 prisoners, thus
fulfilling the German requirements.

Among the prisoners at Pithiviers who had spent more than
a year in the prison were Mr. Tarkowski, Mr. Rado, and Mr.
Nussbaum, all three of whom were on the list for the next
shipment to Germany. As soon as they knew this, Mr.
Nussbaum wrote to his wife: "We are leaving Pithiviers for
Germany. We are clearing the camp to make room for the
women." The letter was dated June 22. He hoped she would
understand the implied warning. But even so there was little
she could do, being a woman alone in a foreign country,
without the means to buy false documents or bribe someone
into helping her.

Anyway where could she go? Since the statute of May 29,
1942, she was conspicuously marked by her yellow star. The
ruling read: "The star is to be worn on the left side of the chest,
clearly visible and firmly sewn to the clothing, by every Jew
over the age of six years. It is to be the size of a man's palm,
have six points, and be made of yellow cloth with a black
outline and with the word 'Jew' written on it in black." This
had become law after the arrest of Mr. Nussbaum, and in
prison he and the others tried to picture their wives and

children so visibly labeled as the legitimate prey of any roundup or other form of persecution. To obey the regulations and wear the star meant giving up all hope of escape; to ignore the regulations meant risking arrest and imprisonment if not deportation. Ironically this uncoveted piece of yellow cloth cost the buyers one coupon of their clothing ration.

A more tragic irony was the involvement of some of the Jews in the preparations for the roundup, without their knowledge. One such case was Mrs. Libers, who had some time before left her name with the UGIF (French Jewish Union) so that she could be contacted if there happened to be any work for her to do. This organization, ostensibly created to help and rescue Jews in need, not only had the approval of the German authorities but was actually founded by SS Dannecker of the Gestapo. Knowing what had been done in Poland and elsewhere in German-occupied territory, he had once written to Berlin: "From our experience in Germany and the protectorates of Bohemia and Moravia, it is clear that by excluding the Jews from a number of spheres of daily life, their segregation into a distinct and separate class follows inevitably."

Thus while the UGIF was supposed by its Jewish members to be a foundation dedicated to the help of their compatriots, it was in fact used by the Germans to facilitate their capture and elimination.

On the morning of July 15, Mrs. Libers had received a telegram asking her to go to the UGIF. By nine in the morning she was at their office, where she found other women who had come like herself in the hope of being given some kind of work or help. There was a job for them, a very simple job: that of attaching small pieces of string to squares of cardboard to make labels. As she worked, Mrs. Libers was filled with increasing misgivings. Who or what were these labels for? To her they looked exactly like the labels that were tied to children when they were evacuated.

Chapter 2

Trapped

A few more moves and the game would be over. Nine thousand men were set and waiting for the signal to go out and hunt down their quarry. The camps were cleared and ready to receive the captured prey.

Yet even at this late stage secret efforts were desperately made to cheat Operation Spring Wind of some of its intended victims. Not all the Frenchmen recruited by the Germans were able to accept the inevitability of the crime. Here and there messages were slipped into mailboxes and warning telephone calls were made. It was a feeble gesture, but those who made it were risking their lives. Women helpers sorting cards at Tulard's office or police inspectors with access to precise information would recognize a name and manage to send a warning in time. Since these were a few exceptions to the general cooperation with the Nazis in their plan, they will be mentioned by name.

As soon as Mr. Kaminsky, a militant communist, heard about the roundup, he told his Jewish friend Mr. Rosenberg what he knew, and the Rosenbergs—father, mother, and daughter— immediately left their apartment and spent the night with friends. Though these were Jews too, the father of the family was a prisoner of war in Germany, and Rosenberg, still trusting in Marshal Pétain's promise guaranteeing the security of the war wounded and the families of prisoners of war, felt he was out of danger in his friend's apartment on the Rue Filles-du-Calvaire.

Already, in May, inspector Dubourq had saved the life of a Rumanian-Jewish neighbor called Kanneman by warning him in time. Learning about a planned roundup of Rumanian Jews at his office, Dubourq had sent Kanneman an anonymous note saying: "Your friends advise you to leave now; tomorrow will be too late." Kanneman understood the warning and left in time.

Another inspector, named Rigal, sent word to a Jewish family called Epstein, though he knew that the father was sick and depressed and it was doubtful that he would act on the warning. In the III Arrondissement inspector Pingenet, who had already put Jews on their guard in preceding roundups, continued to do so before Operation Spring Wind.

The communists, from the information that reached them, mistrusted the intentions of the Germans and printed a pamphlet warning the Jews. This was secretly distributed by members of the Resistance, some of whom did not even know where it came from but at the risk of their lives pushed it under front doors and into the hands of passersby in the street, whispering, "Pass it on."

A copy of this pamphlet reached Mrs. Lichtein. She did not for a moment doubt the truth of what it said, and she was terrified. She decided to sit up that night, so she packed her bags, planning to escape through the window with their daughter as soon as they heard the knock on the front door. They lived on the ground floor and could get away across the courtyard.

Another clandestine paper, called *Notre Voix,* published in French and Yiddish, also gave warning of the roundup that was about to take place, telling its readers to escape or hide and in every way to resist. This issue of *Notre Voix* was brought to the Tselnick's house by some dedicated youngsters, but even after reading it, the Tselnicks found it hard to believe that they were threatened. Rumor had it that no one was ever arrested twice, and Mr. Tselnick had already been picked up by the police in August of the year before, and had spent eighty-seven days at Drancy. He was then released, he knew not quite how or why,

weighing sixty pounds less than before and convinced that he
was the beneficiary of a miracle. So now, not knowing whether
to run away or not, the Tselnicks decided to compromise. They
would remain in the building at 181 Faubourg St. Antoine,
but that night instead of sleeping in their own apartment all
five of them would crowd into a small maid's bedroom on
the fifth floor.

Yet another police inspector, Jacques B., decided to disregard
orders. From the very beginning, when the Germans had
enforced their first measures against the Jews, Jacques had
worried about Paulette Rotblit, a nineteen-year-old Jewish
girl he had known since childhood. They had lived in the same
quarter and used to walk to school together every day. Later
they had dated each other a few times. But they had drifted
apart. In 1941 they had met again, exchanged news and
addresses, and spoken about their friends and relations. As yet
the Jews did not have to wear a yellow star, but they were
already subjected to all kinds of special limitations, so Jacques
asked: "Paulette, is everything all right with you these days? I
mean, because you are Jews, do they make life difficult for
you?" Paulette shrugged her shoulders. "We manage. Don't
worry about us. We've always managed somehow." Jacques
could not tell whether she meant her family or Jews in
general. From the tone of her reply he guessed that she was
irritated and her pride perhaps was injured.

Now, on the eve of Operation Spring Wind, Jacques knew
what was going to happen through his job with the police, and
on July 15 in the afternoon he dialed Paulette's number. By
this time Jews were no longer allowed to have telephones, but
luckily the bureaucratic machine was slow-moving and the
Rotblits' line was still working. When he heard Paulette's voice
on the other end of the wire, Jacques said simply: "It is going
to be a warm night, and there will be thunderstorms. I think
you had better go and sleep somewhere cool." He hoped she
understood and that she would not be at home the next day
when his colleagues knocked on her door.

Although it was not impossible to find a temporary hiding place for the day of the roundup, fleeing Paris was a different matter. For a Jew to take a train involved terrible risks. Apart from ripping off one's yellow star, one had to have false papers which did not have the designation JEW printed on them, since every station was watched, roadblocks were frequent, and the possibility of being asked to show identification papers great. Then even false papers were risky, as they had to be genuine enough to stand the test of a telephone call to headquarters checking their authenticity.

The countryside might seem a good hiding place, but how could these foreigners with heavy accents and unpronounceable names expect to be welcome in a small village. On whose support could they count? They had no money to live on, and there was no work they could do to earn their keep.

Then there was the free zone. Many of the Jews on Tulard's list had tried to cross the demarcation line, but a large number were caught just as they were crossing. Besides it was an expensive undertaking, and the Jews who were left in Paris in 1942 had been drained dry by countless requisitions of their property. But in spite of the danger, during the second week of July, when the city was humming with vague and confused rumors, some Jews nevertheless tried their luck at crossing into the free zone.

One such was Rachel Pronice, a Jewish pianist. She was a lively young woman full of spirit and well suited to living in Paris, which she loved. Her friends called her Ella. She earned her living by giving piano lessons during the day and playing in a nightclub in the evenings. She often entertained friends at her studio at 14 Rue Raffet and was well known in that corner of the XVI Arrondissement. But since she began wearing the yellow star, things had changed. There were people who avoided her and others who even stopped greeting her on the street. She was frightened and decided to leave. Her neighbor, Mrs. Goldberg, a Frenchwoman married to a Jew, who felt secure at that time since her husband was a prisoner of war, describes how Rachel came to leave her cat and a suitcase with

Mrs. Goldberg one morning. She was agitated and depressed but told Mrs. Goldberg that she had found a safe escape route across the demarcation line.

Another person to be alarmed by events was Mr. Kleinberger. On July 15 he left his apartment at 10 Rue d'Hauteville in the X Arrondissement, one of the addresses listed on Tulard's index. The previous roundups had affected adult men only, so Mrs. Kleinberger and her two sons stayed on in the apartment. But as the evening wore on, rumors of mass arrests began to circulate. Mrs. Kleinberger became anxious and went down to confide her fears to the concierge. The concierge sympathized with her and gave her a key, telling her to leave her apartment by the service stairs as soon as she heard a knock on her door, and hide in an unoccupied apartment on the third floor.

Like Mr. Kleinberger, his friend Mr. Abramzyk also left his home that night, the rest of the family refusing the move since they were certain that if there was a roundup it would threaten the grown men only.

From mouth to mouth rumors of the roundup were spread across the city. Inevitably the Linens heard it. Most likely it was their son Nat who brought the news in from the street. From the street because for a Jew wearing a yellow star, there was nowhere to go on a fine evening except the street. Public parks, swimming pools, sports stadiums, gymnasiums, as well as museums, libraries, theatres, and cinemas were all barred to Jews. The same applied to cafes and restaurants—so the choice was between staying at home or going out into the street. There was nowhere else to go. The Linens could hardly remember a time when they were not anxious. Like many others, Mr. Linen believed that he alone was threatened in his family, and he also trusted the promises made by the Vichy government protecting families of prisoners of war. So, leaving his wife and Nat at home in their apartment on Blvd. Beaumarchais, he went to hide at his sister's house, since her husband was a prisoner of war.

At the baker's shop on the Rue des Ecouffes everyone was talking about the roundup. Rue des Ecouffes, Rue du Roi-de-

Sicile, Rue des Rosiers, Rue de la Parcheminerie, Rue des
Blancs-Manteaux, all these streets formed part of the old Jewish
quarter, dating back to the Middle Ages. And since the French
Revolution in 1789, it was to this quarter that Jews seeking
asylum in France had come from every part of Europe. On
Tulard's index these streets occurred more frequently than any
others.

Hearing the conversation at the baker's about the roundup
and that it would include everybody and was planned for that
night, Mrs. Rimmler hurried home to tell her husband. Then
she and her husband went to Mrs. Rimmler's sister, who lived
at 51 Rue Piat in the XX Arrondissement. There too the
rumors were the same. They had to hide, but where? They
visited some neighbors to talk the matter over and were
persuaded to hide with them. Apparently the next-door
building, 51A Rue Piat, was an office building with a garage
on the ground floor; between the second and third floor there
was a small room measuring six by ten feet. Into this they all
crowded, ten people with no room to stretch out—the only
comfortable way to sleep was leaning against the wall, and so
they stood and waited.

In another household the feeling of apprehension bordered
on panic. The Pitkowiczes knew what the Nazis were capable
of. Mr. Pitkowicz himself was a militant anti-fascist of long
standing. His eldest daughter Rosine, who was twenty, and his
eldest son Bernard, eighteen, had joined the Resistance and
both had been captured by the Germans and condemned to
thirty years hard labor. An uncle, Charles Pitkowicz, had been
picked up in an earlier roundup and taken to Drancy; so far,
they had had no further news of him. Convinced that he was
the only one in danger, Mr. Pitkowicz decided to spend the
night in the cellar. His wife and his younger son and daughter
would stay on in the apartment since surely women and
children were safe.

In the same building lived the Epsteins, who had been
warned by inspector Rigal. Mr. Epstein, seriously ill, was
gasping for breath as he struggled with one attack of asthma

after another. He too was sure that he would be the only one in the family who might be arrested: "The women and children are safe, and I am far too sick—they would never dare to take me. Anyway I couldn't run away if I wanted to in this state." So Rigal's warning had no effect.

On the Rue Crespin-du-Gast in the XI Arrondissement, which was to be combed by 246 teams of policemen the next day, lived Mrs. Nussbaum. She had received her husband's letter from Pithiviers in which he told her that he would soon be deported. It was the last letter she was to get from him. She read and reread it. She understood the warning that she herself was in danger but did not know what to do about it. Above all she was obsessed with the thought of her husband's deportation. At the end of the day, she went to visit a cousin living in the same building, and after discussing every possibility the two ladies decided they would sit up that night and not go to bed.

Not far from them in the same arrondissement on the Rue de Vaucouleurs lived the Sienickis. For many days now they had been in a state of extreme distress. Everyone around them was talking about the roundup, and they had remained indoors, feeling slightly more secure inside their apartment. The streets seemed dangerous; at any moment a policeman could stop you and ask to see your papers. Furthermore, their ten-year-old daughter Régine had just come home from the Saint-Louis Hospital, where she had had a mastoid operation. For some days now they had been changing her dressings at home rather than take her to the clinic. It seemed safer somehow.

On the Rue Trévise, Mrs. Pechner was visited by a friend who had come to tell her to run away and hide. Apparently a police officer had told someone that there would be a roundup that night. The Pechners could hardly take in the news, and anyway they had no idea where to go.

That night scarcely anyone slept in the IV Arrondissement. Everyone was in a state of nervous excitement. Like a cornered deer running uselessly in circles, they were all filled with anxiety but could not do anything. Had there been no children, they might have tried something in the way of an escape, but the children were there. The most they could do was pay anxious visits to each other, people on the Rue des Rosiers walking over to friends' houses on the Rue Roi-de-Sicile. As the hours ticked away they comforted themselves as best they could by repeating to each other that a roundup which would put women and children at the mercy of the enemy was inconceivable. It could not happen in France.

Sometime during that night, while last minute telephone calls were being made at the Prefecture to launch the operation, a small team of railway workers at Austerlitz station belonging to the FTP (*Francs tireurs et partisans*) derailed and overturned a locomotive. That night too, Marcel Hartmann, a municipal counsellor who was a communist, was writing his last letter before being executed. At midnight that night, miles away from Paris, in the camp of Mauzac in the Dordogne, a small group of Resistance members, among them the socialist deputy Pierre Bloch, and some English paratroopers escaped from the prison, taking with them the guard who had helped them.

At three in the morning, Rue Nelaton was still buried in the stillness of the night. The soft lapping of the Seine as it flowed by, some two hundred yards away, was clearly audible. But the silence was soon broken by the rumbling of four covered trucks, with small tricolors painted on them, which drove up the street and came to a halt by the dark walls of the Vélodrome d'Hiver not far from the entrance gates. On the wooden benches of each truck were some twenty guards, making four sections in all. Rocked by the motion of the trucks on the way from the barracks to the Vel d'Hiv, they had fallen asleep as they sat, their helmets pulled over their eyes and their hands resting on the bolts of their rifles, held between their knees. Now the sudden brakes had awakened them, and they emerged sleepily from the backs of the trucks. Guns in hand, they swung themselves down, jumping heavily to the ground one after the

other. Then, drawn up behind the four adjutants and the
lieutenant in charge, they entered the Vel d'Hiv. The noise
they made woke several of the people living in the area.
Windows were opened and curtains parted. Later, when day
broke, some of the shopkeepers—a grocer and a bartender—
came over to have a look. But the street was quiet once more.

Four hours later the arrival of the first loads of prisoners
arrested during the night would fill the street with an unusual
amount of traffic and people. Meanwhile the lieutenant inside
was taking his time to carry out his part of the job carefully.
Two posts of two guards each were placed on either side of the
gate, shifts were arranged, and men were assigned to different
parts of the building. Accommodation for the guards was
prepared. In one of the halls, mattresses were unrolled, and
very soon the room had the look of a barracks: helmets and
bags hanging up and rifles leaning against the wall while
resting soldiers, their uniforms unfastened, sat in groups
talking and smoking.

The Police Commissioner of the XV Arrondissement had
sent five squads of eight policemen, and these were stationed in
front of the gates of the Vel d'Hiv. In wartime Paris where,
apart from a few cars running on gas or coal and the bicycles,
there were only *Wehrmacht* vehicles on the streets, these
policemen were going to be dealing with heavy traffic that
would fill all the approaches to the Vel d'Hiv for the next few
days.

In Rue Crespin-du-Gast, Mrs. Nussbaum was still with her
cousin. In the end they had both dozed off. But at four in the
morning a light in the Spienak apartment opposite wakened
them. Through the window they could see the family moving
about and packing their suitcases. The sight startled them out
of their sleepiness and resignation. They must flee at once. But
already it was too late. Somewhere in the neighborhood they
heard loud knocking on a door and the shout: "Open up!
Police!"

Operation Spring Wind had begun.

Chapter 3

Black Thursday

At four in the morning, only two hours before sunrise, it was still very dark. The streets were empty and doors and shutters closed tight. From the outlying suburbs large, heavy trucks were converging on the city, bringing gendarmes, mobile guards, and policemen. This Thursday in July, 1942, was to be remembered as "Black Thursday."*

At pre-established points in the city the trucks stopped and the men from the suburbs were joined by inspectors in civilian clothes. Arrest teams were formed and the instructions read once more. Three or four hundred younger Frenchmen also came to lend a hand. Members of the *Parti Populaire Français,* they wore navy blue shirts and belts and armbands with the initials PPF on them. As the sky paled, everyone was at his post. Depending on the arrondissement, zero hour was either 4 or 5 A.M. In areas where arrests were to be made on a large scale, groups of gendarmes and guards blocked the streets, their guns at the ready. The TCRP buses came to join the police trucks and parked along the pavements waiting for their cargo. The drivers remained in the driving seats except when from time to time one of them would get down to stretch his legs and roll himself a cigarette with some cheap, evil-smelling tobacco.

* The term *Der Fintzerer Donerstig* was first used in a Yiddish tract distributed the very next morning, apparently published by some communist or zionist group, and meant Black or Dismal Thursday. Some eyewitnesses we interviewed said that the name not only described the sinister mood of that day but also was an allusion to the dark uniforms of the police force.

Once they had blocked off an area, the arrest teams, armed with their list of names, would enter the sleeping apartment buildings and knock on the door of the family they wanted. This was happening simultaneously all over Paris: thousands of buildings were being invaded. In some of them so many families were listed that one team of three or four men was not enough, and several teams would be working at the same time at one address. Like some pitiless tide, these uniformed teams would overrun a building, working their way up from floor to floor, banging on doors and shouting, "Police! Open Up!"

Mrs. Dorag, who lived on the Rue Jules-Verne in the XI Arrondissement at that time, described to us what must have been happening in thousands of homes. "During the night of July 15–16 we were awakened by loud knocks on our door. When we opened, there were three men, two police officers and one civilian. They told us to get dressed quickly and take a few belongings and follow them."

The Spienaks had waited too long. The police found all of them—father, mother, and two children—up with their things packed and ready. All they had to do was pick up their cases and go down to the bus. For them this was the beginning of a journey from which none of them was to return.

On the Rue Piat, the Rimmlers and their friends could hear from their crowded hiding place the knocks at the doors and the sound of military boots on the stairs. They also heard people screaming and weeping.

Whenever a door remained shut after the policemen's knock, it meant that a family had escaped. For some policemen who were troubled by the course of events it was a relief to find an empty apartment. All they had to do now was note down that at such and such an address no one was at home. The instructions had said: "Where an individual named on the list has not been arrested, guards and inspectors are to give the reasons for the failure, keeping their report brief and to the point."

On the other hand, there were policemen so intent on the chase that they were disappointed at any failure in their

mission. One went so far as to write in a letter: "If we only had
the necessary authorization, we would ferret out these Jews who
think they can saddle themselves on us." Many were so
conscientious that they forced their way into apartments that
were not opened to them.

In the Friedman apartment, for example, at 233 Rue de
Belleville, the whole family was so fast asleep that they did not
realize what was going on and did not open the door at once.
It was so early that Mrs. Friedman did not feel comfortable
about opening the door. But the police came in all the same,
breaking down the door. Mrs. Friedman's daughter, who was
eight at the time, says she will never forget her mother's tears
and supplications. She was ready to be taken away as long as
they spared the children. But the police would not listen and
gave her ten minutes to get ready.

On the Rue Poitou another mother had the same instinctive
fear of opening the door. She was alone in the apartment with
her two small children. Her husband had already been arrested
and was at the camp at Pithiviers. It may well be that he was
on the train that had left for Auschwitz the night before; at any
rate, he was among the prisoners to be deported at that time.
His young wife was unable to do anything to protect herself
except refuse to answer the door. She waited quietly, but as the
door was broken down by the police, she picked up her two
children and threw herself from the window. The apartment
was on the fifth floor, and all three were killed by the fall. A
similar escape by suicide was found by another woman living
on the Rue de Belleville.

At many addresses, like that of Paulette Rotblit, for instance,
and Mr. Rosenberg's and Mr. Abramzyk's the police came away
empty-handed. The Kleinbergers fled into the empty
apartment on the third floor as soon as they heard a noise on
the stairs and lay there listening, hardly daring to breathe.

The arrests in the suburbs were carried out at the same time
as the arrests in Paris proper. At Ivry the police came to the
home of the Barbanel family at five in the morning. They asked
for Mr. Barbanel, whose name was on their list, and were told

that he was working on a building site and came home only on Saturdays. They then asked for Mrs. Barbanel, who was Polish, and her two eldest sons, who had been born in Poland, but the two boys were not at home. Only Mrs. Barbanel and her two youngest children, a boy of nine and a girl of thirteen, were at home. The inspector said that he did not want the children, since they had been born in France, but if Mrs. Barbanel brought them with her she herself might be released on their account. With the neighbors standing round, the two children said they wanted to go with their mother, and so the three were taken away by the police.

On the Rue Pot-de-Fer in the V Arrondissement, the Goldenzwags, who had a child born in France, were not too perturbed when the police knocked on their door. As he went to open the door, Mr. Goldenzwag said naively, "It will be all right. We have a French child." He was further reassured by the sight of the French uniforms of the inspector and policemen who had come for him. The policemen were chatty and almost friendly: "Pack up your things. You are going to a ghetto near Lublin till the end of the war. After the war you will be able to come back to this apartment."

Perhaps they really believed what they were saying. They asked for coffee, and Mrs. Goldenzwag went off to heat it. As soon as they were ready the father, mother, and four children went downstairs. On the doorstep Mrs. Goldenzwag suddenly fainted. When she came to, the inspector said she could go to a hospital, but she refused. Who would look after the children? A neighbor who was looking on said she would take the youngest daughter, who had been born in France and so was not on the list. He would take her away to the country and look after her. At that early hour Mrs. Goldenzwag was too confused to realize that by keeping the child with her she was condemning it to death. So she refused the neighbor's offer as she had refused the inspector's suggestion to go to the hospital.

Mrs. Lichtein sat up all night so that she would be ready to escape through the window at the right moment. But toward dawn she fell asleep in her chair, her little bundle near her on the floor. The loud knocks at her door at five in the morning took her so much by surprise that she mechanically went to open up before she was fully awake. But as soon as she saw the uniform, she was wide awake and pleaded with the policeman—who was alone, the inspector who accompanied him being busy elsewhere—to let her go. But he told her to hurry up and get ready or else he would call the police. When she heard that grotesque threat, Mrs. Lichtein saw that there was nothing she could say to move him. Taking her daughter by the hand, she followed him.

At Rue de Bondy, Mr. Vistuk had gone into hiding with some French neighbors. But other less generous neighbors decided to give him away as soon as they knew where he was hiding. Meanwhile they watched the movements of the police.

Among the names on the police list for Boulevard Rochechouart was that of Mr. Wallach. Mr. Wallach had long been associated with the resistance against the Germans. Both he and his twenty-one-year-old son Elie were actively involved. Elie belonged to the *Organisation Spéciale,* a group founded by the communist party and later to become the major source of partisans, while he himself worked with Pierre Georges (the future Colonel Fabien) and Samuel Tyzselman at the beginning of the movement. One of the first bulletins listing members of the Resistance executed by the Germans read: "The Jew Tyzselman and Henri Gautherot."

On June 29, 1942, Elie Wallach and another militant, Léon Pakin, had gone to see a furrier called Simon, on the Rue Saint-Antoine. He was known to be working for the Germans, and Elie's mission was to persuade him or force him to stop this treacherous activity. Unfortunately things turned out badly. Simon deafened the whole neighborhood with his shouts, and the two young men had to run. They were chased and eventually arrested on the Place des Vosges.

Pakin's wife was forced to leave her apartment at 18 Rue Chabrol even though she was pregnant, and the very next day the police raided the Wallach apartment even though Elie had moved out of his parents' house some time before. The police

raid coincided with a secret meeting of *Solidarité*.* Besides Mr.
Wallach there were at his house Isaac Kristal, Jacques Kupfer,
Mr. Laizer, and one other militant. The police arrested all five
and took them to Cherche-Midi prison. Later they were handed
over to the Germans, who put them in the Fresnes prison,
where they were "interrogated physically." The two younger
men, Wallach and Pakin, were tortured.

On July 15 the five men were hurried into one of the prison
courtyards by their prison guards and lined up against one of
the walls. There was no doubt in any of their minds that they
had only a few more minutes to live. But this was just a prank
in the German style. They were in fact liberated, and one of
the *Feldwebels* even called out in a friendly tone, "Hope not
to see you again" to Mr. Wallach, who took it as a warning not
to get caught again.

As soon as they were free, all except Mr. Wallach decided to
take no chances and went to stay with friends. Mr. Wallach
returned to his apartment at 108 Boulevard Rochechouart,
meaning to pay a brief visit and then go into hiding. How
could he know that he was in danger again so soon after his
release, and that at six o'clock the next morning the French
police would be knocking at his door again? When they came,
Mr. Wallach managed to slip out of a window into the
courtyard one floor below, and from there he ran to the
concierge of the next building, who hid him in the cellar. His
wife did not think that she was wanted too, and would not have
been able to use her husband's escape route anyway. So she
remained in the apartment and was taken away by the police.

As the city woke up that morning, men on their way to work,
shopkeepers opening their stores, and concierges awakened by
the noise and standing in their doorways to see what was
happening—all were struck by the sad sight of Jewish family
groups walking in silence, the father and mother carrying
bundles and packages and holding their children by the hand.
Slowly the preliminary collecting centers were filled with these

* *Fonds de Solidarité*, a clandestine organization devoted to the help
of the persecuted, from which later developed the UJRE.

disoriented people, and soon the shuttle of buses to the Vel d'Hiv would begin.

The instructions had said that every Jew listed was to be arrested regardless of the state of his health, and no exceptions were to be made on that count. So Mr. Epstein, who had thought his asthma would protect him, was arrested with the rest. Women on the point of giving birth, children with a temperature of 104 degrees, children with measles, scarlet fever, chicken pox, whooping cough, and mumps were all taken along. But the instructions had, for all their detail, overlooked one eventuality—what to do if the person to be arrested had just died. Statistically among so many thousand people it was a probability, and at least three cases, of which one was a baby, were recorded. Not having specific instructions, the police solved the question by wrapping the dead up in blankets and carrying them to the collecting centers too.

In the XVIII Arrondissement, Cité du Pont, Mr. Jablonka was so shocked by his arrest that he had a heart attack. For the police this was a real nuisance. What were they to do with the man who had collapsed on the street and lay there twisting with pain? Finally they carried him back to his apartment, stretched him out on his bed, and left him. Mr. Jablonka lived alone. He had a twelve-year-old daughter, but she was in the country. For two days he lay on his bed, and on July 18 he died in the empty apartment.

July 16 was Bernard Goura's fifteenth birthday. The arrival of the police at his house at five in the morning was an inauspicious beginning to the day, but in any case he was not expecting to celebrate much since his father, Israel Goura, had been arrested three days before. It was a serious business— Israel Goura was not only a Jew but a member of the Resistance too, being the printer for the clandestine movement *Solidarité*. So the police found only Bernard and his mother at their apartment. Mrs. Goura was completely overcome. The police told Bernard he could stay behind, since he had French nationality, but the boy refused to leave his mother. With Mrs. Goura leaning on her son's arm, the two of them went with the police.

In Nogent-sur-Marne, the policemen who came for Mrs.
Rozen were nice, half sympathizing with her and half
embarrassed by their position. In a small town like Nogent
everybody knew everyone else, and to arrest someone you know
is difficult. One of the policemen, Rombeau, was so disturbed
by this that he resigned from the police force a few days later.
This was to be the only resignation in the whole of the
operation.

In a hurry, Mrs. Rozen collected a few things to take with
her. Several times she asked the policemen where they were
taking her, but they could not say. They just told her that she
must hurry. Her son Jean was too young at seven to understand
anything. Hélène, who was thirteen, helped her mother. The
policemen hovered over them, telling them to hurry up. The
neighbors gathered around and looked on. Finally after an
hour they were ready to go. As she went out, Mrs. Rozen heard
one of her ultrapatriotic neighbors say, as she pocketed two
bottles of wine that were left in the kitchen, "Here's something
the Huns won't get."

Another lady, Mrs. Rado, also reported that the behavior of
the policemen who came to arrest her was gentle compared to
the biting hostility of one of her neighbors.

> The hairdresser downstairs brought the policeman up
> to my apartment. He told me that he had come for me
> and that he would be back in an hour and I was to get
> ready in the meantime. I could surely have run away in
> that time, but my husband had been in prison at
> Pithiviers for one year, I had no money, no false papers
> and three children to look after. When the policeman
> came back, he helped me put some things into a baby
> carriage while the neighbors looked on kindly and
> pityingly. Only one woman, who was a flowerseller and
> lived on the ground floor, turned on us with jeers and
> insults. The policeman told her off roundly, shouting
> that it could be her turn next. He really was rather nice.
> He took us to Japy.

The complacent calm with which the French police went
about the arrests, their relatively good behavior, and above all
their confidence-inspiring French uniforms had all been taken

into account by the Germans when they decided to leave the arrests to the French forces of law and order. In many cases the trick worked, and Jewish families who might have been horrified by the sight of a German uniform followed their French captors trustingly. But there also were a number of people who chose to take their own lives rather than be arrested.

In one building on Rue Trousseau in the XI Arrondissement, seven families were arrested at one stroke. The intensity of sadness and misery is difficult to imagine. Mrs. Cymering, whose husband was at Drancy, escaped through a window and climbed onto the roof of the building as soon as she heard them knock on the door. She stood there with her son on her arm while her "captors," as the policemen making arrests were referred to in the circulars, tried to calm her down, telling her not to do anything foolish. Down below in the street a crowd had gathered, among them her neighbors, who tried to reason with her. At 9:30 she jumped, taking her little boy with her. But some firemen had in the meantime spread nets so that neither she nor the child was hurt. They were to die later at Auschwitz with the rest of their Jewish neighbors.

Almost the same thing happened at 58 Rue Crozatier. In that building 110 people were arrested and one person threw himself down the stairwell. As far as we know, not one of those arrested ever returned. A few years ago there was a plaque commemorating this mass destruction of so many former inhabitants of the building. It has since been removed.

It is difficult to find out the exact number of suicides that took place that day. There is the episode of the doctor in Montreuil who killed all his family and then himself by injections. At the Fondation Curie a young intern named Mrs. Jadlowecz killed herself the same way when they came to arrest her a few days later, by injecting 10 ml. of chloroform into her veins. There were several cases of policemen saving Jews whom they found with a gas tube in their mouths when they came to arrest them. They were gassed at Auschwitz only a short time later.

Professor Abrami has calculated that there were 106 suicides and 24 deaths from sickness, two of them women in childbirth, during the course of the roundup. This is less than other estimates, and if one includes the deaths at the Vélodrome d'Hiver, where many of the untended sick died and there were several suicides, it seems a likely calculation.

In a contemporary report, one young man said: "So many suicides . . . they are impossible to count. In the XIV Arrondissement one woman threw her children out of the window, one after the other, and then jumped herself."

In an informer's letter found in the archives of the Gestapo there is the following: "One inspector and one officer, while talking to a concierge, told her that in some part of Paris (Belleville, I think) a mother had thrown her two children from the window and that there had been numerous suicides. This rumor was spread in many different parts of Paris."

In his memoirs, *Les Guichets du Louvre*, Roger Boussinot tells how he saw two policemen supporting a moaning woman on the Rue des Archives. Suddenly she tore herself away from them and ran toward a priest who was walking by. She asked for his help, she clung to his robes, but he went on walking without saying anything and with a look of terror on his face. When the woman followed him on her knees, he leaned against a wall looking as if he were going to be sick. The two policemen caught up with the woman and took her off. Roger Boussinot writes that he has always wondered whether that really was a genuine priest. From his behavior he guesses that it might well have been a Jew dressed up as a priest trying to escape arrest in this disguise.

As the news of arrests spread and people knew what was happening, more and more escapes were attempted, for the most part panicky and unplanned and seldom with much hope of success. People who succeeded in dodging the police barricades on the street never went very far from home; like moths trapped by the attraction of a flame, they could not keep away but returned to pick up some object from their apartment or simply to see what was happening. Every now and then policemen would block a road by standing in a row across it.

Then they would walk slowly down the street, dragging it like a net, allowing only those with no accent, no yellow star, and whose papers were in order with the word ARYAN stamped on them, to pass through. Some children escaped this dragnet by slipping into a corridor and hiding behind a door. But they too had no idea where to go and in the end got caught again. Boussinot writes that he tried to persuade two young fugitives to go with him, but they said they had to "ask Mother" first. Of course. And on the way they bumped into some policemen.

In spite of Mr. Linen's optimistic hopes, his house too was visited by the police. They came at seven in the morning, two policemen in uniform and a young PPF member. They told Mrs. Linen to collect some blankets and enough food for two days and took her and her son Nat with them.

On the Rue de la Bûcherie, Mrs. Soral and her three children —ten, eight, and six years old—were also arrested. Out on the street in front of their building, the inspector, who was alone and waiting for his colleagues to come out of another building, told Mrs. Soral to go and shop for some food at the store. "Don't go too far," he said. "I'll wait for you here by your things." It may have been a hint for her to escape, but Mrs. Soral either did not understand or did not dare to risk it. So she went as far as the bakery with her children, and they all returned with loaves of bread under their arms. The eldest boy remembers the incident clearly, but even had his mother taken the chance, there was little she could do with three children in a quarter swarming with policemen.

At roughly the same time the Pitkowicz apartment was invaded. The policemen there seemed ill at ease as they asked Mrs. Pitkowicz to follow them to the police station of the XVIII Arrondissement with her son and daughter. "You can take a few light things with you," they said.

As she collected some clothes together, Mrs. Pitkowicz felt glad that her husband had gone down to the cellar the night before. He at least would escape. The son, Louis, was also pleased at the thought that his father would be able to flee later when the police had finished with the area. Unfortunately the concierge went down to tell him that the police were in his apartment and his wife and two children were being taken away. So Mr. Pitkowicz came out to give himself up. No doubt he thought that he would be saving his family by this gesture. All his life Louis Pitkowicz has remembered the smile on his father's face at that moment. But his self-sacrifice was useless; the police took the whole family with them.

Leon Goldberg, who was the same age as Louis Pitkowicz, managed to escape and joined the Resistance, where he came across one of the Fingercwajg boys who had done the same thing.

Rue des Ecouffes that morning was a tragic sight. Just for the arrests at No. 22, forty policemen were needed. There were so many children in the building that it looked like an evacuation before a flood. There were the Goldzimmers with three children, the Najmanns with another three, the Sacanis with five, the Schlomènes with three, Mr. Wolfowski with one daughter, and Mr. Zamber with his daughter. The bus that took them all away looked like a school outing. And yet four Jewish families living at No. 22 were for some reason left alone. They could not think why they had been spared. Perhaps the index was not up to date for that building. At any rate, the oversight was corrected a few months later. Every single person living at 22 Rue des Ecouffes was eventually deported. And of the inhabitants of that building, which used to echo with the sound of children playing on every landing, not one returned.

Crowded in the small maid's room where they had hidden the night before, the Tselnicks heard the police arrive. They heard them knock on their apartment door. A neighbor going down the stairs on his way to work, and seeing the police in front of the Tselnick apartment, volunteered: "It is no use knocking there; they are on the fifth floor." So the police went up to the fifth floor, told Mr. Tselnick that they had found out he was there from his neighbor, and took him and his wife and three children away.

At eight o'clock there was a knock on the Sienickis' door. Though they had been locked up in their apartment with their sick daughter for many days now, they went to open without hesitating. They were expecting an Italian friend who had promised to come and take them somewhere safe. While waiting for him they had passed the time packing and changing Régine's bandages. But it was the police, telling them to hurry up and pack. They would not give Mrs. Sienicki time to finish tying the bandage even though she begged them on her knees and the little girl was crying. Through the open door the concierge watched the sickening scene with her arms folded across her chest. On the stairs the Sienickis met their neighbors who were also being arrested. Both families were taken to a preliminary collecting center which had been set up at the police station on the Avenue Parmentier.

The Pechners on the Rue Trévise knew at once what the knock on their door meant, but they had not for a moment suspected that their child of ten, who had French nationality, and Mrs. Pechner were threatened too. So only Mr. Pechner hurried out by the service stairs and hid on a small landing halfway between two floors. When Mrs. Pechner finally opened the door, the policemen told her that unless her husband gave himself up he risked being caught and shot. Before she and her child were taken away, Mrs. Pechner managed to get into the bathroom without rousing suspicion, and through a small window which opened onto the landing her husband was on, she signaled to him that she and the child were going. A heartrending deaf and dumb dialogue followed. Mr. Pechner wanted to come out so he would not be separated from his family, but with her hands Mrs. Pechner told him not to. Then, seeing him hesitate, she forced the issue by letting the policemen take her away. But before leaving she suddenly opened a window and, shouting so the whole quarter could hear her, warned others to get away while there was time. At No. 13 Mr. Presburger heard her shout and escaped. But for Mrs. Pechner, he would have been arrested.

When the police came for Mrs. Abramzyk, they found her alone with her six-year-old son. She wept and begged to be spared. The policemen were embarrassed and moved and

finally gave her a chance to escape. "All right, don't worry,"
they told her. "Get ready, and we will come back for you in an
hour." They had hardly turned their backs when she flew down
the stairs dragging the child behind her. But the concierge had
locked the entrance gate, and nothing, neither tears nor shouts,
would persuade her to unlock it. Neither Mrs. Abramzyk nor
her little boy ever returned. By the summer of 1944 the
concierge understood that they would not come back, so she
took down Marshal Pétain's portrait from her sideboard. It was
the one in which he posed in a three-piece suit with a large dog.

By 11 A.M. the arrests were almost completed. From 11 to
4:30 in the afternoon, the police kept returning to apartments
they had found empty on their first round. They also combed
the streets for runaway Jews, and it was not an uncommon sight
to see these poor disoriented fugitives wandering aimlessly, not
knowing where to go but hoping they would find some means
of escape, being arrested right on the street. A pamphlet of the
time says:

> There are thousands of fugitives. They are hiding with
> friends and neighbors or in cellars. Whole families are
> wandering the streets with their children, sleeping where
> they can at night. From the beginning the French
> population has shown considerable sympathy for these
> unfortunate people. The police continues to try to catch
> up with them, going to their apartments time and time
> again. In some cases the apartments have been sealed from
> the outside. It is the children whose parents have escaped
> who are in the greatest danger.

The next move was to launch the fleet of buses on the dismal
shuttle between the collecting centers in the city and the Vel
d'Hiv, where families with children were to be kept, and
Drancy, which had been prepared for the adults without
children. As the last of the newly arrested Jewish families were
making their way on foot under police escort to the various
schools, police stations, and gymnasiums like Japy, which had
been made into preliminary collecting centers, the first
busloads began moving toward the next stage in the operation.
From 5 A.M. on, Parisians had been shocked and sickened by

the sight of family after family walking sadly along, escorted
by policemen. Louis Pitkowicz told us his family's experiences:

> From our house we walked to the police station of the
> IV Arrondissement. There were four of us—my father,
> mother, my eight-year-old sister, and myself. We were
> carrying our suitcases, two or three hastily packed parcels,
> some bundles, and some blankets. We must have looked
> like emigrants. But we all were wearing a yellow star, and
> passersby realized immediately what that meant. As I
> remember, they would look at us with pity in their eyes.

Mrs. Rado too remembers that sad trek through the streets:

> I had taken my youngest baby's carriage and had piled
> some clothes and a couple of saucepans on it, thinking
> that I would have to prepare food for the children. I
> pushed the carriage from our house in the Rue du
> Faubourg Saint-Antoine to Japy, while the children clung
> to my skirts, frightened and feeling ashamed of our police
> escort. We each had a yellow star on. People stared at us,
> but I could not make out what they were thinking. Their
> faces seemed blank and indifferent. At Place Voltaire
> there was a small crowd, and one woman started shouting:
> "I'm glad! I'm glad! Let them all go to the devil!" But
> she was the only one. The children clung to me tighter.
> As we passed the group, a man turned to the woman who
> had shouted and said, "It'll be our turn next. Poor
> things." She blushed and walked away. The policemen
> told us to walk faster.

In the arrondissements where people had been arrested by
the thousand, one could sense a heavy atmosphere of terror
mixed with unbelief. Where the roundup had affected only a
small proportion of the people, news of what was happening
did not travel so quickly, though even there it spread steadily.
Men going to work, women standing in the long lines
beginning to form in front of the food stores would tell each
other: "They're arresting the Jews. The women and children
too." Many had actually witnessed the departure of a whole
family in tears, or children and parents saying goodbye to each
other, or a suicide. But even by midday no one had an inkling
yet of the vast scale of the operation.

BETRAYAL AT THE VEL D'HIV

At noon the policemen and guards waiting for their relief had a bite to eat at their posts while the inspectors and officers went off to nearby restaurants.

The tone of the police toward the Jews changed completely as soon as they were assembled in the collecting centers. Crowded together with their assorted bundles of luggage and their crying children, they no longer were citizens who had to be persuaded to leave their homes without a fuss, but simply prisoners. Mrs. Rado recalls:

> As soon as we had all got onto the bus, a police officer shouted to the driver and the policemen accompanying us—though the message was intended mainly for us—"If anyone so much as moves or tries to escape, use your guns."
>
> That made me shiver. Being a woman with three small children, I was scared. We had spent most of the day at Japy, and they were now taking us out to the Vélodrome d'Hiver.

Mrs. Mathey Jonais, a nurse who was among the first to come and help as soon as she heard about the arrests, tells of her conversations with the guards at Japy gymnasium. They were mostly very young men from the provinces, mainly Brittany. A few older ones, prisoners of war, had enlisted with the mobile guard in order to get repatriation. Almost all of them said that they would never have joined the mobile guard if they had known they would be given this kind of duty. They admitted that their orders were to shoot if necessary.

"Our instructions are strict," one said. "We are to shoot into the crowd at the first attempt to escape. That is what the machineguns are for. There is to be no doubt about what they are to expect if they try to make a move or decide to resist. They are going to be deported to the salt mines in Silesia."

At Saint-Ouen there was a good haul of Jews, with over six hundred persons arrested by thirty-two inspectors and policemen. They were simple people, mostly dealers in second-hand goods at the local flea market. Since this was vacation time, they were put into the school buildings which had been taken over as a collecting center. For the police this was doubly

convenient, since the police station adjoined the school, and
they could keep an eye on the anxious, milling crowd of
prisoners in the vast schoolyard from the police station
windows. Nearly every one of those six hundred people was to
be exterminated. (In 1965 a commemorative plaque was placed
in the school in their honor, but the text of the plaque
distorted the facts, stating that the six hundred victims had
been arrested by "German occupation troops" when in fact it
had been the Paris police who had done so.)

Everywhere in the collecting centers the Jewish prisoners
waited, worried and with no idea what would be happening to
them. They would count each other in the hope that someone
might have been able to escape. Soon the children began to
complain that they were hungry. By now the collecting centers
were too full to be bearable, and policemen were still bringing
newly arrested people. The commissioner was sweating over his
first report on the operation.

At the police station of the V Arrondissement, near the
Pantheon, where the Goldenzwags had been taken, one woman
was having a fit of hysterics, lying on the ground while spasms
shook her whole body. Around her people screamed and
shouted. Mrs. Soral and her three children were brought from
the Rue de la Bûcherie to this same station. As soon as she saw
the other prisoners, Mrs. Soral realized that something terrible
was going to happen. This was not just a matter of checking
identity papers.

She wished she had taken advantage of the inspector's
kindness when he let her go and do some shopping even though
she knew that with her two youngest children it would have
been impossible to find somewhere to hide. The eldest, Jean,
was ten years old. Standing in the confusion of the collecting
center, she came to a hard decision. Taking the boy aside, she
explained to him what she wanted him to do, and then, as a
group of new prisoners crowded into the door, she pushed him
into the general muddle and watched him work his way out
onto the steps in front of the police station. No one noticed him
as he hurried off down the Rue Soufflot.

Similarly Mrs. Landau managed to slip out of the town hall in the X Arrondissement. She asked for permission to go to the toilets, and then, hiding her yellow star underneath the shoulder strap of her handbag, she walked down some stairs and out into the street.

Mrs. Lichtein and her daughter were taken to a garage on the Rue des Pyrénées which had been taken over by the police. All around there were cars covered with tarpaulins waiting for the end of the war and the end of gasoline rationing. People sat on the running boards, which no car was without in those days. There was only one toilet, and it was outside in a courtyard. Anyone who wanted to use it had to ask permission and would be accompanied by a policeman. In spite of this, one of the women prisoners managed to vanish on the way. So three policemen were ordered to accompany prisoners to the courtyard instead of one. There was the added discomfort of noise; the smallest sound was magnified and echoed under the corrugated iron garage roof. The police added to the already deafening racket by shouting at the tops of their lungs.

"But why do you yell like this?" asked Mrs. Lichtein.

"I have to keep order," a brigadier replied.

From the preliminary collecting centers buses took loads of prisoners to the Vel d'Hiv. Vehicles of every size and make had been requisitioned for the job, and all over Paris one could see this ill-assorted fleet shuttling briskly with its cargo of anxious human beings.

A number of small Renaults belonging to the police rushed in all directions. They had been put at the disposal of the police stations in preparation for Bastille Day on July 14. Apart from the fact that originally Operation Spring Wind had been scheduled for that day, there was some fear that patriotic demonstrations might be staged in the streets. There was an escort of six motorcycles, which were distributed between the IX, X, XI, XVIII, XIX, and XX arrondissements. Ten large police trucks were also used. Four were long Renaults with benches inside, the rest huge Citroens, high-slung and painted midnight blue, opaque and shiny in patches.

But the greater part of the transport fleet was made up of
TCRP buses. There were fifty of them divided between the
arrondissements—Renault buses with central aisles, outside
platforms, and a separate section with leather upholstered seats
for first class passengers. They can still be seen in Paris and
some of the suburbs. Painted off-white and green, with their
round headlights, their squared fenders, and the rectangular
rear-view mirrors sticking out at each side, they look like giant
friendly dogs. Laden with prisoners, they would groan and
creak at every turn while the driver in his flat cap struggled
with the large horizontal steering wheel, hand over hand. On
the outside platforms at the back, policemen stood among the
heaps of ragged bundles. Looking out of the windows with the
sun beating down on their faces were children, their fists and
noses flattened against the glass, their eyes wide open. Even on
this journey they had taken their accustomed places by the
windows as if on an outing and stared out.

Chapter 4

Inferno at the Vel d'Hiv

Outside the Vélodrome d'Hiver, the Rue Nelaton resembled a bus terminal that day. Hundreds of buses jammed with people drew up to the gates all through the day. The drivers waited patiently, perched on their seats while their passengers got off, looking no different from ordinary drivers bringing busloads of sports fans. As soon as one bus was empty and drove away, another would draw up in its place. This rhythm was kept up from morning till night without a break.

Left on the sidewalk, the Jews stood in a daze, their bundles and their children cluttered around them. The families brought to the Rue Nelaton were all families "with children." They were guided and pushed toward the entrance by the police, who were anxious to keep the traffic moving. Inside the swinging doors there were more policemen, an armed patrol keeping watch on the entrance passage. There were guards and policemen on duty everywhere—the expression on their faces forbidding. The guards carried carbines slung over one shoulder and across their backs while the policemen stood with their thumbs tucked into their waistbands. After walking through the doors and the entrance passage, the new arrivals went through another swinging door and came out into the enormous arena of the Vélodrome d'Hiver, taking their first look at the prison which for some time would be their world.

At the beginning the first to come into the vast empty stadium hesitated, not knowing what to do exactly, and stayed near the door. But very soon the whole floor space was filled like a cattle pen. And more buses delivered new loads every ten minutes. By eight o'clock the space inside the cycling track was surging with people. Newcomers were now forced up onto the tiers.

Outside it was a bright summer's day. Inside, under the gigantic glass roof—painted blue for civil defense purposes— a dingy half-light cast a pale greenish hue over everything. Cones of yellow light fell from the electric light bulbs and small projectors which hung from the tangle of girders and roof beams on the ends of long metal rods. At ground level, the two kinds of lighting blended into a wan brightness in which the dust, raised by the ceaseless shifting of the crowds, forever floated. Above, the darkness deepened and turned into impenetrable black as night fell. It took some time for one's eyes to adjust to this slightly spectral light which emphasized the sadness on tired faces, the rings around hollow eyes, and features strained by pain and exhaustion. None of these people knew what was in store for them or even how long they were going to stay here. They settled themselves as best they could. There were about 7,000 of them, of which 4,051 were children. The first impression one got on emerging into this chaotic scene was of being among countless millions.

Normally, when every row in every tier was booked, the Vélodrome d'Hiver would seat fifteen thousand spectators. But this would be only for the length of one sports event. Now whole families, with their belongings and their sick stretched out on the ground around them, had to try and breathe, sleep —in short, live in these cramped conditions. No wonder the place seemed full to overflowing. One thing that all the eyewitness reports agree on is that there was hardly room to move and people were even trodden underfoot. Figures for the number of prisoners who lived through those seven days in the Vélodrome d'Hiver are wildly contradictory. But the very fact of their exaggeration suggests the deep impression made on those witnesses by the horror of so many people crushed together. A contemporary report says:

The Vélodrome d'Hiver must have held about 12,000 persons on the first day. No preparation had been made for them, not even a provision of straw. The prisoners either settled on the benches or sat on the ground. There was no room for them to stretch out. At night the children slept on the floor of the arena. The adults had no choice but to go on sitting on the benches.

One of the prisoners recalls:

. . . and they took us to the Vélodrome d'Hiver. There were thousands of people there already, and we had some trouble finding room to sit. At night we had to curl up tight in order to sleep, and many people screamed in their sleep. It was horrible.

Dr. Didier-Hesse describes his impressions:

When I got there, I was horrified. Why? Because this cycling track, which I had known as a sports stadium, was now absolutely packed with people. What intensified the feeling of overcrowding was that not only every single seat and folding chair was occupied, as at a full house, but the track itself too and the floor of the arena were covered with people lying down.

What would have happened had things gone according to plan? The limit for Drancy had been set at 6,000 persons; beyond that number all prisoners were to be sent to the Vélodrome d'Hiver. Which means that the authorities intended to pack 24,000 into this area. Already, with 7,000 it was overcrowded.

The first day was a day of madness. No food was provided. The people had brought their own provisions—"for two days" was what they had been told. They picked at the kind of picnic food that requires no dishes or cooking. But there was no water to drink and no milk for the children. In no time the air became unbreathable, stinking and thick with dust. One had to shout to make oneself heard. Eyes smarted and throats were parched dry. One of the doctors who got into the stadium reports: "The air was so thick with dust that at times it was impossible to breathe. This also brought on a regular epidemic of conjunctivitis."

For years now, and increasingly since the beginning of the
war, rumors had been spreading from central Europe about
persecutions too horrible to be believed. (Can anyone who has
not experienced them imagine such things?) But the people
who were now in the Vélodrome d'Hiver had come to France
seeking asylum—to France because it was the land of freedom,
of equal rights and respect for human life. These rumors could
never threaten them.   On July 16, 1942, however, the brutal
truth was glimpsed. It was accepted with reluctance. No doubt
one of the reasons it took so long to penetrate was the fact that
the policemen who had made the arrests were French
policemen. But though at first the reality of their situation was
only confusedly grasped, there was no doubt now in anyone's
mind that they had entered a world of disaster. All around
them the forces of law and order kept the stadium sealed off
from the outside world. Mrs. Dorag says: "There were
policemen at every exit, and they seemed indifferent and
unmoved."

For the policemen the most unpleasant part of the business,
the arrests, was over. The die was cast. As far as the policemen
were concerned, it was no longer their responsibility. It was the
destiny of these poor people. The attitude of the police was to
become more and more indifferent, more cynical and brutal. In
this stadium the fate of 7,000 people had been decided, and the
eighty armed guards made sure that there was no relenting.
The gradual hardening in the attitude of the police and the
terrible conditions of their prison made it clear to the prisoners
that whatever the fate in store for them, it would be hateful.
Any illusions, any fragments of hope that might have subsisted
in the hearts of these uprooted Jews, crumbled at the touch of
reality.

As soon as they realized that they were trapped, many gave
way to despair. One doctor who worked there told us: "I shall
always remember one old grandmother sitting on a folding
chair, her hands resting on the embroidered apron covering her
knees. She did not move: she would not speak though I
addressed her in several languages. It is a haunting picture—

she seemed a personification of the silent pain and crushing inevitability of her fate."

For others, their despair broke out in fits of hysteria. They screamed and lost all self-control. Dr. Didier-Hesse remembers one family in particular: "The father, about forty years old, just sat hugging his knees, his hands limp, his expression lost. His Polish wife wrung her hands and moaned, while the daughter, a child not more than eight years old, hung on to her mother trying to kiss her and whispering words of comfort to her in French."

At times there were waves of mass hysteria. For instance, a round of applause suddenly crackled, starting in a dim corner of a stand and spreading throughout the immense stadium. For no reason people clapped their hands and looked at each other with tears in their eyes, their nerves breaking. After a few minutes and just as suddenly, the clapping died out. For a second there was a hush of complete silence, and then the continuous hum of background noises started up again. At other times there would be sudden shouts and cries of: "Set us free! Set us free!"

Right from the first day, the Cathala sisters, who were sent by the organization called *Solidarité* to take stock of the situation, and who did manage to penetrate into the stadium, predicted that "these people will go out of their minds." They were not far wrong. The report mentioned earlier also cites the case of one young woman who was driven insane and could not stop screaming. One doctor congratulates himself for having been able to send back at least one poor madwoman and her victim, a small boy she was beating to death, battering his head with a bottle.

Then there was the little boy who would not let go of the skirts of a Red Cross nurse, Mathey Jonais, but clung to her screaming and making faces. "His mother told me that he was an abnormal child. It had been tragic. She had given thanks to God when the baby's life had been saved at birth. But later, when the boy's abnormality began to show, she realized that it was a curse. Meanwhile the child was hungry, and he howled just like a wolf on the verge of starvation."

One woman, either because she was insane or because she wanted to take her life, threw herself on the ground and leaning on her arms banged her head on the cement floor. Bystanders watched her for a while. Then she was overpowered and taken to the center of the arena. A medical report reads: "We had to tie down the insane, men and women, to stretchers and hide them from the rest of the crowd. Our orders were to treat them as shams."

One woman slashed her wrists with the splinters of a broken mirror. By the time someone noticed what she had done, she had fainted from loss of blood. A tourniquet was applied, and she regained consciousness, but realizing where she was, she began to scream. They had to tie her down to a stretcher. Whether the motive was madness, a cool appraisal of the situation, or despair, there were many attempted suicides.

Coming out of the toilet, an unspeakable mess of filth used by thousands of prisoners, Mrs. Toukarski was so overcome that she decided she could not endure it any longer and quietly started climbing over the parapet, intending to throw herself down, while her young daughter watched her. A cousin held her back just in time.

In all there were about thirty attempted suicides, ten of them successful. For the most part people threw themselves from the topmost tier into the arena. They would fall onto the track below while the crowd backed away screaming. They were picked up, wounded, gasping, dead or dying.

One social worker wrote to her mother: "They fling themselves at us and beg us to put them out of their misery. 'Kill us. Only please don't leave us here.' Or 'For God's sake, give me an injection. I want to die.' " Another social worker, Mrs. Tavernier, remembers: "One of the prisoners standing next to me suddenly started to shake me by the shoulders quite roughly, at the same time screaming, 'Why don't you and the rest of your kind get on with it and kill us? Kill us! Aren't you ashamed?' Then he stopped and his arms fell to his sides again."

On the third day a whole delegation of mothers followed by their scampering children went up to one of the guards and calmly asked to be killed there and then, with their children, rather than be left to live in that confinement. The guards sneered. These people were exaggerating.

The children too reacted—in their own way. Talking of the Warsaw ghetto, one writer says: "The worst, the saddest and most unforgivable crime, was that before they took the children's lives they stole their innocence." At the Vélodrome d'Hiver 4,051 children began to lose their innocence. It did not happen immediately, but then one does not age in a second.

André Baur, one of the directors of the UGIF, says that he was surprised and overwhelmed to see "children running about in the center of the arena teasing the guards, whose orders were to chase them back onto the tiers."

Miss Monod, who rushed to the scene at the first hint of the roundup, describes the striking contrast between the children playing on the track and their parents sunk in utter despair. The sadness of the adults was probably what most affected the children. They tried to cheer and comfort their parents with little loving gestures, changing roles with them in this unnatural situation.

If a child cannot understand the meaning of despair, one emotion that is familiar and almost constant in him is wonder. These children could not understand what had happened. There they were, they and their parents, punished and put into prison. Why? Dr. Weill-Hallé is haunted by one memory: "I shall never forget one little girl. She was sick. With her eyes glued to my face, she was begging me to ask the soldiers to let her go. She had been a good girl all year; surely she didn't deserve to be put in prison."

What the doctor did not know is that this was exactly the reaction of the children in Belzec that same spring and summer. According to one witness, Rudolf Reder, as they entered the gas chambers, the first to go in whimpered: "Mother, it's dark, it's so dark, and I was being so good."

Only one photograph taken of the Vélodrome d'Hiver at that time survives. It has been printed often. It shows people standing in crowds on the central part of the arena or squatting

along the cycling track. Above all one notices in the center of
the picture a gendarme crossing the track briskly. Kepi,
leggings, jodphurs, and crossbelt—clearly a French uniform.
His air is busy and military, but no French policeman should
have had any business here.

   This snapshot is worth a closer look. No one knows who took
it, but it bears witness today to what happened. One woman
seems to be looking into the camera; she is pregnant, obviously
so. On the slope of the track there are people sitting, knees bent
and their heads buried in their hands. Others are stretched out
on their sides or curled up with their heads resting on some
package. In the foreground is a suitcase. Further off an old
woman with her hair pulled back off her forehead seems to be
rocking herself. One recognizes the women's fashions of the
time: hair in coils, turbans, boleros, leg of mutton sleeves, and
the wide, shiny patent leather belts. In the center of the picture
the tragic face of a child looks out. Behind him sit two women
leaning against each other. Nearby are two sisters, both of them
darkhaired, tucked into one blanket.

   Despite the desperate conditions, there were among the
uprooted thousands who had that morning begun their long
journey toward death many whose stubborn will to survive was
only intensified by the chaos in the Vel d'Hiv. And some rose
even to the culmination of courage and love which consists of
separating oneself from a favorite child in order that it might
escape and live. Mrs. Lichtein, for example, could not forgive
herself for falling asleep that night and being surprised by the
police. At least her daughter should not suffer through her
weakness. So she went with the little girl as near as she could to
the scuffle and agitation around the entrance gates and
encouraged her to try and get out onto the Rue Nelaton. As the
little girl wound her way between the guards, one of them
called her back. She replied that she had not been inside the
Vel d'Hiv but had only come to get some news of her family.
And so she slipped away.

   The Pitkowiczes, whose father had thought he could save
them by giving himself up, were also in the Vélodrome d'Hiver.

Here in the harsh reality of their prison they suddenly understood that their hopes had been wishful dreams. Throughout the morning they wandered up and down that mad circus trying to glean some scrap of definite information, but every hint that they were given only confirmed their suspicions—their situation was really serious. Louis Pitkowicz, who was fourteen years old, decided he had to get out. When he told his parents, they both reacted strongly, his father approving his plan while his mother was against it. It troubled her to think of him alone in Paris. He was too young. There would be no one to look after him. But in the end Mrs. Pitkowicz gave way and agreed to let him go. Though the thought must have crossed their minds, neither Louis nor his parents knew that when they said goodbye, this would be for the last time. They would never see each other again.

Mrs. Linen's reaction was much quicker than that of the Pitkowiczes. When the police came for her and her son Nat, she instinctively threw a coat over her son's shoulders to hide his yellow star. Her fears only increased as they rattled toward the Vel d'Hiv in the bus, and in the confusion of being unloaded and shepherded toward the entrance gates she pushed her son away from the crowd, whispering, "Quick, hurry and get away." Nat himself has told us how, finding himself on the pavement with only the protection of his coat which hid his star, he walked away from the Vel d'Hiv, going where the road took him. He could see the Seine not far ahead. Near the gates he passed a woman looking out from inside the stadium. It was Marianne Lichtein. Having just watched her daughter slip out, she was waiting for a suitable opportunity to wander off herself.

Ida Nussbaum was fiercely regretting having refused her concierge's offer to look after her little son. It had been a nightmarish vigil before the police came, but now that she saw what was going on in the Vel d'Hiv she realized that she could rely on no one to save her. All her former hopes had been illusions. The guards would not hesitate to take children away from their mothers, and if they did leave them together it would be so that they might be killed at the same time. She decided that she must try to save herself and her baby. Not knowing precisely what she would do but filled with determination, she started to go downstairs with her son Bernard in her arms. She was fighting her way against a stream of newcomers carrying their bundles up the stairs. At each landing the guards asked her where she was going. She improvised: "With the baby on my arm I couldn't take all my things up at once. I left a few packages downstairs. I want to go and get them." The guards on duty in the midst of this chaos allowed her to go down, and she got as far as the entrance gates. There are witnesses' accounts of guards who were seen actually weeping while working at the Vel d'Hiv. So many different sources say this that it must be credited. But it is only fair to record that in general the attitude of the police was "icy and indifferent," as Dr. Vilenski, one of the general practitioners who came to help at the Vel d'Hiv on the 16th, summed it up.

Obstinately Ida Nussbaum waited in the shadows. Then, sliding forward unobtrusively, she stood near one of the policemen guarding the entrance. Just two yards away was the street and freedom. On the other side of the street, a lady stood in the doorway of a building watching the flood of people going into the stadium. Her eyes met those of Ida Nussbaum. If only she could get as far as that doorway, she would be safe. All she had to do was cross the road. Little by little, the young mother moved forward. It seemed an eternity. Each step brought her nearer to safety. The lady across the street did not take her eyes off her for a second. All around the hubbub of police and prisoners was continuing as before. Ida Nussbaum was within two yards of the lady's doorway when a hand fell on her shoulder. She almost choked as her hopes collapsed.

"What are you doing here?"

Her reply was prompt: "It is more than an hour since they said they would give us food. I have nothing for my baby, and I was coming to get something for him to eat."

The French lady's eyes suddenly filled with tears, and she brought some bread and biscuits for the boy. The policeman

took Mrs. Nussbaum by the arm and led her back to the
entrance of the Vel d'Hiv, telling her that she was to go inside.

"Please, please let me stay outside just a little longer. My
baby needs fresh air—one can hardly breathe inside. Also I am
waiting for my mother and the rest of my family. Please let me
stay."

All around the giddy procession of buses and prisoners laden
with bundles was continuing without interruption. Soon Ida
Nussbaum's relatives appeared, some cousins, an uncle, and an
aunt. It was to be their last meeting. Seeing Ida leaning against
the wall, they asked her what she was doing.

"Nothing. They let me air my baby for a while." Then in a
whisper, "I'm trying to get away. For Bernard's sake."

For three hours she was to stay there with the baby on her
arm, watching for a chance to escape. Suddenly there it was—
the changing of the guard at lunchtime. Every detail of those
few minutes is indelibly impressed on her memory:

> I was getting so tired I began thinking of giving up.
> Bernard was clutching me round the neck and kept
> saying: "Let's go upstairs, Mommy. I want my Teddy.
> Let's go upstairs." But then everything changed. The
> guards were gathering into a group; a bus arrived
> bringing more policemen. It was midday and they were
> changing shifts. The new policemen were shaking hands
> with the men they were replacing, and no one was paying
> any attention to me. I slid along the wall holding the
> baby tight against me so that he hid my yellow star. My
> heart was beating and my mouth was dry. I walked
> straight ahead. A policeman caught up with me and
> shouted: "Move along, you're not allowed to stand
> around here. Move on!" I walked on without turning
> around, my heart drumming so hard I felt it was going
> to burst. I still don't know if the policeman did that on
> purpose, pretending not to notice that I was escaping, or
> whether I was lucky and really managed to escape on my
> own.

As the Vel d'Hiv was filling up, arrests continued to be made
elsewhere in France and Western Europe. There were
roundups in Bordeaux, Tours, Dijon, Saint-Malo, Nantes, and

La Baule. At Bordeaux, like Paris, the French police were to
make the arrests, which had been scheduled at first for July 13
or 14. Arrangements had been made for a convoy to leave
Bordeaux directly for Auschwitz on July 15. Then it turned
out that in the whole area there were only 150 alien Jews, and
Roethke canceled the convoy. Excusing himself before
Eichmann, Roethke said quite bluntly: "I had very little time
and could not find enough Jews to make up the number for a
convoy." Eichmann was nevertheless displeased. On July 14 he
telephoned Roethke. (We have a record of this call as Roethke
made a memo of it in duplicate, sending one copy to
Dannecker, for his information, and putting the other in the
file called "Transportation of the Jews.")

> The SS Obersturmbannfuehrer (Eichmann) stressed
> that it was a question of prestige and that the negotiations
> with the Ministry of Transport in Germany had been
> long and difficult before permission had been finally
> granted for the convoys and now Paris was canceling one
> of the trains. This had never happened before, and the
> incident was to be regretted. Eichmann was not anxious
> to report what happened to SS Gruppenfuehrer Muller
> because he would be blamed himself, but he was
> wondering if it were not better to drop France altogether
> as an evacuating territory.
> I asked him to do nothing, explaining that the
> cancellation of that train had not been the fault of my
> office. Furthermore Section IV J of the Gestapo had not
> realized that there were only 150 alien Jews in Bordeaux
> until it was too late. As soon as the figure came through,
> I telephoned the Central Security Office in Germany. The
> rest of the convoys would leave France on schedule.

This whole exchange is so typical that one can imagine it as
part of one of the usual melodramatic films about the German
occupation. Nothing is left out: the two Nazi officers in uniform
at either end of the Berlin-Paris telephone line, their high
peaked caps decorated with eagles, one shouting his
disapproval, exploding with anger and then coyly wondering
whether he should not drop France altogether; the other
humbly excusing himself and begging his boss not to do

anything. *"Ja wohl, mein Obersturmbannführer."* They both knew what was meant by "evacuation" in this context. It meant the treatment, the final solution.

So on the morning of the sixteenth some ninety alien Jews, all of them poor, walked across Bordeaux with their bundles to go to the Saint-Jean Station. With them were the policemen who had arrested them.

Similar scenes were taking place in the whole of provincial France. At Bordeaux and at Rennes the French police went to the houses to make the arrests. In the other towns, Rouen, Châlons, Dijon, Nantes, Saint-Malo, La Baule, it was the German gendarmerie who for some reason undertook the job. And outside France Operation Spring Wind was taking place in the whole of Western Europe. In Holland the Commission for Repatriation of the Dutch Government summarized the operation as follows in a report: "July, 1942. The round up. Jews are being dragged from their houses, collected at the Zentralchelle für Judische Auswanderung, and transported to Westerbork." In her hiding place, Anne Franck was to wait until March, 1944, but Operation Spring Wind rustled past her door.

In Belgium too:

> The month of July saw the beginning of a tragic series of systematic mass roundups which were the first step on the route to the extermination camps. Suddenly, in the night, whole quarters were cordoned off and a whole army of SS headed by Gestapo members hunted out the Jews, going into each house, checking the papers of every person they came across, and interrogating householders about the whereabouts of Jews in their buildings. Amid scenes of painful emotion men, women, children, and old people were torn from their beds and, regardless of their sobs and cries, heaped into trucks that had been brought for the purpose.

This extract comes from a report of the Belgian government. It goes on to say:

> The synchronization was perfect . . . whether one turns to Eastern Europe or to the West. It is interesting

to note at this point that the deportation of Jews from
Belgium and Western Europe generally coincided almost
exactly with the Master of the German Reich's decision
to wipe out the ghettos of Eastern Europe. The mass
deportations from Belgium date from July 22, while those
from Warsaw date from the same month, July, of that
year.

At around three o'clock in the afternoon Louis Pitkowicz
edged his way right up to the entrance gates of the stadium,
waiting to try his luck and get away. There was a double row of
guards, and the regular beat of the patrol on the Rue Nelaton
was interrupted only at each changing of the guard for a very
brief period. But Louis was lucky. Soon after he reached the
gates there was a disturbance which gave him his chance to run
away. A group of women had crowded around the policemen at
the gates begging them for water.

"Our children are dying of thirst. Can't you do something?"

More women joined them, and soon there were about a
hundred or more. Children were crying and howling, hanging
onto their mothers' skirts. They pleaded more urgently but to
no effect. The guards, glowering from under their helmets,
turned about and tried to hold back the wave of angry women
with their rifles.

"Look, there's an open grocery!"

In one surge they all pushed and struggled forward, bumping
into the guards, holding onto them and overwhelming them
completely. Driven by their maternal instinct, they did not
even try to escape, they merely wanted water for their thirsty
children. They raced across the road to the open shop. Though
for a moment there was the wildest confusion, not one of the
women got away. They all returned under escort of the guards
but triumphantly clutching bottles.

Louis took his chance and, tearing off his yellow star with one
quick movement, he rolled it into a tight ball in his fist and
stuck his hand in his pocket. He mingled in the crowd of
Jewish women and police for a moment, then walked away as
if he were a local boy who had been caught up in the muddle

because he happened to be there at that time. He walked with beating heart into the narrow Rue Nocard, which led to the Seine—the same road Nat Linen had looked down a short while before. There was a mobile guard at the bottom of the road, marching up and down with a gun on his shoulder, but Louis walked past him without faltering.

After the escape of her daughter, Mrs. Lichtein continued to hang about the entrance. She had noticed Nat Linen's escape and made several attempts to get away herself, but every time the guards caught her at it. "Get inside if you don't want to be locked up," one of them shouted. She went up to another of the guards and pleaded: "Let me go. What difference does it make to you, one prisoner more or less?" The policeman shrugged his shoulders, but it seemed to her that he might be moved. "Get inside, go on inside," he said, but as he said it he turned away, almost as if he were ready to overlook her next move. Mrs. Lichtein felt encouraged and decided not to take notice of him but walk away since no one else seemed to be paying any attention to her. She walked up the street mechanically and utterly numb. She passed a doorway crowded with women looking out.

"Please let me in. Please hide me."

"No, no, no one is allowed in here. Don't stand there, go away."

Their faces were white and opaque with fear. But luckily there happened to be a street sweeper standing nearby, with his broom and cart, wearing the municipal uniform. He smiled at her. Nothing more. But that smile probably saved the panic-stricken woman. At least one person was on her side. She whispered to him to stay near her and then walked on, reassured and encouraged and somehow feeling protected by the sound of his footsteps behind her. When she finally arrived at the elevated railway, having safely crossed an army of gendarmes with no difficulty, she summoned her courage and turned to look back at the street sweeper. He was smiling and lifted his hand briefly as if to say good luck.

In the city the arrests were slowing down, but the police were still chasing out fugitives.

One hour after Mrs. Soral's little boy had escaped from the police station on the Rue Soufflot, his absence was noticed. The police reacted as if some homicidal maniac had got loose. Two inspectors were immediately dispatched to Mrs. Soral's house in the hope that the boy might simply have walked home. His mother waited tensely for their return. In fact, the police had guessed right. Like a frightened animal not knowing where to turn, the boy had gone home, but the concierge had quietly led him away from the house. The concierges of Paris played vital roles in the lives and sometimes deaths of the Jews that day. Mrs. Soral was relieved to see the two inspectors return empty-handed and grumpy. Her son was safe.

Dr. Robineau remembers another escape from the Vel d'Hiv:

> The entrances to the stadium were watched by the French police, who zealously carried out their duty to prevent any escapes with no thought for the prisoners themselves. I had finished my work with the sick and came away revolted by what I had seen and worn out. On the platform of the metro station I noticed a little man whom I recognized as one of the prisoners I had examined in the Vel d'Hiv a little while before. He had been suffering from acute hernia, which I managed to relieve a little. Seeing his instinctive start back when we exchanged glances, I smiled. He winked back at me. In his hand he carried a small case which no doubt contained all that he considered precious. I have often wondered how he was able to find his way out of that well-guarded inferno.

One young mother and her son were actually helped out of the Vel d'Hiv by a policeman named Louis Petitjean. He had been so overcome with remorse after arresting them that he had gone to the Vel d'Hiv to rescue them.*

* For documentation of the incident see *Nouveau Candide*, No. 317 (5/22/1967).

Chapter 5

The News Spreads

The rumors which had for some days been circulating through the city took substance in the early hours of the morning of July 16 and became fact as the sinister round of arrests began to be made. Then, as prisoners were marched to the local centers and driven off to the Vélodrome d'Hiver and Drancy, the news shook the whole of Paris, its echoes reaching the furthest corners of the capital.

The news affected people at every level. It was the only subject of conversation in shops, at café tables, at work, in offices. Everyone was worried about friends or relatives. One question at least could be answered immediately—where all these people were. The Vélodrome d'Hiver was mentioned again and again. Some people had actually been there and seen the inside of the sports arena in its new guise as a prison. Though the Dantesque scenes they described seemed hardly credible, the sound of people weeping could be heard in the streets around the stadium.

On the Rue du Docteur-Finlay a Citroen workshop for manufacturing gears had windows overlooking a small inner courtyard of the Vel d'Hiv. The only water tap to which the prisoners had access was in this courtyard, and the sight of the long line of people waiting for their turn to drink, only a few of them possessing some kind of receptacle to drink from, shocked the Citroen workers who crowded round the windows.

The former Citroen employee who described the scene to us says that the memory still bothers him. From the windows they

threw food down into the courtyard, and soon, as the families
and friends of the unfortunate people inside learned about
these convenient windows, they flocked to the Citroen
workshops with packages which they gave to the workmen.
During their lunch hour the men would try to take them into
the stadium, but as often as not they were prevented by the
guards.

Later many Parisians actively tried to express their
indignation and shock at this bestial operation and to show
their sympathy for its victims. When the full extent of the
crime was known, many notable personalities, leading
organizations, and the different political parties took a stand
against the roundup and openly voiced their protest. But at
this early stage, during the first few hours and days, every
Parisian had to decide for himself, without the guidance of
anyone else, what to do and how to react to the events.

One member of the National Front, Myriam Novitch, who
was later to cover the trials of war criminals in Germany for
the Institute for the History of Ghetto Fighters in Israel,
decided she could help by preparing baskets of food and fruit
with a friend for the prisoners. They even found oranges,
which were a priceless rarity in those days when everything was
scarce. At the gates to the stadium, however, they were not
allowed in.

Naturally the militant Jewish groups were among the most
concerned and in particular members of Solidarité, who felt
especially close to the sufferers, not only because they were
themselves Jews but because in many cases they had friends or
relatives among the prisoners at the Vel d'Hiv. This made them
feel all the more frustrated at their powerlessness in the face of
the efficient German machine.

One of the more important members of Solidarité, Alfred
Cukier, did what he could by helping to draw up a list of Jews
threatened by the operation in order to warn them. The
Solidarité movement was vigorous with dedicated members
ready to risk danger and undergo hardship. Mr. Cukier
described to us how on July 16 he had an appointment with

Sarah Vronsky, liaison agent of the movement, who also was
his sister-in-law. They had arranged to meet at the Sully Bridge.

> We were to meet as if by chance. I was to go up to her
> and say good morning. But when I saw her coming
> toward me, her eyes red and her whole face wet with
> tears, I could not help murmuring to her in Yiddish,
> "What's the matter?"
> "The roundup," she said. "This morning I was
> supposed to go to Rue Charlemagne and I saw everything.
> The street was swarming with cops and every single Jew
> was taken away. Those who were unable to stand up
> without help were taken away on stretchers." She burst
> into sobs and I put my arm around her shoulder and led
> her away. As soon as she calmed down a bit, I left her,
> asking her to try and collect as much information as she
> could. I had other engagements, but little by little as the
> day passed we found out what was going on.
> I decided to go to the Vel d'Hiv myself. As I came out
> of the La Motte-Picquet metro station, I noticed the busy
> traffic and the frequent TCRP buses loaded with luggage,
> eiderdowns, pillows, and blankets. That was disquieting
> in itself, and I walked on toward Grenelle. I could see
> dozens of policemen in uniform and doubtless there were
> more in civilian clothing. I did not get too close since I
> was what we used to call "illegal" and the police would
> have been only too glad to catch me. It was risky being
> there at all so I looked on from a distance. I watched the
> poor anxious people hurrying in and out of the building.
> I even saw one Jew, wearing a yellow star, present a paper
> before being admitted, no doubt a member of the UGIF.
> None of the *Solidarité* members dared be caught with
> such a pass, and the irony of it all made me angry. It was
> essential for us to know what was happening inside so
> that we could let others know.
> Finally we asked two young social workers, introduced
> to us by Dr. Alex, to help, which they did in every way
> they could. They were the Cathala sisters. Not wasting a
> moment, they got into the stadium that same day as social
> workers. Late in the afternoon I went to their house to
> hear their report firsthand. They had been shaken by
> what they saw. They said the air was unbreathable inside
> the stadium and the stink so strong it choked them.
> Prisoners had to relieve themselves wherever they

happened to be. They had seen many people lying
prostrate on the ground without moving and others
acting hysterically as they began to lose their reason.

Besides the Cathala sisters. *Solidarité* sent two other women
into the Vel d'Hiv. They were the wives of prisoners of war and
theoretically protected for that reason. Their names were
Hélène Kro* and Tonia Zabuski. There was a third lady,
Felah Decargan, whose husband was an "Aryan." These three
women would go up to the gates of the stadium laden with
baskets of food as often as twenty times a day in the hope that
the guards would let them in, which they sometimes did.

Others went even further. For example, there was one group
of young students who decided they must do something as soon
as they heard the warning rumors. They tried to organize a
rescue service. Except for Roger Boussinot, their names are still
unknown. Roger was a student at the Sorbonne, where in
between classes he and a friend, a Catholic Boy Scout called
Favard, used to enjoy serious discussions in which each showed
off his ability to argue and reason. On one such occasion Roger
had declared that he was always for the pursued, never for the
pursuer. It was a quotation from some author which he took as
his motto. Now as Favard told Roger about the rumors of the
impending roundup, he reminded him of that motto. This was
the time to put it into practice. We have Roger Boussinot's
account of the group's activities on the morning of July 16.

"We were about twenty altogether, and we figured that if
each of us managed to rescue three or four Jews, taking them to
some safe hiding place, we would have saved 200 people by the
end of the day."

Unfortunately it was much more difficult than they had
imagined to achieve this. Roger Boussinot told us that he spent
the whole day dodging the police, the PPF, and the armed
guards in a vain attempt to save a few of the victims.

That same morning one of the teachers in a public school of

* Hélène Kro, who belonged to the Resistance, was to throw herself
from a window some time later when policemen of the Vichy government
came to arrest her.

the IV Arrondissement, Sylvia Barberet, though the school was
on vacation, could not stop thinking of the little Jewish
children who came to her class with a yellow star sewn onto
their black pinafores. They too would be threatened by the
roundup. Dressing hurriedly, she ran to the addresses she knew
and collected any of her pupils she found at home and took
them somewhere safe, thus saving their lives.

As well as individual efforts, there were the organized efforts
of the well-known charities. Foremost among these were the
Quakers. Their name was familiar in Europe at that time
wherever there were people suffering or in need. Often those
who received help from the Quakers were not clearly aware
what they stood for; for many, especially the children, they
were associated with a dim memory of an English breakfast and
represented abundance and comfort. They deserve at least the
tribute of a description of their good work in this account since
they worked quietly without advertising their beliefs so that
many people did not know whether they were a religious sect
or a charitable organization. They never tried to convert those
they helped, but intervened where they were needed gently and
efficiently.

No one seems to know how the Quakers found out about
Operation Spring Wind, but they were at the Vel d'Hiv from
the very first day. On the morning of July 16 the only
provisions to be found at the stadium were the gift of the
Quakers: twelve cartons of biscuits. A ridiculously inadequate
amount, but they meant that someone worried about the
welfare of the prisoners and that was a lot in those days.

As soon as the French Red Cross was alerted, doctors and
nurses were sent to the Vel d'Hiv. Miss Monod, who was
attached to the Red Cross as a social worker, was enjoying a few
days' rest with her family at her father's parsonage in Saint-
Germain when she was summoned. Mrs. Gillet of the Red Cross
in Paris telephoned her on July 16 and told her that women
and children were being arrested and taken to the Vel d'Hiv.
She was being asked to go to the Vel d'Hiv since she was
familiar with the Jewish problem. She was indeed familiar with

the suffering of the Jews, having worked at the camp at
Pithiviers for a whole year.

So she rushed to the Vel d'Hiv, presented her papers, and
was allowed in. What she saw terrified her. The noise, the
overpowering smell, and the madhouse atmosphere bewildered
her. She was struck by the carefree playing of the children in
contrast to the pain and despair on the faces of the adults, and
the sight of the guards, huge men, strong and healthy, their
paunches held in by their belts and their rifles ready, standing
guard over toddlers not three feet high. Miss Monod's job was
to provide help for the families; as soon as she found out from
those in charge of the stadium that all these prisoners were to
be sent on to the camps of Loiret, Beaune-la-Rolande, and
Pithiviers, she left for Loiret. She knew that Pithiviers was
being cleared to make room for the new arrivals, but apart
from deporting the men to accommodate the women and
children, nothing had been prepared for the reception of the
new prisoners, and the children especially had many needs.

Another Red Cross worker, Suzanne Bodin (who was later
deported and died at Ravensbruck) organized the medical help
for victims of the Paris roundup. She called nurses and alerted
doctors who usually lent their services to the Red Cross, and
tried to fight her way through the red tape to get permits for
admission to the Vel d'Hiv. In spite of the obstacles Dr. Tisne
of the Prefecture put in her way, Suzanne Bodin managed to
collect a team of twelve nurses, who for the next eight days
devoted all their time to the prisoners in the Vel d'Hiv.
Working in three shifts of four nurses each, they would appear
at their appointed times, as punctually as if they were clocking
into an office.

One of the nurses, Mrs. Mathey Jonais, was a kindly lady
nearly sixty years old at the time. She had volunteered as a
nurse in 1914–18 and again in 1939–40, and had been wounded
in both wars since she served with the ambulances on the
battlefront. One of her favorite expressions was that she had
seen much in her life and would be seeing plenty more. Later
she joined the Resistance and was arrested by the Gestapo in

June, 1944, and deported to Ravensbruck. There she remained until she was liberated in May, 1945. In 1965 Mrs. Mathey Jonais celebrated her eightieth birthday. Twenty years after the events of the war her comments were:

> I shall never get over the feeling of despair and helplessness that filled the Vel d'Hiv. I still have nightmares about it.
>
> I remember going to the Vel d'Hiv and getting off the metro at the La Motte-Picquet station. We all wore dark blue capes and veils over our heads then. People came up to us asking if we would take messages to their families inside. Of course we said we would, but only very rarely did we manage to find the people we were to give the messages to. Someone gave me a bottle of cough syrup "for Daddy," someone else asked for news of a daughter. In order to stop this petty traffic, we were forced to go into the building in one group.

These nurses and the social workers, not more than fifteen women in all, finding themselves in the middle of an inferno, did all they could think of to alleviate the general misery. One of the social workers, Mrs. Tavernier, went as far as protesting to the Prefect, saying, "There are times when I am ashamed of being a Frenchwoman." A few doctors later joined the nurses.

When the *Secours National,* the French national emergency service, arrived at the Vel d'Hiv on the first day, it was not allowed access to the stadium. The *Secours National* was founded by the Pétain government after the defeat of France and the occupation by the Germans, its name purposely different from that of the prewar *Secours Rouge.* As an organization it had shamelessly appropriated Jewish property, and so the whole visit to the Vel d'Hiv seemed hypocritical, though on the second day the provisions brought by the *Secours National* were taken in to the prisoners.

The members of the UGIF had gambled on some sort of compromise with the Germans, and now they found themselves again at the heart of a new, acutely tragic situation. They had known that preparations were being made for a roundup. They had employed Mrs. Libers and the other women on the job of making labels for the deportees the night before the raid. Mrs.

Libers said later that by the seventeenth she and the other helpers realized that the UGIF had been aware of the impending arrests when it employed them for the work on the labels. Another witness told us that the roundup had been discussed at a meeting of the UGIF, in the headquarters of the organization on the Rue de la Bienfaisance, on July 14. Being powerless to help in any other way, the members had decided they would have to limit themselves to giving medical aid.

During the afternoon of July 16, André Baur, Secretary General of the UGIF, visited the Vel d'Hiv with two other leading members, Mr. Katz and Mr. Musmik. As soon as he appeared inside the stadium, he was booed and insulted. In front of him were seven thousand people, over half of them children, heaped together without beds or even straw, with no food or water. He could smell the dreadful stench, which reached right to the glass roof. For him this was the beginning of the painful realization that his policies had failed. Later André Baur, his wife, and four children were deported to Germany, none of them ever to return.

Dr. Didier-Hesse was one of the medical team to be sent by the UGIF into the Vel d'Hiv. As soon as he heard what was happening, he hurried to the UGIF headquarters and asked to be assigned to the Vel d'Hiv. He was told that even if he had not volunteered, he would have been recruited anyway, since the need for doctors and medicines was urgent. Unable to help otherwise, the UGIF was doubly anxious to do everything possible to provide adequate medical aid for the prisoners. Even so they were hampered by the regulations: authorization both from the Prefecture and from the Germans was necessary for entry into the stadium, and there was a strict rule that only two doctors could be present at the same time.

Armed with an impressive *ausweis* printed in German and signed by Roethke, and another pass written on the letterhead of the Commission for Jewish Affairs, signed by Duquesnel and stamped with the emblems of France, Dr. Didier-Hesse was allowed into the Vel d'Hiv on the evening of July 16. His colleague, Dr. Loewe-Lyon, was already at work there.

It is difficult to imagine the extremity of the needs of the

Jews in their ill-equipped prison. There were the critically ill to be removed to hospital, there were women in labor, there were people suffering from contagious diseases who had to be separated from the rest, there were cases of insanity requiring sedatives, then there were babies howling for milk, and countless minor emergencies to be met. It did not take Dr. Didier-Hesse long to size up the situation. Making a list of the most urgent necessities to bring with him the next day, he left to prepare for the next day's work.

After the first thorough raids fewer and fewer arrests were made. The police was now merely double-checking the addresses that had yielded no victims on the first round.

As soon as Nat Linen had passed by the armed patrol on the Rue Nocard, he walked on like a sleepwalker, looking neither right nor left. He was only fifteen years old, and he had to look after himself in a hostile city. He walked toward the Seine, to the old Passy bridge and up the steps into the metro station. He whispered to the woman at the barrier that he had no ticket and no money. She hesitated for one instant but then let him through.

He had decided to hide with the family of a non-Jewish schoolfriend named Elbode, even though he knew the parents were right-wing in their sympathies. To a young Jew in Nat's position, the difference between right and left was especially significant and could mean the difference between being helped and being betrayed. But he knew the Elbodes and trusted them. They welcomed him, looked after him, and so he was saved.

Like Nat Linen, Mrs. Lichtein's daughter walked along the road aimlessly until she came to the metro. It seems that all the runaways had the same reflexes, and so when Mrs. Lichtein in her turn managed to get away, she ran into her daughter at the Etoile metro station as if by some miraculous coincidence.

When they found each other, they decided to go to the house of a Spanish friend, an exiled republican, who lived in Paris with his wife. To do that they had to take a train to Nation, back in the direction they had come from. It was an elevated metro which passed very close to the Vel d'Hiv. As the train

crossed the Seine at Passy, the two women looked at the river
below them. Soon they could see Boulevard de Grenelle. There
was quite a crowd. The train stopped at Grenelle station, where
some policemen and some Germans got on.

As the train moved on, the eyes of every passenger were on
the street scene below. In the crowd, the shiny helmets of the
armed guards were visible; there were the buses with large
white reserve tanks lashed to their roofs, bringing more Jews
to the Vel d'Hiv. Though the metro was crowded, no one
spoke. Mrs. Lichtein and her daughter, even though they were
traveling in an ordinary car and not the last one in the train,
which was reserved for Jews, felt self-conscious and were certain
that everyone was looking at them. Surely they were mad to
have come back to this area. But they reached Saint-Jacques
station safely and, after a short walk along the Boulevard, came
to their friends' house at number 29. The sculptor La Torre
and his wife Gilberte Davos greeted them warmly, but Mrs.
Lichtein, who had been under extreme nervous strain all day,
suddenly broke down.

When he got back to the city, Louis Pitkowicz returned to
his parents' apartment. There he wandered through the empty
rooms thinking of his family at the Vel d'Hiv. On an impulse
he rang the bell of the apartment next door where one of his
friends lived. His friend's parents had also been arrested, but
he and his older sister had managed to hide, so the three
children kept each other company. For three days they waited
for something to happen to solve their predicament, daring
neither to move nor make a sound nor even stand near the
windows. And all the while they worried about their families.
The food that had been left in the apartments soon ran out,
and they were forced to do something since they obviously
could not go on hiding in the empty apartments. Louis finally
decided to go to the house of a former schoolfriend who lived
in the VI Arrondissement, where the Pitkowiczes used to live
and where Louis used to go to school. At 3 Rue du Four, Mr.
and Mrs. Haut, his schoolfriend's parents, did not hesitate for
a moment but invited him in and looked after him.

From the moment she entered the Vel d'Hiv, Ida Nussbaum

had a presentiment of what was going to happen, and from then on she had only one thought in her head: to save her baby son. She regretted not having accepted the offer of her concierge to look after him, but now she had succeeded in escaping from the Vel d'Hiv. After rounding the first corner of the Rue Nelaton, she hurried into the nearest café and asked the lady at the counter for some water for her thirsty baby. The owner of the café seemed to have guessed her plight and took her and the child into a back room, expressing her sympathy. Then she brought two plates, some bread, and milk and water. The little boy was comforted, and his mother began to feel less tense. She asked whether she could use the telephone and called some neighbors, asking them to tell the concierge what happened and to tell her to come and get the child.

As she replaced the receiver, she noticed two policemen in uniform standing outside the café, talking with the owner of the café. Was she being betrayed? Impossible! It could not be true! She no longer cared what happened to her; she lacked the energy to resist. As long as someone came for the child in time, she would accept whatever happened to herself.

On the other side of the shop window the owner of the bistro and the policemen were still talking. Ida Nussbaum froze where she stood, not daring to move. She focused her attention on a small notice glued to the glass pane but was all too aware of the two uniforms beyond the glass. They were now coming into the café. They walked straight up to her but did not look hostile. One of them pointed to the yellow star on the breast pocket of her coat.

"It would be a good idea to take that off."

She had forgotten all about it. The policeman took a penknife from his pocket and cut the thread holding down the six points of the Star of David. "That's better," he said, slipping the scrap of yellow cloth into Mrs. Nussbaum's pocket. Both policemen looked friendly and smiled. They were both young.

"We'll be on duty until three o'clock. Until then you're safe here, but don't move. After three, get away—only take care, don't stay in Paris. Go to the country."

In their hiding place, the Kleinbergers were visited several times by their concierge, who kept them up to date with events. Toward evening she moved them to a better hideout she had prepared in the cellar.

The Rimmlers too, after many anxious hours, were called on by a Polish lady of their acquaintance, who took them to another refuge. There were thousands of Jews like these who had gone into hiding, not knowing where to go next, worried about friends and relatives, often in such a state of panic that they gave themselves away. A contemporary description of the terrible atmosphere that Thursday night gives some idea of the strain under which these fugitives lived.

> At this moment there are several thousand Jews hiding in Paris, their condition resembling that of hunted animals. They cannot stay with the people who offer them shelter, because they don't want to expose their helpers to reprisal. They cannot return to their own homes, since these have been sealed off by the police. They have no means of existence, and they will soon be unable to buy food because their ration cards will no longer be valid. Among them are mothers drifting in the city with several children, sleeping in a different place each night, young girls with no idea where to look for refuge, and who will have one of two choices tomorrow—to die of hunger or fall into the hands of pimps. Suicide or prostitution.

Mrs. Soral's little boy was among the lucky ones. Wandering between La Maub' and the Rue de la Bûcherie, he came across some friends and was rescued. He survived.

At nightfall the gates of the Vel d'Hiv were closed, shutting in the stench, which, of all the physical discomforts suffered by the prisoners, proved to be the most difficult to bear. It was the most degrading. It was worse than the hunger and the thirst and the sleepless nights on cement or wooden floors. From the first day this pestilential smell settled over the place, and it is striking how all the accounts of eyewitnesses mention it and agree on its pervasiveness and overpowering quality.

The Vel d'Hiv had been sealed. The swinging doors on the Rue Nelaton were opened only to let in the Jewish prisoners as they arrived and then quickly shut again. Apart from the doors, there was not one opening or ventilation shaft in working order. The hot July sun fell on the glass roof of the stadium with the weight of lead. Although there was a brief thunderstorm during the afternoon of the sixteenth, and rain pattered on the roof of the Vel d'Hiv in large drops, the atmosphere inside remained heavy and hot. With thousands of people living, breathing, and perspiring in that furnace, one's first impression on entering was that the air inside had a different density from the air outside.

For the use of all the prisoners there were ten lavatories and about twenty urinals. Half of these were cordoned off almost immediately because they had windows overlooking the street and could therefore be used as an escape route. Only those lavatories with barred windows or that were too high above street level to be of any use as a way out were left open, and for seven thousand people these were obviously too few. It took up to an hour or an hour and a half of waiting in a line to get a turn at using the available facilities. By the end of the morning all the lavatories were blocked and the urinals overflowing. Inside the lavatories people had to sit on filth. And, to make things worse, there was no water.

Women who were indisposed had no means of staying clean. It was also impossible to wash babies and small children. Diapers had to be left dirty and fermented. The adult prisoners were depressed and humiliated to discover how helpless they were in the face of their most elementary needs. They would try to suppress and control themselves as long as they could, then in shame and despair would have to relieve themselves, often in public. Here and there an old man would be holding up a coat to hide the shame of a squatting woman. Young girls would try to move a little way from the vicinity of their family. The survivors obviously did not enjoy describing the details of this ridiculous and shaming torture, but not one of them omitted to mention the horror of it when describing the Vel d'Hiv. For eight days, seven thousand people were locked into a closed building without water and without sanitary conveniences. One would liken them to animals in a cage except that even animals' cages are kept clean.

There were pitiful sights on every side. Reduced by their needs, old men and women would stand near a wall or even stay where they were to relieve themselves, since what are usually called "comfort stations" had become too foul to go near. It is hardly credible that all this was happening in Paris and before the vigilant eyes of French guards, gendarmes, and policemen. In all the eyewitness reports we collected, the description of the sanitary conditions recurs like a refrain. In one doctor's report there is the following:

> It would take a whole book to record the heartbreaking sights I came across during my shifts at the Vel d'Hiv. Just to give some idea of the standards of cleanliness, I will mention one incident. I was prescribing the appropriate medicine for some prisoners who were suffering from constipation when the nurse who worked with me exclaimed that I was not doing them a favor by giving them the medicine. When I asked her why, she told me that not only were the toilets inadequate, but by now they were blocked and absolutely unusable and furthermore could not be repaired. I checked her information and found it to be true. In short, crowded together by the thousands, the prisoners did not have, or at any rate no longer had, any latrines that they could use.

This unbearable violation of human dignity was cruelly felt by the prisoners, and we now know that it was not merely the result of neglect by the authorities, but was consciously contrived to break their spirit. Mrs. Nussbaum told us:

> In the middle of the morning on the sixteenth, my cousin's little daughter asked to go to the lavatory. The two of them went off, leaving the other daughter with me and my son. We were on the fourth tier, and they had to go downstairs. Half an hour went by, then an hour, then an hour and a half, and still they had not come back. More and more people were arriving, and we had to squeeze closer. I noticed some small children urinating where they stood. I began to get worried, but just then I

saw them coming back. My cousin spoke to me without looking at me: "You know how sick I am. Well, there is one thing left for me to do—jump down and kill myself. It's unbearable, I'm sick, the lavatories are out of order, there's nowhere to go, we'll all be dead soon anyway——" With that she made a run for the railing to throw herself down, but I caught her and held her back.

All through the next seven days the situation deteriorated. Even the guards began to complain. Urine began seeping down the steps, and the smell was atrocious. The guards could not bear it; this was the only protest they were to make.

On top of everything there was the incessant noise; under the glass roof of the building the thousands of voices were magnified by the echoes and sounded like a busy railroad station. Screams, loud sobs, or despairing cries would rise above the general hubbub so often that no attention was paid to them. From time to time the loudspeakers would crackle to announce some item of news, give instructions, or call out a name.

Drancy was no better. According to plan, the men and women unaccompanied by children were taken there, the first buses arriving at eight in the morning. Not all of them came from Paris; many came from the suburbs. For collecting small groups of prisoners, ordinary police cars were used. Hélène Rozen, who was arrested with her mother at Nogent, remembers the police car that took them to the Vel d'Hiv making a detour via Drancy to drop a newly married couple who had been picked up at St. Maur.

Throughout the day buses came and went in relays—an endless procession. Thousands of persons were brought and unloaded in the Drancy courtyard. Four tables were set up in the yard at which the prisoners' names were registered as they went into the camp. Very soon the clerks doing this job, who were themselves prisoners from previous roundups, found they could not deal with the volume of incoming traffic. There was the further difficulty of sorting Jews from Aryans. Many non-Jewish women, some of them Frenchwomen, had lied in order to be allowed to go with their husbands. Not that it did them much good, since at Drancy men and women were kept in separate parts of the prison. With a burning sun beating down on the open yard and bundles of luggage piling up everywhere, there was complete chaos.

That same night at Arras, a young man of twenty-four was writing a last letter in his prison cell before facing a German firing squad. His name was Joseph Delobel, and he was a communist and a member of the Resistance.

> Arras, July 16, 1942
>
> It is not without pain that I write these last few lines to you in the name of all my comrades. . . .
> . . . Our victory is certain. Nazism and Fascism are on the verge of dying, never to return. Comrades, friends, I bid you goodbye, assuring you that like all our friends in suffering, we shall face the executioners with our heads held high.
> Dear parents, be brave. Goodbye.

Chapter 6

Toward the Final Solution

On Friday, July 17, the second day of the roundup in Paris, Himmler, head of the Gestapo, went on a tour of inspection at Auschwitz. This death factory was about to process some new material, and he had to make sure that it was in working order. It seemed at that time that nothing and no one in Europe was able to put a stop to the "final solution." Germany was at the height of her power. The military communiqués issued by the Fuehrer's General Headquarters were one endless boast of victory. Germany's advance was proceeding at a lightning pace—not only on the Russian front (Sebastopol fell on July 2) but also in North Africa, where Rommel's divisions threw back the British after taking Tobruk on June 22. On July 12 the military communiqué read:

> German troops and their allies, supported by the admirable Luftwaffe, have defeated and completely destroyed the enemy in an offensive which took place west of the Don between June 28 and July 9. After the capture of Voronezh on July 7, the Don was reached south of the city and commanded along two hundred miles of its course, where several bridgeheads have been established.

On July 22 there was news of victory in the action in North Africa around Alamein, "where the British have lost 1,200 prisoners and a considerable number of tanks." Meanwhile on the Russian front: "Rostov in flames is being attacked from the west, north, and east." One sentence of the dispatch ran: "A large German force is rapidly advancing on Stalingrad."

This was the first time that Stalingrad was mentioned in a bulletin of the Nazi General Headquarters, and at the time no one dreamed that the fighting around that city, which was to start the following October and continue until January, 1943, would sound the death knell of the German army.

The Auschwitz Notebooks give a clear account of Himmler's visit:

> On July 17, SS Reichsfuehrer Himmler arrived at Auschwitz for a tour of inspection. This was his second visit. There to guide him were Gauleiter Bracht and SS Obergruppenfuehrer Kammler. Attended by his hosts, Himmler made the rounds of the entire camp, looking into the agricultural installations, the building sites, the laboratories, the experimental plantations at Rapsko, as well as the nurseries and forestry school. Afterwards while inspecting the camp at Birkenau, he watched the extermination of a whole convoy of Jews who had just arrived. He was present throughout from the unloading of the train to the selection of prisoners fit for labor, the extermination by gas in Bunker 2 of those judged unfit, and finally the clearing out of the bunker.

The convoy mentioned in this passage from the Notebooks was a load of 2,000 Dutch Jews who arrived on July 17. Of the 1,303 men and 697 women, 1,251 men and 300 women were considered fit for labor and the remaining 449 who were too weak to work were gassed ("wurden vergast") . It was their execution that Himmler watched. The Notebooks continue:

> That evening Himmler attended a reception given in his honor by Gauleiter Bracht at his home in Kattowitz. He arrived at the party with the commandant of the camp, Rudolf Hoess, and Mrs. Hoess and the head of the agricultural installations at Auschwitz, SS Obersturm-bannfuehrer Dr. Caesar.
>
> On July 18, Himmler toured the municipal camp, the kitchens, the women's camp, occupying blocks 1–10, the workshops, the stables, the "Canada" buildings, the slaughterhouses, and the guards' barracks.

The word "Canada" mentioned in the report requires explanation: it was the prisoners' nickname for the buildings in which the prisoners' belongings, taken from them on arrival at the camp, were collected and sorted. In 1943 the "Canada" buildings occupied no less than thirty-five huts. Special teams of deportees were assigned the task of sifting the vast quantities of assorted property, ranging from old clothes to gold wedding bands, jewelry, gold fillings torn from the jaws of the dead, eyeglasses, and even toys left behind by the children. Except what was appropriated by the SS guards on the spot, all gold and silver was sent to the bank of the German Reich. Watches went to the central office of the Economic Administration of the SS at Oranienburg, and the eyeglasses to the Health Department. Objects of daily use such as handkerchiefs, suitcases, knapsacks, bristle brushes, combs, etc., were taken to the office in charge of spreading German culture. The report of Himmler's visit continues:

> In the women's camp Himmler asked to be present while one of the women prisoners was beaten. He wanted to observe the effects of the punishment. Seeing the state of the woman after the beating, he declared that from then onwards physical punishment of women prisoners could be administered only with his own personal authorization. At the end of the tour, Himmler spent some time with Hoess in his office and made a few suggestions. He asked that the construction of the Birkenau buildings be speeded up and that the method of exterminating Jews unfit for work be perfected. Then, in recognition of Hoess's achievements so far, Himmler promoted him to the rank of Obersturmfuehrer.

This visit is vividly remembered by one of the survivors of Auschwitz, André Montagne. He had been working at Birkenau for a week, on the construction of the barracks which were to make Birkenau such a gruesome annex of Auschwitz, most of the buildings being used as gas chambers and crematoria. It was hard work, under a fiery sun with nothing to drink and only a thin soup for food, though the working day lasted twelve hours. In his words:

> I remember the day Himmler came to Auschwitz. It was sometime in the middle of July. The rollcall that

evening took an unusually long time. We had to stand
at attention for three hours in absolutely straight lines.
The silence was eerie. The SS and Kapos in charge, all of
them criminals convicted by common law, did not allow
the slightest movement on our part. If anyone collapsed
from sheer exhaustion, he was soundly punched and
kicked and dragged off to a nearby building, where if he
had not already succumbed to their rough treatment, he
was finished off.

I did not actually see Himmler. I did not dare to risk
turning my head to have a look. All I saw between the
shaven heads of the prisoners standing in front of me, for
just a moment, was a group of VIP's in black or green
uniforms, some with a broad red stripe down the sides of
their pants, which distinguished them as superior officers.

While Himmler was visiting Auschwitz on July 17, the
roundup was continuing in Paris. Led by Hauptsturmfuehrer
Roethke himself, the Germans went to have a look at the Vel
d'Hiv.

Roethke's nickname for it was "the birdcage." The image,
typical of the morbidly fanciful Nazi imagination, described
the place exactly since the Jewish prisoners, like wild birds
blindly fluttering against the sides of a cage, were confused and
panicked as they realized how firmly they were caught in their
huge and well-guarded prison. There were some who would
not give up, but frantically searched for some loophole or some
oversight of the guards which would permit them to escape. All
too often the attempts were made too late.

As he watched them, Roethke knew only too well that they
had already been condemned to death. And yet he and the
other Germans gave permission for some of the more critically
ill to be transferred to the Rothschild hospital. It would seem
irrelevant to cure someone who was about to be executed
anyway, but it was part of the German method (which they
called *Tarnung*) purposely to lead their victims to draw the
wrong conclusions. By letting a few of the sick prisoners get
treatment in a hospital, the impression was created that the
Germans were acting in accordance with normal human
conditions, and therefore there must be some hope that this

horror would end. This treacherous system was practiced at all levels, throughout the operation and right up to the edge of the mass graves before the victims were shot and to the very doors of the gas chambers. Anyway there was no escape. Runaways or survivors were merely temporarily reprieved; they would be caught in the end. At the Rothschild hospital the sick prisoners from the Vel d'Hiv would be well within reach of the German authorities.

The Germans had relied on the French to carry out the arrests, and this visit by their officials was merely to check that everything was proceeding as planned. The UGIF doctor, Dr. Didier-Hesse, advised one of the visiting German officers whom he met in the Vel d'Hiv not to go up into the tiers of the stadium. He feared for his safety, given the emotional state of the Jews. The doctor obviously still had some illusions about the intentions of the Germans. He would have done better to let the officer go up.

In a memorandum addressed to Knochen and Oberg, dated July 18, 1942, Roethke gave the score of victims for Operation Spring Wind.

> The roundup of alien Jews residing in Paris which took place on the sixteenth and seventeenth of this month resulted in the following number of prisoners:

Men	3,031
Women	5,802
Children	4,051
Total:	12,884

> One striking feature in these numbers is the high proportion of women. This discrepancy in the number of women compared to that of the men captured is probably due to the fact that no women had been arrested during the earlier roundups, and also to the fact that anticipating a roundup similar to the ones before, more men had felt the need to go into hiding than women.

Roethke goes on to criticize the behavior of the French populace during the roundup:

> There were many instances of French bystanders expressing pity for the Jews who were being arrested.

> They reacted particularly to the arrest of Jewish children. The transport of Jewish families was not effected with due efficiency in many cases, so that the non-Jewish population noticed, and people gathered into small crowds to talk about the event.

The SS knew perfectly well that it was voluntary indiscretions that had alerted those Jews who had escaped arrest. They would now use informers and take their revenge.

> The IV J office of the Gestapo has received information from a variety of sources that a considerable number of alien Jews marked for arrest had been warned of the impending roundup and had consequently been able to go into hiding in time. It appears that some members of the French police force had betrayed their trust and in many instances warned the very people they should have arrested, advising them not to spend the nights of the sixteenth and seventeenth of July in their homes. The wealthier Jews in particular had been helped in this way. We have asked our informants to bring us concrete examples with exact details incriminating the officers in question, but we have not so far received this information. The truth of the rumors, however, cannot be doubted.

Roethke was not disappointed. There were in fact numerous betrayals. For example, the following report was found in the dossiers of the Gestapo, describing the escape of Rachel Pronice.

> Around six o'clock on Friday, July 17, a group of French policemen went to 14 Rue Raffet to arrest some alien Jews who lived there. An inspector and an officer of the peace started talking with the concierge, mostly about the roundup, dwelling on the inhumanity of the operation and describing the desperate reactions, citing a number of suicides that had taken place as a result and in particular the story of one woman (living in Belleville, I think) who had thrown her two children out of the window, preferring to kill them rather than be separated from them.
> Moreover this rumor was spread in many quarters of the city. Note that in the same building on Rue Raffet, a Polish-Jewess who taught the piano had left a couple of nights before the arrival of the police and had tried to

escape into the free zone, obviously because of some
warning she had received.

This document is typewritten and unsigned. In the margin
are notes in German in Roethke's handwriting: "About the
events of 16 and 17" and near the details of Rachel Pronice's
escape: "According to my sources, she should be at Pithiviers."

Thus the smallest hint was carefully checked and acted upon.
The informers' pains were never wasted. Their information
was usually correct and promptly put to use.

On the reverse side of a piece of paper with the letterhead
"Maurice O., Pearls—Precious Stones—Rue de Châteaudun,
TRUdaine" another informer wrote down his observations
about the evening of July 16 and sent them to the Gestapo.
According to this man, all the heartbreaking episodes that took
place in Paris had been staged by the French police.

> The police has been at the bottom of the whole
> business and very successfully handled the arrests in such
> a way that the French onlookers would be moved to pity
> the Jews and hate the Germans. In fact one heard nothing
> but insults and anti-German shouts from the people who
> walked behind the convoys (*sic*) of Jews. The police
> omitted nothing that might rouse sympathy for the
> Jewish cause. Women were left waiting outside the
> collecting centers, and their weeping and crying made
> one feel one was in front of the Wailing Wall.

It was an anonymous informer also who betrayed Mr. Vistuk
when he hid in some neighbors' house, most likely giving them
his milk coupons in return:

> Most Jews hid in their neighbors' houses, though some
> went considerable distances from their homes. The
> Vistuks, for example, who live at 76 Rue de Bondy, were
> not at home when the police called for them. Yet after
> their disappearance their milk ration continues to be
> collected from the dairy on the ground floor of their
> building, where they are registered. The fact that their
> supply of milk is fetched for them by a Frenchwoman
> suggests that they must be hiding nearby.

The stench of hate and cowardice that emanates from these
faded documents is sickening. Prompted by the basest motives,

these traitors became murderers during those terrible days in 1942, using silent weapons of paper which would result in large-scale bloodshed with no consequences to themselves.

Despite all this, the Nazis were far from satisfied. Roethke continues his memorandum as follows: "Though 9,800 people were arrested by the French police on the first day of the roundup, on July 17 only a fraction of this number were taken, as was to be expected. The total for the second day was around three thousand people."

On the whole, the yield of the operation was below the German expectation which, as we said above, had been set at 28,000 persons for the Paris area. It will be remembered that Paris was but one small section of the grand plan elaborated at the Berlin conference under the name of the Final Solution. The conference had been scheduled for December 7, 1941, but it had had to be postponed because of events of more immediate importance which took place that day: the Japanese attack on Pearl Harbor and the entry of the United States into the war. It was finally held on January 20 at 56–58 Grossen Wannsee Strasse in a vast and comfortable drawing room which also served as an office. The members attending had been summoned by Eichmann on Heydrich's instructions, Heydrich having been appointed to this mission by Goering. While a huge log fire roared in the fireplace, the members defined the Final Solution. According to the minutes, "The Final Solution of the Jewish problem in Europe would affect eleven million people. A list of numbers per country follows." In that catalogue, which was put in alphabetical order, starting with the Ancient Reich (of Germany) and ending with the USSR, the figures for France were:

France, occupied zone	165,000
France, unoccupied zone	700,000

A little further on, the minutes continue:

The pattern of the Final Solution of the problem should be the transfer of all Jews, under a reliable escort, to the East where they are to be attached to the Labor Service. There the healthy adults are to be divided into

working gangs, men on one side and women on another,
and taken to build roads. It goes without saying that a
large proportion will quite naturally be eliminated by
their physical unfitness at the beginning. The survivors
at the end of the work project, who will also be the
strongest among them, will have to be given suitable
treatment at the conclusion of the operation.

The "treatment" mentioned in the minutes of the conference
is more exactly explained elsewhere, and there is no doubt that
it was understood to mean execution.

We have the following comments in the minutes concerning
France and the drawing up of a list of Jews as the first step
toward their evacuation: "No difficulties are expected in either
the occupied or the free zones of France over the taking of a
census of Jews with a view to their evacuation." It is obvious
from this sentence how much confidence the Nazis had in the
complicity of the Vichy government. Later, Eichmann was to
give the following account:

> When the rest of the members attending the conference
> left, Heydrich, Mueller, and Eichmann stayed on in the
> conference room, comfortably stretched in deep armchairs
> in front of the fire. It was a relaxed and intimate occasion,
> Heydrich smoking while all three sat looking into the
> fire. . . .
> The three of us stayed on alone. I was offered one or
> two glasses of brandy, perhaps more. Heydrich explained
> to me how he wanted the official report to be worded.
> Then we each went home, and I sat up at my desk to write
> the report.

We know now that the five months from January to July,
1942, were enough for these experts in mass murder to work
out to the last detail their plans for France. The figures
mentioned in the minutes of the Wannsee conference of
January 20 had been corrected and modified to 260,000 to
280,000 Jews in the unoccupied zone and 180,000 Jews in the
occupied zone.

After the roundup of July 16 and 17 in Paris and provincial
cities in the occupied zone, the attention of the German

authorities turned to the unoccupied zone. One thing to be
remembered at all events is that *every single Jew* in France was
threatened.

> In accordance with the orders of Reichsfuehrer SS,
> addressed to the Gestapo office IV B 4 by the head of
> Service IV on June 23, 1942, all Jews domiciled in France
> are to be deported as soon as possible.

Meanwhile, the plan was to arrest fifty thousand Jews in the
free zone for a start. Preparations and the first steps for the
roundups had already been made.

Though some disappointment was felt among the Germans
about the results of the Paris raids, there was no real anxiety,
since a death sentence had been passed on all Jews in Europe
as well as those living in France. There was no fear that anyone
would escape. Europe had been sealed off from the rest of the
world for all practical purposes. The only front was far to the
east. For the rest, Switzerland was cut off by her mountains,
Franco's Spain too had a mountainous border, and neutral
Sweden was a long way off in the north. Furthermore the
program of deportation and extermination had been designed
to take the minimum time, given the material handicaps such
as the capacity of the camps (Birkenau was not yet quite ready)
and the transportation problems. Transportation was one of
the weak points in the plan, and it was vital to the success of
the operation that all convoys travel with maximum loads.

The Pétain government, far from condemning the German
action, shared in their enthusiasms and their anxieties. In this
context two documents must be quoted in their entirety. They
need no further comment. The first is a letter written under
the letterhead of the Ministry of the Interior of the State of
France, signed Gallien, head of the Cabinet, and stamped with
the emblem of Pétain's government. The letter is in German
and addressed: *An den Befehlshaber der Sicherheitspolizei und
des SD im Bereich des Militärbefehlhabers in Frankreich, z.
Hd von Herrn SS Obersturmführer Röthke.* The subject of
the letter is a report of the course of action recommended to

the prefect in charge, by Gallien, in order to speed up the operation. His instructions follow:

> As you no doubt know, the occupation forces intend the departure of trains deporting Jewish prisoners from the camp at Drancy to take place at regular intervals. I therefore enclose for your convenience a timetable for trains leaving during the month of August. The occupation forces attach the greatest importance to the punctual departures of these trains and require that every available place on each train be occupied. For this reason it is essential that there should be no slowdown in the pace of arrests and that the number of prisoners agreed upon (32,000) be handed over to the *Befehlshaber der Sicherheitspolizei*. I urgently ask you to let me know the following:
>
> 1. The number of arrests made so far in the unoccupied zone.
> 2. The average rate of arrests you expect for the future.
> 3. The maximum number of arrests you can hope to make.
>
> I would further like to inform you that Obersturm-fuehrer Roethke's latest instructions are that all Jews arrested in the occupied zone are to be sent to the camp at Drancy, where their deportation East will be arranged by the German authorities.
> You will be sent further details with the dates for the transfer of Jews to Drancy.
> I take the liberty of stressing the necessity for a prompt reply to this letter.

Near the stamped emblem of the Vichy government, there is a note in Roethke's handwriting referring to Gallien as an imbecile.

The second document is dated July 23, 1942, and written by Darquier de Pellepoix (Commissioner for Jewish Affairs) to Pierre Laval, who was head of the government at that time. A copy of the letter in German survives, with handwritten marginal notes by Roethke, who seems to have been a painstaking worker.

> In compliance with the agreement made between the representatives of the German authorities in charge of

Jewish affairs, Colonel Knochen and Captain Dannecker, and the representatives of the French government, Mr. Bousquet, Secretary of State for the Police, and Darquier de Pellepoix, General Commissioner for Jewish Affairs, the Commission for Jewish Affairs was to deliver to the German authorities 32,000 Jews, men and women, 22,000 from the occupied zone of France and 10,000 from the free zone. These people were either alien Jews residing in France or French Jews originating from certain foreign countries. The orders of the German authorities were carried out on July 16 and 17 with the result that a total of 8,890 persons—3,095 men and 5,885 women—were arrested in Paris and its suburbs.

At this point there is one of Roethke's handwritten comments correcting the figures listed by Darquier de Pellepoix. The note reads: "Plus 4,000 children, total 12,884." The letter goes on:

This total is far below the figure expected on the basis of the census lists at the Prefecture of Police. One factor to be taken into consideration is that while on the first day the arrests were carried out more or less successfully, on the second day the proportion of Jews to be arrested who were absent from their homes was 66 per cent. Also, as a result of indiscretions on the part of certain police officers, a number of Jews had been warned of the raids and had managed to cross secretly into the free zone.

I have met with members of the occupation forces today and could see that they were very dissatisfied with the results of the roundup.

The German authorities have set aside especially for that purpose enough trains to transport 30,000 Jews. It is therefore necessary that the arrests made should correspond to the capacity of the trains. It would be opportune to put into immediate effect whatever measures are necessary to arrive at the arrest of 32,000 Jews, which is the number agreed upon by the French government.

I take the liberty of proposing the following supplementary measures:

1. The arrest of all alien Jews or those originating from the countries listed previously who have fled into

the unoccupied zone, holding them in readiness for
transportation.

2. Since the Germans do not object, one could equally
arrest Belgian and Dutch Jews, in fact all foreign Jews
not possessing passports issued recently and clearly valid.

3. If after the arrest of Jews described in 1 and 2 above,
the agreed total of 32,000 has not been reached, it might
be advisable to make up that number by arresting Jews
of French nationality whose naturalization does not date
back further than January 1, 1927.

I would like to stress that these absolutely essential
measures are to be applied immediately in order to fulfill
the promise made by the French government to the
German authorities.

The adding up of numbers of prisoners and the working out of
statistics was to take several days, though the French officials
concerned had put their energies to the task on the second day
of the roundup.

However, one urgent problem remained, for which an answer
had to be found immediately. What was to be done with the
4,051 children who were crowding the Vélodrome d'Hiver?
Were they to be deported with their parents?

Chapter 7

The Death of 4,051 Children

Avenue Foch in Paris is the avenue of the Boulogne woods. In July the large chestnut trees that line it are heavy with leaves and, depending on the time of day, throw shadows on the lawns or the façades of the buildings.

At ten o'clock in the morning on July 17, seven men were sitting in conference around a large table in a second-floor office at number 31. The green baize covering the table was checkered with patches of sunlight filtering through the leaves of the trees outside the windows. Two of the seven, seated at the head of the table, were Germans: Roethke, in civilian clothes, and SS Sturmbannfuehrer Hagen in military uniform. Facing them sat five Frenchmen in civilian clothes. Leguay, the general delegate of the police, François and Tulard from the Prefecture of the Police, Darquier de Pellepoix and his general secretary Gallien. Ashtrays were scattered over the table, and the air was thick with tobacco smoke. Leaning over, Gallien offered Roethke a light.

There was just one item on the agenda for that meeting: What was to be done with the Jewish children who had been arrested? No decision had yet been made. On July 10 Dannecker had cabled his boss, Eichmann, in Berlin asking whether "children under sixteen years of age could be deported after the fifteenth convoy." The answer was still being awaited. The problem became all the more delicate as President Laval, speaking for the Vichy government, had already stated his position on the question. And it was not a very creditable position. In order to understand and fit such a serious decision into its context, one must go back and reconstruct the preparations for the roundup. Between the conference at Wannsee Strasse and Black Thursday, a whole series of questions arose, closely linked together, which one should consider in their chronological order.

On May 5, Reinhardt Heydrich himself came to Paris to install Karl Oberg as Supreme Commander of the SS and of the police in France. At the Hotel Ritz, Oberg was introduced to René Bousquet, Assistant Director of the Police, to Hilaire, Assistant Director of the Administration of the Ministry of the Interior, to Fernand de Brinon and to Darquier de Pellepoix. Among other subjects, the solution of the Jewish problem was discussed, and it is difficult to imagine that Heydrich, who had presided over the Wannsee conference, should not have hinted what the Final Solution was.

The night before, May 4, Dannecker raided the Rothschild hospital, where a number of Jews lay sick. Throughout the visit he held a revolver in his hand. The reason for this visit was understood much later when, as a prelude to Operation Spring Wind, these patients were deported to Germany.

On May 12 or 13, wasting no time, Dannecker was already making inquiries of General Kohl, head of ETRA (the military railroad transport) about the possibility of providing means of transport. Assuring Dannecker of his anti-Jewish sentiments, Kohl promised to do his best to provide the necessary number of coaches for the transport of at least ten thousand or twenty thousand Jews.

After some correspondence, a preparatory meeting was scheduled for June 11. It was from then onwards that the operation began to be put into practice. Meanwhile Heydrich had returned to Prague, where on May 28 he was fatally wounded by members of the Czech resistance; he died of his wounds on June 5. So the operation which was being set up was given his name—Operation Reinhardt. One of Heydrich's last acts, on May 18, had been to rule that "persons of even partly Jewish descent were to wear the yellow star of David," and to cable this decision to Paris.

On June 11, 1942, Dannecker, who was well informed on the Jewish question in France, met with Mr. Asche and Dr. Zoepff, the heads of the Jewish sections in the Hague and Brussels, at the office of the Security Service of the Reich, in Berlin. At this meeting three decisions were reached:

1. To deport fifteen thousand Jews from the Low Countries, ten thousand from Belgium, and one hundred thousand from both the occupied and free zones of France.

2. To send three convoys of deportees East each week.

3. To ask the French government to pay seven hundred Reichsmarks for every Jew deported.

On June 12 or 13, Dannecker again opened the question of transport with the *Service des Transports des Chemins de Fer à Paris*. Here he met with a great disappointment. Although General Kohl had previously undertaken to provide the transport Dannecker had requested, owing to the development of the military situation on the Russian front, the *Service des Transports* was no longer able to guarantee the necessary convoys. There was a shortage of railroad cars, and those that remained were barely enough for the transport of 350,000 French workmen needed by Gauleiter Sauckel for the STO. In a period of just a few weeks, the Wehrmacht had demanded thirty-seven thousand freight cars, eight hundred passenger cars, and one thousand locomotives for its Eastern Front. Regretfully, Dannecker noted: "The railroad cars were so urgently needed that there was no time to load them, and they therefore went to Germany empty."

After this overwhelming drain on the means of transport available, it was impossible to establish a precise program of deportation until the transport arrangements had been reorganized. The authorities needed trains; at the same time they had to have enough deportees to fill them. Losing no time, Dannecker called Darquier de Pellepoix for a meeting on June 15. Pellepoix, as French Commissioner for Jewish Affairs, promised Dannecker "several thousand Jews from the free zone."

On the same day Dannecker wrote a "technical note to Knochen about the transport of the Jews, submitting the latest

arrangements he had made." In order to "avoid any
interference with the movements of the French workmen in
Germany" (the STO, that is), he discussed only the
"transplantation," as he called it, of the Jews. "In this way
whole families would be deported, and they would be allowed
to hope that their younger children, under sixteen years of age,
would be sent to join them later."

So at that stage the question of deporting the children was
not even raised. On the other hand, Dannecker decided to
summon a meeting of the police and the Security Service
(*Sicherheit Dienst*) to issue orders for the roundup of Jews in
the provincial towns of the occupied zone. In his opinion, there
were some twenty-six thousand Jews to be arrested in that area.

In a report to Knochen informing him of these decisions,
Dannecker also confirmed that during the interview he had
with the French Commissioner for Jewish Affairs on June 15,
Darquier de Pellepoix had assured him that the Germans could
count "on several thousand Jews from the free zone who would
be handed over to us for deportation." On June 16 Dannecker
cabled the Chief of Security Police at Orléans, telling him to
make preparations for the deportation of prisoners at Pithiviers
and Beaune-la-Rolande, in order to make the necessary room
for the new arrivals.

On June 26, 1942, a new circular letter was issued to all those
concerned, giving practical detailed instructions about the
actual arrangements for deportation. In this circular, it is quite
clear that children under sixteen were not to be included
among the victims of the roundups. Nor were Jews originating
from countries then at war with Germany, or from neutral and
allied countries, to be arrested.

Finally, the departure of each convoy was to be announced
by telephone (PASsy 54–18) or by telegram, detailing the size
of the convoy and how many women were traveling. A number
of these telegrams have been found. We also know that during
the inspection of the concentration camps at Oranienburg,
which took place three times a week, information about the
convoys was transmitted to Hoess, the director of the camp at

Auschwitz, so that he could prepare for their reception.

On June 27, Dannecker met Dr. Zeitschel of the German embassy in Paris and told him that he needed fifty thousand Jews from the free zone for deportation. Dr. Zeitschel immediately instructed Counsellor Rahn to mention this to President Laval. Dannecker was in fact counting on twenty-six thousand Jews from the occupied zone outside Paris, twenty-two thousand to thirty thousand Jews from Paris, and the necessary fifty thousand to make up a total of one hundred thousand from the free zone. Counsellor Rahn and Pierre Laval met that same day.

On June 30 the meeting with the police and the Security Service which Dannecker had planned, concerning the arrest of Jews in the provinces, took place in Paris. There were eight people present; the representatives from Nancy and Poitiers did not come. At this meeting the latest instructions were issued, and among other things it was decided that in doubtful cases the French definition of Jew would be used, as it was much wider than the German definition. On the same day, Eichmann came from Berlin to talk with Dannecker in Paris. They worked together all day, putting final touches to numerous practical details. From an account of this meeting one learns that throughout their session neither Eichmann nor Dannecker lost sight of their objective for an instant, namely that "all Jews domiciled in France were to be deported as soon as possible and that pressure should be brought on the Vichy government to increase the rate of deportations to three convoys per week."

On July 2, a council of ministers was held at Vichy, during which the question of deportations was mentioned. Darquier de Pellepoix stated the promises he had made to the Germans, and Laval too reported the questions that Rahn had raised on June 27. The council of ministers was presided over by Marshal Pétain, and no one made any objections.

On July 2 the commissioner for the XII Arrondissement, together with the members of the Police for Jewish Affairs, made arrangements for the arrest of all the patients at the

Rothschild hospital. The roundup of the sick was completed in the early hours of the morning of July 3 and was the prelude to Operation Spring Wind.

July 4 was an important date in this affair. On that day all the detailed instructions for the Paris raids were issued by Dannecker, who confirmed that the French police would carry out the arrests alone. At the same time the commissioners of each of the arrondissements were asked to take personal responsibility for the arrests in their own sectors.

On the same day, the summit meeting already mentioned took place on Avenue Foch, with Dannecker, Knochen, and Schmidt representing the Germans and Bousquet, Darquier de Pellepoix, and Dr. Wilhelm (from the General French Delegation for occupied territories) the French.

In the evening Laval met Knochen in Paris. Knochen informed him of the decisions taken earlier in the day, and Laval approved them. It was probably at this meeting that the French president made the proposal which surprised even the Germans. As was already mentioned, during their meeting on June 27, Counsellor Rahn asked Laval to see that fifty thousand Jews were provided by the French in the free zone, for deportation, and told him of the planned arrests in the occupied zone, stating that the lower age limit had been set at sixteen years. Now the head of Marshal Pétain's government, obviously finding the German plans too humane, was proposing to deport the children under sixteen as well.

The Nazi Dannecker himself was so surprised that he sent Eichmann an urgent telegram on July 6: "President Laval has proposed that children below the age of sixteen be included in the deportation of Jewish families from the free zone. The fate of Jewish children in the occupied zone does not interest him."

It was Laval's suggestion which, while it astonished Dannecker, prompted him to ask Eichmann whether he agreed to the deportation of children under the age of sixteen after the fifteenth convoy. Meanwhile events took their course. On July 7 the meeting of the special committee was held, and on July 16 Operation Spring Wind was launched.

Now, on July 17, the second day of the roundup, the children in question were making their presence felt. They filled the Vel d'Hiv with their howling and could be heard all over the quarter. Weeping, crying, complaining, they were hungry and thirsty and drove their mothers wild. They were quite a nuisance, and the meeting taking place at Avenue Foch had been called to decide what was to be done with them. Some answer to the problem had to be found. Finally Darquier de Pellepoix made a suggestion: "Why not put all the Jewish children from Paris and the suburbs in children's homes run by the UGIF?"

It was not a bad idea. That way the children would be within reach, so to speak, and under control. But it did not meet with unanimous approval. The French policemen, with François and Tulard at their head, on the contrary voted for immediate deportation. Why hesitate when Laval had given them the freedom to do what they wanted? Darquier's compromise was suggested by the indecision among the Germans themselves. They had not yet received instructions from their superiors and were still waiting for a reply from Berlin. It was not their fault if Vichy had forestalled them.

At this point Roethke interrupted to say that it would be wiser to wait for a decision from Germany. Meanwhile it was decided that the children would be left with their parents for the moment. The Jewish families would be transferred to Pithiviers and Beaune-la-Rolande with the children, and from there the parents would gradually be taken to Drancy for deportation. Later, if Berlin accepted Laval's suggestion, the children would follow. There was in fact no doubt in anyone's mind that the message from Berlin would favor the deportation of the children. It was just a matter of waiting a few days or even a few hours. One or two points were then cleared up, and a few tasks relating to the fate of the prisoners arrested on July 16 and 17 were divided among those present.

The French police were put in charge of the transportation of the Jews from Pithiviers and Beaune-la-Rolande to Drancy. They would also be in charge of the supply and the organization of the convoys, which would be taken care of by the national railroad service (SNCF). Between Drancy and the German border, the French police would provide an escort of one officer and twenty gendarmes per convoy, supported by eight German *feld-gendarmes* and one German officer.

The UGIF was not left out in the distribution of duties; to them fell the "medical care" for the prisoners.

The meeting ended at 11:30, the Germans accompanying the Frenchmen to the door and saluting them with a "Heil Hitler." On the sundrenched pavement they parted, each going off to his car, a large Hotchkiss or Viva-4 Renault, under the eyes of the German sentry.

On July 29 Eichmann telephoned from Berlin: Yes, the children could be deported. Making a record of this telephone conversation, Dannecker said: "I have discussed the question of the deportation of children with SS Obersturmbannfuehrer Eichmann, and we came to the conclusion that as soon as it was possible to resume convoys to Germany, we would send children as well."

It seems clear that it was Eichmann who fulfilled Laval's wishes, and yet during his trial he said:

> The French police had arrested the children with the rest of the Jews. That is why we were immediately contacted and urgently asked what was to be done with these children. In reply I answered what you find here. . . . If you take this document by itself without considering any others, you will get the impression that I decided offhand what was to be done with the children, as if I was in a position to make that decision. And yet it will be clearly demonstrated by a document originally numbered 64, which is the text of a telegram, showing that the IV B 4 section in Paris had turned to me as early as July 10 to tell me of the arrest of the children and to ask what was to be done with them, were they to be deported or not. The very fact that eleven days passed between the decision and the order proves that the question had been passed through the usual channels to the highest competent authority. On the eleventh day, when I had been informed of the final decision on this

question, I passed on the order to Paris by telephone. It should be noted that Mueller himself was not qualified to make a decision on the matter. I will further point out that in spite of the fact that Himmler's order stipulated explicitly that all Jews without exception were to be deported, Bureau IV judged it necessary to make inquiries about whether this order applied to the children.

So Laval and his police made a firm proposition. Eichmann or Himmler made a decision on it, and as a result the children were deported. Of all those who went to Germany, not one returned.

Chapter 8

Seven Days in the Vel d'Hiv

Operation Spring Wind had been launched at four o'clock in the morning of July 16. On the seventeenth the raids continued. While the authorities on the Avenue Foch sat discussing the fate of the arrested children, the police carried on with the work. Teams of policemen would make their way up the stairs of marked addresses, knocking on the doors. But the day before had been a revelation—people's eyes had been opened to the truth, and their illusions had been dispersed. So few arrests were made on the second day that Roethke complained bitterly. On the other hand, there still were people who could not believe such things possible.

At 12 Boulevard de la Villette, in the XIX Arrondissement, lived a veteran soldier, Mr. Faynzilber. He had lost a leg in action and had been awarded the Croix de Guerre. Filled with apprehension, he sat in his small apartment on July 17, waiting. Hopping on one leg, he found it difficult to look after his two small children, a boy of four and a girl of six. His wife had been arrested the day before and was now at Drancy. And he was left with the children to care for. Heaving himself along on his crutches and with the two children dragging behind him, Mr. Faynzilber had made his way from Boulevard de la Villete to Boulevard Haussmann and the offices of the Federation of Amputees. His son Lucien was too young to wear a yellow star, but the girl had to wear one, while Mr. Faynzilber's own decorations were the stump of his amputated leg, his military cross, and the yellow star. At the offices of the federation for the war wounded, he was very kindly received. The people there, shocked and overcome with shame when they heard his story, immediately sent the following letter to Darquier de Pellepoix:

July 16, 1942

Mr. Faynzilber, a veteran soldier of the 25th regiment of the *Marche Etranger,* is still recovering from an amputation for which he needs daily medical treatment. He cannot move without crutches and lives alone in a fourth-floor apartment. What makes his case particularly distressing is the fact that he has two very young children to look after. We would be grateful if you could kindly try to obtain the release of Mrs. Faynzilber, the wife of this brave invalid, by applying the special ruling which apparently grants the right to regain their freedom to Jewish women married to prisoners of war.

The reply came on July 23:

I gave your letter of July 16 my closest attention. I cannot give you a favorable answer since the occupation forces forbid any show of favoritism.*

Darquier de Pellepoix, who wrote this letter, did not even take the trouble to bring the case to the attention of the Germans. As a matter of fact, there were a few instances of wives of prisoners of war being liberated on the first day, mainly due to the general chaos. Later on August 15, Roethke himself declared that these women had been released without his knowledge and there would be no repetition of such releases. Mr. Rosenberg's appeal was similarly received when he was arrested on July 17.

Warned of the roundup by Kaminsky, Mr. Rosenberg took his wife and daughter to stay with some friends on the Rue des Filles de Calvaire. They thought they would be protected in this house, since the father of the family was a prisoner of war. Other refugees came for shelter in the same belief and spent the night in the small apartment. The prisoner of war's wife

* Mrs. Faynzilber never came back. Mr. Faynzilber himself and his daughter were deported later and also disappeared. Only the little boy, Lucien, survived, and we were unable to trace his whereabouts until 1964.

was particularly worried about her small child; she could not rest but went out for news on the morning of the seventeenth. The rumor she heard, which was partly true, said that veterans and those with military decorations had been freed.

Hearing this, Rosenberg decided that since he himself had been awarded a military cross and would therefore be protected, there was no point in imposing on his friend's wife or breaking the law by going into hiding. Returning to his home at 11 Rue Commines with his wife and daughter, he found the door of his apartment broken down. So they had come to look for him. Still he thought that once he explained his position and showed proof of his decoration, everything would be all right, and he asked the concierge to go and fetch the police. This kind of naive trust is exactly what the Germans had counted on for the success of their operation.

Soon an inspector, along with a policeman in uniform, came from the police station of the III Arrondissement. His name was Noel. After making some sarcastic remarks about the situation, he cast a withering glance at the photograph of Rosenberg in the uniform of an infantryman, taken in 1939, and at the military cross pinned to its frame.

"Since you're a veteran and since your daughter is French, we'll let you leave her with friends—if you have any friends who are ready to look after her, that is," he conceded grudgingly.

All the neighbors offered to take in the thirteen-year-old girl, and she was eventually entrusted to the Gaillards. Mrs. Rosenberg kissed her daughter goodbye, giving her last-minute bits of advice. That was the last they saw of each other. From the police station the Rosenbergs were taken to the Vélodrome d'Hiver in a police truck.

"It was only when I entered the Vel d'Hiv that I finally understood what was happening to us," Mr. Rosenberg said later. "There had never been a chance that I would be freed. But by then it was too late."

The UGIF also deplored the fact that:

It has been impossible to obtain the release of descendants or relatives of prisoners of war or of soldiers who fell either in this war or the last war.

It is shocking that the occupation authorities have refused to release children of French nationality who were arrested at the same time as their parents on July 16 and 17. They consistently refuse to regard them as French citizens even though they were born in France and are indisputably French in the eyes of the law.

By one o'clock in the afternoon of July 17, Operation Spring Wind had ended. The buses took their last loads to Drancy and Vel d'Hiv with engines grunting and puffing almost as if they were tired and impatient to get back to their depots. The siege on the quarters with the heaviest Jewish population was lifted, and gendarmes, policemen, inspectors, and militant members of the PPF, having completed their mission, returned to their barracks, offices, or sections. The sentries who had been borrowed for the operation were able to resume their watch over the buildings occupied by the Germans.

In the happy prewar days, when the Vel d'Hiv was associated only with sports contests, one of the competitions was referred to as "the infernal six-day round." The same expression would apply very aptly to what was about to take place in the same arena during the seven days after the roundup. It was a succession of every kind of moral and physical suffering. The prisoners were to experience every aspect of despair after their initial numb stupefaction.

They had been brought to this place by French policemen on the orders of French officials to suffer and be sent to their death after being carefully chosen from a clearly defined class of citizens—alien or stateless Jews. This was the first step in the persecution of the Jews. Most of them were women, children, and older people, since the majority of adult male Jews had already been rounded up in previous raids.

For some years now—in some cases as many as ten, twenty, or thirty years—these people had been anxiously wanting to become integrated and form part of the French population. Many bonds attached them to their adopted country: children born in France and brought up like French children, marriages, betrothals, friendships, and neighbors, etc. Yet many retained traits which set them apart, in some cases an accent, in others some tradition or custom.

When they were told that they would be persecuted in France as they had been elsewhere, they would not believe it. Many, even though they believed the rumors of the impending raid, did not know what to do about it. It was not enough to be warned. Things were not that simple. However courageous, daring, provident, and efficient they might be, their heavy accent would betray them at every turn. In France they had no family ties, no network of relations who might help, no country cousins who might put them up. And, having escaped, how would they survive? How could a Jewess alone with her children to look after, and no papers, find work and live in occupied France, which had become a police state? And beyond the practical impossibility of escape, their fighting spirit and resolution were undermined and weakened by their great disillusionment. They had come to France because of an ideal image they had had. Like many other foreigners, the Jews had been coming to France since the beginning of the century almost as if on a pilgrimage to the land of freedom. If the French themselves . . . what could they do? So their difficulties were not merely of a practical, geographical, and economic nature, but also spiritual. Some disappointments can leave a man weak and spent.

Among the first to be moved to pity were some doctors who decided to devote their skills to lessening all this misery. In spite of André Baur's request on behalf of the UGIF, neither French nor German authorities would allow more than two doctors to work in the Vel d'Hiv at the same time. And when Gallien paid a brief visit to the "bird cage" on Sunday, July 19, he confirmed this ruling. So in compliance with the orders of the Prefecture and the Germans, two doctors only were on duty at the Vel d'Hiv at any one time. A system of shifts was worked out between the ten doctors or so sent by the UGIF, among whom were Dr. Weill-Hallé, Dr. Loewe-Lyon, Dr.

Inside the Vel d'Hiv, July 16, 1942. This photograph is described on pages 50–51.

PREFECTURE DE POLICE

Direction de la
Police Municipale

ETAT - MAJOR

Ier Bureau-A

PARIS, le 13 Juillet 1942

S E C R E T

CIRCULAIRE Nr. 173 - 42

à Messieurs les Commissaires Divisionnaires, Commissaires
de Voie Publique et des Circonscriptions de Banlieue.
(En communication à Direction P.J. - R.Gx - Gendarmerie
et Garde de Paris.)

Les Autorités Occupantes ont décidé l'arrestation et le rassemblement
d'un certain nombre de juifs étrangers.

I - PRINCIPES.

A - A qui s'applique cette mesure ?

a) catégories:

La mesure dont il s'agit, ne concerne que les juifs des nationalités
suivantes:

- Allemands
- Autrichiens
- Polonais
- Tchécoslovaques
- Russes (réfugiés ou soviétiques, c'est-à-dire "blancs" ou "rouges")
- Apatrides, c'est-à-dire de nationalité indéterminée.

b) âge et sexe:

Elle concerne tous les juifs des nationalités ci-dessus, quel que
soit leur sexe, pourvu qu'ils soient âgés de 16 à 60 ans (les femmes de 16 à
55 ans).

Les enfants de moins de 16 ans seront emmenés en même temps que les
parents.

Dérogations:

Ne tombent pas sous le coup de la mesure:

- les femmes enceintes dont l'accouchement serait proche
- les femmes nourrissant au sein leur bébé
- les femmes ayant un enfant de moins de 2 ans, c'est-à-dire né après
    le Ier Juillet 1940
- les femmes de prisonniers de guerre
- les veuves ou veufs ayant été mariés à un non-juif
- les juifs ou juives mariés à des non-juifs, et faisant la preuve,
    d'une part, de leurs liens légitimes, et d'autre part, de la
    qualité de non-juif de leur conjoint

./...

Reproduction of the first two pages of the circular from the Prefect
of Police of the Vichy government concerning the organization of the
roundup. (Translation on pages 279–281.)

- 2 -

‡ les juifs et juives porteur de la carte de légitimation de l'union
Générale des Israélites de France, carte qui est de couleur
bulle ou jaune claire
- les juifs et juives dont l'époux légitime est d'une nationalité non
, visée au paragraphe a)
- les parents dont l'un au moins des enfants n'est pas juif.

Dans le cas où un membre de la famille bénéficie de la dérogation,
les enfants ne sont pas emmenés, à moins qu'ils ne soient juifs et âgés de
16 ans et plus.

B - Exécution:

Chaque israélite (homme et femme) à arrêter fait l'objet d'une fiche.
Ces fiches sont classées par arrondissement et par ordre alphabétique.

Vous constituerez des équipes d'arrestations. Chaque équipe sera com-
posée d'un gardien en tenue et d'un gardien en civil ou d'un inspecteur des
Renseignements Généraux ou de la Police Judiciaire.

Chaque équipe devra recevoir plusieurs fiches. A cet effet, l'ensemble
des fiches d'un arrondissement ou d'une circonscription sera remis par ma Direction ce jour à 21 heures.

Les équipes chargées des arrestations devront procéder avec le plus
de rapidité possible, sans paroles inutiles et sans commentaires. En outre, au
moment de l'arrestation, le bien-fondé ou le mal-fondé de celle-ci, n'a pas à
être discuté. C'est vous qui serez responsables des arrestations et examinerez
les cas litigieux, qui devront vous être signalés.

Vous instituerez, dans chacun de vos arrondissements ou circonscriptions, un ou plusieurs "Centres primaires de rassemblement", que vous ferez
garder. C'est dans ce ou ces centres que seront examinés par vous les cas dou-
teux. Si vous ne pouvez trancher la question, les intéressés suivront momen-
tanément le sort des autres.

Les autobus, dont le nombre est indiqué plus loin, seront mis à votre
disposition.

Lorsque vous aurez un contingent suffisant pour remplir un autobus,
vous dirigerez:

a) sur le Camp de Drancy les individus ou familles n'ayant pas d'enfant
de moins de 16 ans

b) sur le Vélodrome d'Hiver: les autres.

En ce qui concerne le camp de Drancy, le contingent prévu doit être
de 6.000. En conséquence, chaque fois que vous ferez un départ pour Drancy,
vous ferez connaître le nombre de personnes transportées dans ce camp à l'
Etat-Major qui vous préviendra lorsque le maximum sera atteint. Vous dirigerez
alors les autobus restants sur le Vélodrome d'Hiver.

./...

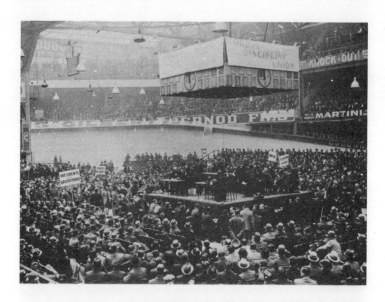

Before the war the Vélodrome d'Hiver was the scene of political assemblies (ABOVE) and sports events (BELOW: preparations for a boxing match).

The camps of Gurs (ABOVE) and Beaune-la-Rolande (BELOW) were
intended for the internment of Spanish Republicans. Later the Jews—
first foreign, then French—joined them there.

Some of the victims of July 16 and their executioners. ABOVE: Mr. Faynzilber (LEFT) lost a leg in the service of France in 1940. When Jews were ordered to wear a yellow star, he had himself photographed wearing his Croix de Guerre and Military Medal and holding hands with his daughter (older than six and required to wear a star) and his son (not yet old enough to wear it). Mr. Faynzilber hoped, as a war veteran, to save his wife from deportation. Mrs. Nussbaum (CENTER) was arrested but escaped from the Vel d'Hiv with her child. Rachel Pronice, a pianist, was warned and left Paris before the roundup. She was arrested at the demarcation line and disappeared without a trace.

BELOW: The order to execute Operation Spring Wind came from Heydrich (LEFT) —seen here with Himmler (AT LEFT IN BACKGROUND) — and was implemented by Eichmann (CENTER). Shortly afterward Heydrich was assassinated by a squad of Czech paratroopers (PHOTOGRAPH OF FUNERAL AT RIGHT). But the roundup took place as planned.

RÉCIT DES TRAITEMENTS INFLIGÉS AUX FAMILLES JUIVES
DANS LA RÉGION PARISIENNE À PARTIR DU 16 JUILLET 1942.
-=-=-=-=-=-=-=-=-=-=-

Ce récit est loin d'être complet. C'est peu à
peu qu'en arrive à savoir ce qui se passe par
les confidences des rescapés, des infirmières,
même des gendarmes qui gardent les camps.

LES ARRESTATIONS

C'est le jeudi 16 Juillet que les inspecteurs et gendarmes français, le plupart du temps accompagnés de jeunes dorictistes, ont commen-
cé à frapper aux portes des Juifs désignés sur leurs listes.

La nouvelle se répandit en ville comme une trainée de poudre ;
et un sauve-qui-peut général s'en suivit. Tous ceux qui le pouvaient
s'enfuyaient, à peine vêtus, cherchant asile chez des voisins français,
chez des concierges, dans les caves et les greniers. Certains ont sim-
plement refusé d'ouvrir leurs portes. Là où les portes ont été ouvertes,
ça parfois forcées, on vit se produire des scènes déchirantes. Des femmes s'évanouissaient, des enfants hurlaient et beaucoup de ces persé-
cutés eurent recours au suicide. Une mère a jeté ses quatre enfants
par la fenêtre, d'un quatrième étage, puis s'est précipitée elle-même
dans le vide, pendant qu'on forçait la porte. Une petite fille de 10
ans affolée a sauté du cinquième étage. Dans un logement qu'on a for-
cé, les gen'armes se sont trouvés en présence d'un homme qui tenait
dans la bouche le tuyau du gaz et qui était à moitié asphyxié. Une jeune femme de 24 ans s'est fait mutant. À Montreuil, un médecin s'est sui-
cidé avec sa famille au moyen de piqûres. Des faits analogues se sont
répétés les jours suivants.

Aussitôt pénétré dans un logement, la police a déclaré les Juifs
qui s'y trouvaient en état d'arrestation. Ils ont reçu l'ordre de se
préparer en hâte, on leur a permis d'emporter quelques objets indispen-
sables, et des vivres pour deux jours. Certains n'en avaient pas, ou
fort peu. Ils étaient condamnés à jeûner complètement les deux premiers
jours. kxxpxi

La police, ayant reçu l'ordre de ne pas prendre en considéra-
tion l'état de santé des personnes inscrites sur les listes, a emmené
non seulement des malades graves, mais aussi des morts. Un enfant mort
la veille a été emporté dans un drap. On a pris des femmes et des enfants à partir de deux ans, des femmes enceintes dans le 7ème, 8ème,
et même 9ème mois, des malades tirés de leur lit, et portés sur des
chaises ou des civières ; une femme paralysée a été emmenée sur une
chaise roulante. Des vieillards de 60-70 ans n'ont pas été épargnés.

Mais c'est surtout la razzia des enfants qu'il faut souligner.
C'est à partir de deux ans que les enfants ont été considérés comme
aptes pour les camps de concentration. En principe, les enfants français devaient être épargnés, en réalité, la majorité des enfants arrêtés est de nationalité française. Dans plusieurs cas, en l'absence des
parents, on a pris des enfants de 6, 10, 12 ans, la preuve en est que
quelques enfants français arrêtés seuls ont été relâchés après trois
jours de détention. Une jeune femme est venue demander des renseignements au sujet de sa soeur âgée de 10 ans qui se trouvait au Vel d'Hiv.
On emmène même des enfants malades avec 40° et 41° de fièvre, atteints
de rougeole, de coqueluche, de varicelle, de scarlatine et même de
typhoïde. Quelques-uns ont été envoyés à l'Hôpital Claude-Bernard. Les
mères désespérées se dressaient en vain entre les policiers et leurs enfants malades. Dans nombre de cas on a arraché de force les mères de
leurs petits ; on les a enlevées tantôt par force, tantôt par ruse.
Les cris et les pleurs remplissaient les rues. Les voisins, les pas-
sants ne pouvaient s'empêcher de pleurer.

Reproduction of the first Resistance tract denouncing the arrests of
July 16. (Translation on pages 282–283.)

In 1945 George Horan, a deportee, published some engravings, based on life sketches, entitled *On the Brink of the Jewish Inferno*. This one shows the arrival of the children at Drancy.

Drancy: On the outside the barracks look like middle-class apartment
buildings (ABOVE). Inside is a different story . . . (BELOW). Internees
arrive in increasing numbers from 1942 on (ABOVE). Among them are
many young people who have not yet lost all hope (BELOW).

MINISTÈRE
DE L'INTÉRIEUR

ÉTAT FRANÇAIS

DIRECTION GÉNÉRALE
DE LA
POLICE NATIONALE

PARIS   le 26 Septembre   1942

P. N. Cab. A N   876

LE SOUS - PRÉFET
Délégué dans les Territoires Occupés
du Secrétaire Général à la Police,

à Monsieur l'OBERSTURMFÜHRER ROTXE
31 bis, Avenue Foch
P A R I S.

Je vous confirme ma communication téléphonique de ce
jour :

Un convoi venant de zone libre et composé d'environ
80 à 90 Juifs étrangers, passera la ligne de démarcation à
Vierzon le 29-9-42 à 22 H 41.

Départ de Vierzon le 29-9-42 à 23H24.
Arrivée au Bourget-Drancy le 30-9-42 à 4H49.

Je vous prie de vouloir bien prendre les dispositions
nécessaires pour que la Feldgendarmerie soit avisée de ce convoi.

P. le PRÉFET
Par autorisation

Reproduction of a letter from a Vichy delegate in occupied territory
informing Roethke of the "delivery" of a convoy of Jews by Vichy to the
German authorities. Roethke's notes are at lower right. (Translation on
page 284.)

One of the Jewish patients at the Rothschild hospital; most of them
will be deported.

ABOVE: Some of the women and children arriving at Auschwitz station will be taken immediately to the gas chambers. The abbreviation SNCF can be seen on the car. BELOW: Some women are judged "good for service" and escape death temporarily.

ABOVE: "Selection" on the platform of Auschwitz station. At right the
column of men considered fit for forced labor; at left the column of
women, children, and the sick who will go directly to the gas chambers.
BELOW: A deported mother has looked after her children all the way to
Auschwitz. They are sent together to the gas chambers.

Children at Auschwitz, photographed by an SS.

Vilenski, Dr. Didier-Hesse, and Dr. Benjamin Ginsbourg. The
Red Cross sent Colonel Robineau, Dr. Comby, Dr. Milhaud,
and Professor Vaucher. In the center of the arena they set up
a kind of first-aid post.

On the seventeenth, Dr. Didier-Hesse returned laden with
all he could lay hands on in the way of drugs, hypodermic
needles, cotton wool—and also napkins and bits of string. The
Red Cross nurses had suggested these as a comfort for the
women who were indisposed, since there were no toilets and no
water. The assortment of medicines was piled on two tables
that had been pushed end to end. But the medical supply was
limited: rubbing alcohol, mercurochrome, insulin, and the
universal panacea, aspirin. A small spirit lamp was used to boil
the water for sterilizing the hypodermic needles in a small
enamel pan.

Nurses and doctors worked with dedication. Among their
patients were the sick or the wounded, people who had tried
to escape or commit suicide when they were arrested or who
had tried to kill themselves in the Vel d'Hiv itself, by throwing
themselves down from the top tiers. They lay on the ground
with fractured limbs. There were others with serious diseases.
In the medical reports one comes across the following:

> I saw a number of cases of ulcers or cancer of the
> digestive tract; the patients often had diagnoses from the
> most distinguished surgeons and hospitals, and several
> were due for operation the week of their arrest. A few
> women had attempted suicide before being brought to
> the Vel d'Hiv. Cases of TB wandered around spreading
> germs, and one shudders to think of the number of small,
> less resistant children who must have been infected in
> these unhygienic surroundings. Other pulmonary cases,
> who were unable to get the necessary treatment, braced
> themselves for a relapse of their disease. . . .

There were kidney attacks, heart attacks, and miscarriages. Dr.
Didier-Hesse tells of "one man whom I found sitting on the
ground, his skin livid and his face distorted with pain. Beads of
sweat stood on his forehead, and he was clutching his chest. I
asked him whether I could help. He replied in German that he

himself was a doctor, that he was having a heart attack, and no
one could do anything for him. I gave him an injection of
coramine."

Then there were the minor ailments to attend to: dizziness,
faintness, slight skin infections, and colds. The smaller children
were particularly troubled with breathing difficulties and upset
stomachs. At least a hundred of the 4,051 children had been
taken from their houses sick, some at the height of a fever,
others suffering from mumps, measles, chicken pox, whooping
cough, or scarlet fever. The police had brought them with the
rest. Some attempt was made to isolate them by putting them
in the closed spectators' boxes around the track. There,
wrapped in blankets, shivering and feverish, or swollen and
disfigured with rashes, frightened, coughing, and vomiting, the
little ones cried their lungs out while the older ones tried to
quiet them.

Not much later, there were epidemics in the camps at
Beaune-la-Rolande and Pithiviers. Doctors like Dr. Weill-Hallé
were already thinking of the possibility of the spread of disease.
Weill-Hallé had spent his life working with BCG, the anti-
tuberculosis vaccine. His anxiety was understandable but
entirely useless. Eight weeks later, nothing was left of 4,051
children except some ashes in Poland. One of the writers of
this book plunged his hand into these ashes when he went to
Poland on a pilgrimage and found, among minute fragments
of bone, a miniscule bone from a baby's finger.

The doctors tried to obtain permission for the evacuation
of the most critical and the contagious cases but the rules were
strict, and Jewish doctors were not qualified to make decisions
anyway. The only doctor whose opinion on serious cases was
accepted was Dr. Tisne of the Prefecture. But he was rarely
there and had to be reached by telephone, which complicated
matters further. Moreover he was seldom helpful. Miscarriage
with profuse hemorrhage was not considered serious enough
for evacuation, nor was a heart attack, nor an attack of the
kidneys. It was a matter of luck or chance if any patient was
allowed out. Somehow Dr. Didier-Hesse managed to get a man

with an amputated leg released, and he left, leaning on his
daughter.

Thanks to the intervention of Dr. Comby and Dr. Robineau,
the madwoman and the little boy she had stunned with a bottle
were taken out.* Dr. Vilenski saw one woman on the point of
giving birth and thinks that she was allowed out. She might
well be the pregnant woman who appears in the photograph.
On the third floor Hélène Rozen and her brother watched their
mother, who was sick. When she lost consciousness, she was
taken to the infirmary; after three days, thanks to the devotion
and cunning of one of the nurses, she was transferred to the
Rothschild hospital. The children left with her and were sent
to the Lamarck Center for Jewish Children.

Two other children escaped—a girl of eight and her brother
of three. Their name was Friedman. They were taken to the
Rothschild hospital after a nurse had pretended they were
suffering from mange.

The director of the municipal police, Hennequin, reported
the following:

> I was told that about fifty Jewish prisoners were dying
> and had been left without treatment, stretched on the
> ground in one corner of the stadium. Though my orders
> were not to allow anyone in the service to enter the Vel
> d'Hiv, I let the Commissioner of Police from the XV
> Arrondissement go inside to confirm this information and
> take the necessary humane steps that the case demanded
> if it were in fact true. As soon as François found out what
> I had done, he informed the Germans that I had been
> encroaching on their territory. The SS immediately
> threatened to arrest me and the Commissioner from the
> XV Arrondissement if it turned out that the Jews who
> had been hospitalized as a result of my interference were
> not considered sufficiently sick when examined by a
> German army doctor of their own choosing. The threat
> did not have much effect on me since it was obvious
> without any medical training that the Jews in question
> were truly dying.**

* Recognizing himself as the boy involved, Leon Ickowicz wrote to us.
So we know that he was saved by the intervention of the two doctors.
** Deposition before Judge Zoussman on 1/3/1948.

So much for Hennequin's testimony to his own humanitarian standards. Colonel Robineau also tried to insist that the seriously sick prisoners be transferred to a hospital, and he was told simply: "If you like the Jews so much, you will be allowed to share their fate."

Most of the victims of Black Thursday were sent to Drancy, the Vel d'Hiv, or to the camps in the Loiret; a very small number, twenty or thirty in all, were transferred to the Rothschild hospital in Paris. The Germans and the doctor from the Prefecture, Dr. Tisne, were not very understanding and would not allow any more, though the nurses and doctors battled to get as many of the sick into the hospital as possible. Only cases of heart failure and cases needing surgery were considered serious enough for hospital treatment. There were prisoners with acute appendicitis, peritonitis, burst ulcers, and some of those who attempted suicide inside the stadium, with fractures. Among them was Mrs. Rozen, who was suffering from a heart condition and whose children had been put into the children's home on the Rue Lamarck. Mrs. Friedman and her two children were taken to the hospital together.

Rothschild hospital was hardly recognizable during the occupation, surrounded as it was by rolls of barbed wire and guarded by gendarmes and policemen. It was hardly a normal hospital since the patients treated there were to go on to the extermination camps. And most of the doctors and nurses were hardly acting normal, since they did their best to prolong their patients' illnesses and so justify a longer stay at the hospital. From December, 1941, the Rothschild hospital had become in effect a prison-hospital for the Jews. The Prefecture of the Police and the Prefecture of the Seine had jointly taken over two wards, which they used for the critical cases among the prisoners at Drancy.

The hospital was cleared in preparation for the roundup just as Beaune-la-Rolande and Pithiviers had been emptied for the Jews who were about to be arrested.

At six o'clock in the morning of July 3, the hospital had been surrounded by French uniformed and plainclothes policemen, while the commissioner in charge informed the director of the hospital that he had to hand over all patients who had come from Drancy. Professor Robert Worms remembers that morning all too well:

> Among the sick there were patients suffering from bilateral tuberculosis, arteriosclerosis, and extreme heart failure. One young man was afflicted with a severe form of diabetes, another was at the height of an alarming heart complication, still another had jaundice and kidney trouble at the same time, a war casualty was in unbearable pain after an amputation, a case of prostatis needed treatment twice a day, while in the surgery ward there were prisoners convalescing after recent operations. One had been operated in the stomach the night before.

The clearing of the hospital was conducted at a brisk pace, the policemen involved taking no notice of the groans of the sick, whom they jostled without cease, even going to the extreme of striking them. Only those who were so sick that they were on the verge of coma were permitted a stretcher. Lacking clothes, they were all taken off in nightshirts and pajamas. Some were driven away in police vans handcuffed to each other. In one hour the hospital had been cleared.

The hospital pharmacist, Mr. Dupont, even now cannot keep himself from breaking into sobs when he recalls the scene: "One or two of the policemen seemed moved, and I remember one in particular who looked as if he was going to collapse, but mostly their expressions were hard and forbidding. And none of them bothered to answer when I asked what was going to happen to these sick people."

What happened was that one of them died on the way to the camp. Several more died at Drancy in the following few days. The rest were put onto the first train to leave Drancy after the roundup of the sixteenth and seventeenth of July—a convoy which arrived at Auschwitz on July 21, where 375 of the deportees who were not strong enough to work were killed in the gas chambers.

For those who had been allowed to leave the Vel d'Hiv for health reasons, their stay in the hospital was merely a brief respite. But even a short time could be used for an attempt to escape. For example, Mrs. Friedman spent several weeks in the hospital. Her children were there too but in a different ward, the ward for contagious diseases; during that time the two children were rescued. Mrs. Friedman's daughter, Mrs. Guen, now a married woman with children of her own, told us:

> My brother and I owe our lives to Miss Claire Heyman, who still works at the Rothschild hospital as a social assistant. To us she has always remained "Aunt Claire."
> I remember being looked after at the Rothschild hospital and being unable to leave our ward to visit our mother, who was in a different part of the hospital. As soon as we came out of quarantine, we went to see her, but she was not well. One morning we were not allowed to visit her; we were told that she was very sick indeed. The next day and the days that followed, the same thing happened. But my brother, who was only three years old at that time, rushed to her bed in spite of the nurses who tried to hold him. They had to tell us then that mother had left for Drancy. My brother ran through the hospital and out into the garden at the back and threw his arms around a tree. He hugged it so tight we could not get him away, and he kept calling "Mother" without stopping. After that he fell seriously ill. He had a tumor on the brain, and I sat up with him every night. I was only eight years old, but I was like a little mother to him. The nurses scolded me for sitting up all night. When he recovered, Aunt Claire looked after us.

Neither Mrs. Friedman nor her husband, who was already at Pithiviers, came back.

Mrs. Rozen also was taken to Drancy and from there to Auschwitz when she left the hospital. Her children, Jean and Hélène, remained at the center on the Rue Lamarck.

Thus a small number of prisoners were temporarily evacuated to the Rothschild hospital. Thanks to the general chaos, seven or eight wives of prisoners of war were also admitted on the first day of the roundup.

On July 19 about twenty people were admitted in equivocal circumstances. The people in question were men and women in possession of labor permits issued by the Germans. Where the permits were genuine, they belonged to workers employed in the garment trade and furriers' workshops; both these industries recruited their staff largely from among alien Jews. The UJRE, which was then newly organized and had a great following among the Jewish workers, took a firm stand on the subject, namely, encouraging the workers to sabotage the workshops and intimidate the owners, whether they were Jewish or not. At the same time, possession of such a labor permit was for many the only way to earn a living legally. Needless to say, a lively trade in these certificates was run by the "Aryan" owners of the workshops. But it is only fair to add that there were some who gave them away out of sympathy for the unemployed Jews.

So, on the nineteenth, when policemen from the Prefecture came to the Vel d'Hiv (after complaints had been made to the Germans by the owners of garment workshops who found that they were without labor as a result of the arrests) and called out the names of the establishments that needed their employees back, all those who owned labor permits, whether genuine or false, tried to get out. There were arguments, and a few people smuggled themselves out on a fake document; others were not so lucky. Among those who succeeded were Mrs. Rado and Mrs. Dorag.

On the second day of Operation Spring Wind, the General Secretariat for Youth, which was then headed by Georges Lamirand, began sending its young members to the Vel d'Hiv. One of the tasks generally performed by these young people was the clearing of bombed sites, and their presence in the Vel d'Hiv was the result of a similar kind of concern. Dressed in a semi-uniform consisting of blue shirts, blue berets, and sometimes white gaiters, they set about their work without hesitation; it was their good deed for that day. But not all of them were tactful, and there were mixed feelings among the prisoners about them. Indeed they were mistaken for members of the PPF or army cadets by quite a number of people. Hélène Rozen, who watched them at work, says that she was struck by the coarseness of their manners while talking with older people.

Mr. Sienicki also complains that "they were rough and would
not let us get up or move from our places."

There were far more violently negative reactions to their
helping in the Vel d'Hiv in the *Au Pilori* newspaper. In the
July 23 issue, under the headline "Our Children Servants to the
Jews," one read:

> We have just received an astounding news item. At the
> instigation of the French Red Cross, and with the
> agreement of the Undersecretary of State for Youth, Mr.
> Lamirand, Mr. Henim (assistant to the head of the
> Commission for Youth Work, Mr. Roscouet) has given
> formal orders to various Youth Centers in the Paris region
> to send groups of their members, mere children of fifteen,
> to the Sports Palace (known as Vel d'Hiv) at Grenelle
> Boulevard, where several thousand Jews have been
> dumped. Their work consists of cleaning out the vast
> building, clearing up after the Jews, emptying dustbins,
> carrying the sick on stretchers if necessary, storing and
> distributing provisions, etc.
>   For two days several Youth Centers have submitted to
> this shameful work, but protests have already begun, and
> today a number of Youth Center organizers have refused
> to allow the young French boys entrusted to them to be
> subjected to such hateful servitude. . . .

One of the young men in question was so overcome by what
he saw that he wrote about it to one of his friends. Whether he
intended his friend to spread the information or not, it was
passed on:

> On Thursday evening I was given orders to report to the
> Vel d'Hiv. Next morning I went. There were about
> fifteen thousand Jews there. It is something so terrible,
> so diabolical, it seizes you by the throat so that you can't
> even cry out. I shall try to describe it to you, but multiply
> everything I tell you by a thousand, ten thousand or a
> hundred thousand and you will still only know a fraction
> of the truth. . . .

He goes on to describe what we know already. Very
conscientiously he corrects his impressions and brings the
information up to date:

In order to stick to the exact truth in this account, I would like to make some corrections, mainly that although fourteen to fifteen thousand people were arrested, only about six or seven thousand were kept in the Vel d'Hiv. That is the most detailed information I have to date, August 10th.

The appearance of the Youth Movement members gave Albert Goura an idea. He had been brought to the Vel d'Hiv with his mother, an uncle, an aunt, and his cousins, the Baums. Right from the first day, Albert Goura and Bernard Baum had resolved to do something. They tried their luck with the young Pétainists. Their instinct was right.

For money, they were given some uniforms, and that evening, July 17, dressed up as French youth workers, they had no difficulty in slipping out. They went home to their apartments on the Rue Maur and, after stocking up on food and drugs, *returned* to their families in the Vel d'Hiv. With no thought for themselves, they concentrated on helping their relatives and friends. Behaving as responsibly as grown men, they devoted themselves to fulfilling their duties toward their families, as yet unaware of what the future held in store for them.

Chapter 9

The Days That Followed

The second act of Operation Spring Wind took place in the free zone of France. As will be remembered, the Germans were claiming fifty thousand Jews from the unoccupied territory and had outlined the method for the roundup there. The Vichy government, which controlled the area, zealously complied with the demands of the Germans. Trains had been scheduled for the deportation of the Jews, and it was essential that they be filled to capacity. The roundups in the occupied zone had not yielded the number of prisoners anticipated, so the figures would have to be made up by finding a maximum number of deportees in the free zone. As a start, the poor people already in the concentration camps would be handed over to the Germans, then new raids would be staged to refill the camps and arrive at the total expected by the Germans.

Meanwhile the occupation forces decided to obtain detailed information on the proceedings. At the July 4 meeting in Paris, Bousquet had confirmed "that during the recent council of ministers, Marshal Pétain, the head of state, as well as President Laval, had agreed to the deportation of all stateless Jews in both occupied and free zones, as a first step." At the same meeting Bousquet had decided on the deportation of Jews already in prison in the free zone. At which point Dannecker suggested "an inspection of the camps before the delivery of the prisoners to the Germans." When Bousquet objected that such a step would infringe on the sovereignty of the government of the free zone and was therefore unthinkable, he was told:

Germany's readiness to take over the Jews living in France, in spite of being involved in a war, was more than a simple action. It showed their wish to solve the Jewish problem on a European scale. He was not to imagine that it was an easy thing for Germany to allow such large numbers of Jews to enter the country; but regardless of the difficulties, she had determined to solve the problem.

Finally, Bousquet had to admit that he could not refuse a preliminary inspection of the Jewish goods (*Judenmaterial*) by a German delegate.

This passage is quoted from Dannecker's minutes.

So on July 10, accompanied by Schweblin (the French head of the anti-Jewish police in the occupied zone) and provided with a letter of introduction addressed to all Prefects by the Secretary of State for Police, Dannecker and SS Unterscharfuehrer Heinrichsohn left by car on a tour of southern France. On their return they expressed their delight at the efficient organization of the journey and the exemplary reception given them by the French. From Milles, near Aix-en-Provence, they went to Rivesaltes, near Perpignan, and to Gurs in the neighborhood of Pau. At each stage of their journey the representatives of Pétain's government made platitudinous, servile speeches. The Commissioner of Police at Grenoble declared that he "thought it of vital importance to imprison all Jews," the head of police in the Nice region said that "he would be grateful for the removal of all Jews from his area," while the head of the Périgueux police said "that a swift solution of the Jewish question through deportation was highly desirable." At Marseilles the local head of the Francists complained that on July 14 there was a large gathering of Gaullists demonstrating and shouting "Vive de Gaulle." On July 19, as Dannecker's car was passing through Périgueux, a Frenchman of Alsatian origin, named Spitzer, yelled out "Dirty Hun!" loud and clear. He was immediately arrested, and the Prefect of the Dordogne region apologized to Dannecker.

While this incident marred Dannecker's tour on the nineteenth, the first convoy of Jews arrested on July 16 left Drancy for Germany, and the first batch of prisoners from the

Vel d'Hiv were put on a train at Austerlitz station to go to the camps in the Loiret. That same day also, Ernst Jünger, a well-known German writer, strolled among the graves in the Père-Lachaise cemetery, jotting down for posterity his impressions and reflections as an officer in occupied territory:

> Paris, July 19, 1942
>
> Afternoon at Père-Lachaise. I wandered in the midst of the tombstones with Camilla.
>
> This cemetery is very beautiful, especially where it is abandoned and overgrown. I thought of the legions resting there. No space is sufficient to contain the ever growing armies of the dead: they should try a different way. There would be room for them in the hollow of a nutshell then.

Coming back to Paris, he went on:

> I returned to Paris by winding roads. Every time I look at the winged genius of the Bastille, with his torch and the ends of a broken chain in his hands, I experience an increasingly vivid sense of an extremely dangerous and far-reaching force. He gives the impression of speed and calm at the same time. In him one sees the spirit of progress exalted, already enjoying the triumph of future struggles. Just as the working people joined with the merchants to create the spirit of the Bastille. . . .

On Saturday, July 18, at the corner where Rue Saint-Antoine meets Rue des Tourelles, three members of the FTP belonging to the P2 division in Paris threw a hand grenade at a German recruiting center. All three were deported and only one returned: Paul Tillard.

On July 23, the day the last of the Jews left in the Vel d'Hiv set out on their long journey, Roland Delval, member of the FTP, arrested by two policemen, Hennion and Gadenne, on May 5, 1942, was brought to trial and condemned to death. On the same day, the guillotine was set up in the yard of the Santé prison in Paris, and its gruesome knife beheaded another member of the FTP, named Dalmas. He had been arrested by the police in May, 1942, during a demonstration in the Rue de Buci.

The next day, July 24, the two young men mentioned earlier,

Wallach and Pakin, were condemned to death. They were shot
at Mont-Valérien prison three days later.

Once the immediate danger was over, those who had
succeeded in finding a safe hiding place set about fortifying
their precarious position. The free zone of France became a
center of attraction. That it was in any way safer than the
occupied zone was mere illusion. Pétain's police and his
gendarmes were straining to hunt down fugitives. At the same
time arrangements were being made for large-scale roundups.
And on the demarcation line itself, the Germans were
patiently waiting for the unsuspecting runaways.

Leaving Paris as best they could from the closely watched
railroad stations, without identity papers, risking arrest at any
moment, the Jewish fugitives piled onto the trains by the
thousands and came to try their luck at the demarcation line.

After being warned by a telephone call from her former
school friend, as was described above, Paulette Rotblit had left
her home. She knew of a good "contact" and had in addition
been able to procure some "reliable false documents" for
herself and for her mother. On July 25 the two women took a
train at Austerlitz station and before the end of the day arrived
at the address they had been given: a hotel at Rochefoucauld.

To the "guide" who introduced himself to them, they had to
pay the agreed price of sixty dollars per person. They found
themselves in a group of about eighteen adults and some
children, all fugitives. Following the young man, they crossed
some fields and walked along a path, the men carrying suitcases
or holding small children in their arms. Not a word was spoken.
For them it was an anxious moment. They had placed their
lives in the hands of this young man and had also given him
most of their savings. All that remained to them were the
clothes they wore and the few belongings they carried. In their
hearts they were deeply distressed, with just a spark of hope.
They walked for less than a quarter of an hour.

"Suddenly we came to a turn, and there in front of us was a
group of Germans in uniform waiting, with a truck parked
nearby. I turned around," Paulette Rotblit told us, "and I saw

our 'guide' walk off, raising his hand in greeting to the soldiers. The Germans began herding us toward the truck, pushing at us with their guns to make us get in. We had been caught and handed over to the enemy. The women wept, and the three men in our party had the wild look of madmen in their eyes. They were beginning to realize that they were lost, and this last treachery, coming at the very moment they were hoping to be saved, had knocked them out. Not completely, though. One of the women pushed her son toward us, whispering, 'Save him, save my child, say he is with you.' Both my mother and I looked so un-Jewish that even our fellow fugitives mistook us for non-Jews. Moreover, we had very good false documents, while the rest of the party had nothing. Some still carried their yellow stars tucked in their pockets."

Back in Rochefoucauld, the captured fugitives were locked in the town granary, which served as a prison. During the eight days they spent there they carefully sewed what was left of their money into the lining of their clothes. But a few weeks later, at Auschwitz, the Sonderkommandos systematically went through these same clothes and found the money. These savings ended up in the treasury of the Reich to increase the funds of the Reichsbank.

After eight days, Paulette and her mother, passing for non-Jews, were released with the little boy whom they pretended belonged to them. Everyone else was taken to Drancy. When they got to Paris, Paulette took the child to an address she had been given. A few days later, at the beginning of August, she and her mother managed to cross the demarcation line, this time with the help of an honest guide. The little boy also was taken across some time later and joined his father, Mr. Blumenfeld, who had set himself up as a watchmaker in Pau. Mrs. Blumenfeld was deported and died at the hands of the Germans.

On leaving her studio in Rue Raffet, Rachel Pronice had confidently told Mrs. Goldberg that she had "contacts." Not hearing any further news of the young piano teacher, Mrs. Goldberg assumed that she had crossed the demarcation line.

"Then one morning," Mrs. Goldberg told us, "I was called to an office near Place Saint-Augustin [most likely the UGIF on the Rue Bienfaisance]. It was run by Jews. I was already frightened at being summoned at all. When I got there, I was rather brusquely attended to by some unpleasant people. One of them handed me a crumpled piece of paper with scribbles on it. 'Here is news of a woman who is going to be deported,' he said. It was Rachel's writing—a hurried scrawl on a scrap of paper. 'I'm writing about the tobacco. They caught us. We were betrayed. Love, Rachel.' She must have given this note to a bystander, and it found its way to the UGIF. I never heard any more from Rachel, and after a time I gave her suitcase to her sister."

For those who succeeded in crossing the line, the difficulties were only beginning. There were those who were penniless and had nowhere to go. They would be still in a state of shock after a harrowing escape and would remain where they were, vulnerable in their belief that they were safe just because they had crossed the famous demarcation line. They were still unaware that on this side of the line there were people on the lookout for them, gun in hand, that there were barbed wires to catch them and delivery papers all ready. They crowded into every village—four hundred at Confolens, two hundred at Chasseneuil, and as many at Chabanais, for example.

Simone de Beauvoir, who had just crossed over herself with Sartre, wrote: "At Navarreux, the hotel was full of refugees. Unlike us, they had not crossed the border by choice. Most of them were Jews and obviously under strain."

At Romazières, a kindly hotel keeper put them up and fed them free of charge. On the other hand, in Limoges the price of hotel rooms suddenly became three times as expensive as usual. But there were people who volunteered to help these unhappy Jews, among whom there were unaccompanied children, like the sons of the writer Pierre Créange. The whole Créange family had been caught by the Germans on the demarcation line. Risking everything, the eldest boy had said, pointing at his parents, "We don't belong to this lady and gentleman. We don't even know them." Taking their cue, the parents joined in the cruel charade, and the two children were allowed through while Pierre Créange and his wife were taken away between two policemen. Neither parents nor children looked back; they had to play their parts.

The volume of the migration across the line created extra work for the Germans guarding it. On July 30, the customs post at Vierzon cabled Paris to report that thousands of Jews were trying to cross the line clandestinely, and reinforcements were needed.

Meanwhile in Paris it was a heartrending weekend. People were frantic as they discovered the disappearance of those they loved and made desperate attempts to release them. For example, Mr. Barbanel's family was arrested while he was at work. He found out what had happened from the neighbors. Twice more he heard news of them and then nothing. Someone brought him a letter his daughter Thérèse had thrown from the train. He never saw her again. All that remained to him of his family were papers drawn up at the town hall in Ivry relative to their disappearance and death.

From these documents it is clear that the death sentence had been firmly signed from the moment they entered the French camp, some two or three weeks after they had been arrested. The official language is dry, but the facts are eloquent. These papers were drawn up in 1946, on the new letterhead of the Ministry for War Veterans, Republic of France.

The minister declares:

The disappearance in the following circumstances
of Adolphe Barbanel
born August 9, 1933, in Paris XIII:
Arrested July 16, 1942,
Held at Beaune-la-Rolande and Drancy
Deported August 19, 1942, to Auschwitz, Poland.

The disappearance in the following circumstances
of Thérèse Barbanel

born January 10, 1929, in Paris XII- Seine:
Arrested July 16, 1942,
Held at Beaune-la-Rolande
Deported August 7, 1942, to Auschwitz, Poland.

The dates for the mother are the same.

The death certificates issued by the Ivry Town Hall read:

This is to certify the death on August 19, 1942, at Drancy,
of the Barbanel child and the death on August 7, 1942,
at Beaune-la-Rolande of Thérèse Barbanel.

Mr. Barbanel told us how after the Liberation he had rushed
to the police station at Ivry, saying, "Tell me—where is the
policeman who took my children from me?" An inspector
replied, "Oh, those—they were Nazis. They are no longer here.
We don't know what happened to them."

For some days the Rimmlers stayed with their friends at
Bures, not daring to leave the house. Then Mrs. Rimmler
decided to return to Paris and their home on the Rue des
Ecouffes to find out what had happened.

As mentioned above, this particular building suffered an
extraordinary number of arrests. Out of eleven families, seven
were taken away—fourteen adults and nineteen children. Four
families had been left, and Mrs. Rimmler found them stunned
and unable to understand why they had been spared. There
were the Blachmans, a father and three daughters (the mother
was in a hospital) ; the Rubins and their two sons; Mrs.
Chanowski, who lived with her son (her husband had already
been deported) ; and the concierge, Mr. Benkimoun and his
wife, who had also been left behind. But they were not
forgotten. On February 7, 1943, the policemen came around a
second time. Only Clara Chanowski returned of those arrested
in 1943. She was the sole survivor of the forty-four people at 22
Rue des Ecouffes, since everyone taken away on July 16, 1942,
had disappeared.

Mr. and Mrs. Rimmler, who were then both twenty-five years
old, now own a clothes shop on the Rue du Roi-de-Sicile, a
hundred yards away from their former home. They still cannot

pass by the building at 22 Rue des Ecouffes without a sigh at
the memory of the laughter and shouts of twenty-two children
who were still alive on the evening of July 15, 1942. Mrs.
Blachman, who was in the hospital when the second raid on the
building took place, lost her reason on finding out what had
happened to her husband and her three daughters. She died a
patient at the Sainte-Anne hospital.

On August 13 another meeting took place at Avenue Foch.
This time, besides Roethke, the general delegate of the French
police Leguay and his assistant, Commander Sauts, attended.
Leguay confirmed that the Jews were being rounded up in the
free zone and submitted a timetable for the convoys. He was
asked to start forwarding the children, as there now was room
for them, thirteen trains having already taken full loads of
adults to Germany. Indeed, from now on, Jewish prisoners
from the free zone were handed over to the Germans with their
children, "in the proportion of five hundred children to every
seven hundred adults. The orders of the RHSA forbade
convoys consisting solely of children."

Leguay was told what Laval already knew, "that this
operation had been planned as a permanent solution and
would in its final phases include Jews of French nationality."

Trainload after trainload of prisoners were delivered to the
enemy, with the time the train crossed the demarcation line and
the expected time of arrival efficiently relayed ahead. The
police cleared the camps, only to fill them again with Jews who
would fill the next train. We have an eyewitness account of the
departures from the Milles camp near Marseilles:

> Parents had been given the option of leaving children
> between the ages of five and eighteen behind if they
> wanted to,* and seventy children were to be separated
> from their parents, who were due for deportation. On
> Monday we watched the children's departure. It was a
> heartrending moment as they were put onto the train

* In the free zone, Laval's heartless proposal to deport all children was
implemented much later.

with their meager luggage. The younger ones, not understanding the purpose of this separation, would cling to their parents, crying and refusing to let go. Those who realized how much their parents were suffering tried to control their feelings. Mothers hung onto the doors of the departing cars. Even the guards and the policemen found it difficult to hide their emotion. The adult prisoners' expressions were bitter and resigned. After all they had been through, they seemed to have been drained of the strength to fight against their destiny.

While the parents were handed over to the Germans, the children were sent to children's homes run by the UGIF, from which they too were eventually almost all picked up. Meanwhile the adults were being deported:

> Prisoners picked out for deportation were then lined up and shepherded onto a train on a nearby track. Like the first train, it was made up of freight cars in which a little straw had been scattered. An armed guard stood by each car.
> The deportees quietly obeyed the orders they were given, carrying or dragging their luggage behind them. The attitude of the police, which had been one of relative reserve the day before, for some reason changed at this point, becoming more brutal. Guards would harass the lines that did not advance at the pace they wished them to, and would underline their shouts with kicks with their heavy boots. One captain of the gendarmes was even seen to punch one of the prisoners. Noticing this and other similar incidents, a Protestant minister who happened to be on the spot lodged a complaint with the police. . . .
> Every now and then a piercing cry would shatter the uncanny silence of the camp: some prisoner, unable to take any more, would have tried to kill himself by slashing a vein or taking poison. There were eight attempted suicides in one day.

Captain Annou of the gendarmerie wrote the following rather cold report for the attention of the Regional Prefect, Cheyneau de Leyritz, at the Prefecture of Cahors:

> The special train of September 1 carried a mixed load of men, women, children, old people, and some sick and

disabled, who were left to their own devices once the train
started moving.

. . . Crushed together, they sat on the straw, which was
damp with urine. The women were desperate because they
were forced to relieve themselves in front of strangers.
People fainted from the heat and the oppressive odor and
could not be treated. . . .

The sight of this train made a strong and unfavorable
impression on the non-Jewish French population who
chanced to see it, especially in the stations.

Scenes like this were taking place all over the occupied zone,
but the climax came on August 26, 27, and 28. On August 27,
Leguay was again called to Avenue Foch to report. With his
aide, Sauts, he was received by Heinrichsohn, and the
"September program" was discussed. Leguay complacently
announced that "on September 1, 2, 3, and 4, there would be
one train per day, each bringing a thousand Jews from the free
zone." Heinrichsohn's assessment of the progress of the
operation in the free zone was recorded in his minutes:

Leguay could not give us any exact information, as the
roundups of the nights of the twenty-sixth and twenty-
seventh are not yet over. These raids are widespread in
the free zone, since in Bousquet's estimate it is preferable
to make the arrests in one thorough operation rather than
a series of isolated minor ones, which would give the Jews
a chance to hide or escape to neutral countries over the
border. Currently the French police, the gendarmerie, and
the Wehrmacht are coordinating their forces for the
success of the operation. We shall have exact figures
tomorrow or the day after, and only then can Mr. Leguay
give us details regarding future deliveries.

On Friday, August 28, 1942, the number of Jews
deported will have reached twenty-five thousand.

At this session the representative of Marshal Pétain's
government complained that the Germans, by allowing
information about the roundup in southern France to be
published, were making the work of the police much more
difficult.

While Leguay was in session with the Germans in Paris and

raids were continuing in the south, for the rest of France it was summer vacation time. In her clandestine *Lettres Françaises,* Edith Thomas described the convoys, French trains with the initials SNCF painted on their sides, made up of cattle cars with a full load of deportees except for the last car, a comfortable passenger coach carrying the escort of thirty French gendarmes and their officer, all perspiring in their beige summer uniforms. Inside the freight cars, the prisoners were crowded around the small window, gasping for a little air to breathe. On their way to Drancy, or rattling to the German border, these trains shuttling their loads of Jews would pass other trains full of French holiday-makers. It was August.

Roger Boussinot, who had spent the entire day on the sixteenth trying in vain to rescue some Jews, was now going home to his parents' house for the holidays. He says that he was already preparing himself to enjoy the carefree sunny days ahead of him. He felt that a corner of green country and the coolness near the water were all that he wanted to occupy his mind with. He was late because he had stayed on to try and help the Jews on the sixteenth.

> The first person I met was the mayor.
> "Hello there," he said, embracing me. "Your parents were expecting you last night. What's the news? What are they talking about in Paris? What is the latest there?"
> I put down my suitcase, feeling a little hot but pleased at this reassuring, affectionate welcome. . . .
> "Nothing," I said. And I meant it.

Two young middle-class girls from the VII Arrondissement, Benoîte and Flora Groult, were keeping diaries at that time. On June 7 they indignantly recorded the first appearance of the yellow star and described the reaction of one of their schoolfriends, who made himself a yellow star and wrote "philo" across it. They and their girlfriends decided to do the same. But on June 9 Daddy told them not to wear their home-made stars—there had been arrests. On June 15 one of the girls passed her written examination. On June 8 the other

wrote admiringly of the Russians: "What a nation! Kharkov
has been taken, but there are always more towns and more
steppes!" On June 10 the yellow star comes up again. One of
the girls at high school, Hélène Schwartz, was wearing it. . . .
On June 15 a philology examination at the Sorbonne; June 25,
the defeat of the Russians at Sebastopol and the British at
El-Alamein. There were no entries for July 16, 17, or 18.

On August 2 they were on vacation in the Berri country and
stayed there until August 27, when one sister is mentioned as
having waited for the other—at Austerliz station.

While vacationers were enjoying themselves in a small tourist
village in the Haute-Loire, a few kilometers away, at Tence, a
Jew committed suicide as the police came for him.

In the Protestant church at Chambon-sur-Lignon the
Reverend Trocme preached a sermon which was remembered
by a Jewish refugee:

> The people in their Sunday best were crowding at the
> church door. My father, even though he was not very
> devout, felt uncomfortable about going into a Christian
> church. I sat with my mother in the front row. The pastor
> began to speak. He spoke of the Jews who were being
> persecuted. I can't remember now exactly what he said,
> but I know that he was appealing for help for the Jews,
> in every way possible, since what was being done to the
> Jews was shameful, and it was everyone's most urgent
> duty to put a stop to it. After the service a lady played the
> piano. She had come to give a recital "in aid of the
> persecuted Jews." In the large and brightly lit white-
> painted church, the notes of the "Appassionata" burst
> out. I cannot hear it now without associating it with the
> memory of that day. Sitting in the front row, my hand in
> my mother's hand, I could feel her grip me from time to
> time. Looking up, I could see only her profile, her straight
> neck, her hair caught up in a chignon, and the pearl she
> always wore in her ear. I could see she was crying, so I
> started crying too. The minister spoke some more. We
> were not alone. All the same, both my mother and my
> father died at Auschwitz.

In the surrounding farms, many Jewish refugees and
especially children were welcomed and looked after.

On July 16 and 17, as we have said, 4,051 children had been arrested by the police in Paris. The roundup then spread everywhere else. Some children escaped, some were left behind and had to fend for themselves. Others ran away and were in hiding while the police hunted them like rats. Still others were looked after by various people; there were runaways in every village all over the country. It was around these children that most emotion centered. François Mauriac, Edith Thomas, and a thousand others were moved by the pitiful glances, from behind the glass of bus-windows and behind the wire of police trucks, of children on their way to the camps. Mrs. Vidal has told us about one load of children whom she saw leaving Saint-Sulpice and whom she will never forget. As for the others, the ones who escaped and now were alone and disoriented, their survival depended on the support of the people around them.

But the Germans were thorough and intended to catch them too. Laval, speaking for the Vichy government, had undertaken to hand them over, and true to his word, he had them hounded out by his policemen. They were not safe even in hideouts arranged for them by priests.

At Lyon, 284 Jewish children had been left by their parents in the care of the church, before being deported. Father Chaillet hid them by entrusting them to French families he knew. When the Prefect, Mr. Angeli, summoned the archbishop and demanded the children, he was disappointed. Father Chaillet would give away nothing, and the families he had chosen kept their trust. So the Vichy police arrested Father Chaillet himself.

The Resistance published a pamphlet on the subject, titled "You shall not have the children."

The Prefect, Mr. Angeli, acting on the orders of the Germans, has been demanding that 160 Jewish children aged between two and sixteen be handed over to him. These children were put in the care of Cardinal Gerlier by their parents, whom the Vichy government has already betrayed to Hitler. The cardinal has told the Prefect:

BETRAYAL AT THE VEL D'HIV

"You shall not get the children." A struggle between the Church of France and the police has started.

Fellow Frenchmen, whatever your political opinions, whatever your beliefs, listen to your consciences and don't let innocent children be delivered to the executioners.*

Whatever the people's reaction, the Vichy government did the Germans' bidding, and Ambassador Bergen was able to cable Berlin on September 14:

The French government has ordered the arrest of all priests who hide Jews wanted for deportation, or help them escape deportation by any means whatever. Several priests from the Lyon diocese have already been taken into custody, some because they supported and spread the message of protest spoken by their archbishop and others because they refused to give up the Jewish children in their care.

At 11 Rue Commines the Rosenbergs' daughter, who had been left with the Gaillards when her parents were taken away, was looked after by these neighbors throughout the occupation. Hélène and Jean Rozen, who had been permitted to leave the Vel d'Hiv with their sick mother, were put into the children's center on the Rue Lamarck while their mother received treatment at the Rothschild hospital for a while before being transferred to Drancy and from there to Auschwitz. The Rue Lamarck center was one of the children's homes run by the UGIF and where at this time children orphaned by the deportation of their parents were collected and kept in cold storage, so to speak. That is, they were listed with the police and were permanently at their disposal. Some were temporarily farmed out to French families. Though the families willing to look after the children were kind and devoted, they were far too few, and most of the children stayed at the center. Hélène Rozen remembers:

I was thirteen and the oldest among the children. It may sound boastful to say this, but I was very much in demand. We would be lined up in a row, and our

* Quoted by Henri Amoretti in *Lyon Capitale 1940–1944* (Editions France-Empire) .

prospective foster families would walk along the line
looking us over carefully and then point out their choice.
"I'll take this big girl," said one lady, indicating me. I
threw my arms around my brother and said that there
were two of us and I didn't want to be parted from my
brother, who was only eight years old and needed
me. . . . I fought like a lioness. Eventually I had the
good luck of being sent to a wonderful family named
Delore, who took the two of us.

Taking in children, hiding them, rescuing them, and helping
them escape became an urgent task of the first importance, in
which many people became involved. There were private
efforts, often anonymous, but there also were whole networks
which were organized for the purpose and which were to have
their martyrs. It was dangerous and very difficult to forge
documents, to set up and support secret refugee centers for
hundreds of children in a country run by the Germans as
France was at that time. Children were smuggled across the
Alps and the Pyrenees into Switzerland and Spain by brave and
devoted young people. Two such smugglers, Mila Racine and
Marianne Cohen, paid for their heroism with their lives. Both
were shot. Other organizations involved in the rescue of the
children were "La Sixième" (Section Six of the EIF—
Eclaireurs israélites de France), the SERE (Service
d'Évacuation et de Regroupement des Enfants), and the OJC.

Father Devaux and Father Chaillet, working with Pastor
Vergara, organized a rescue service, and roughly eight thousand
children were successfully hidden by them. Of these, only
one thousand were claimed after the Liberation, no one from
the others' families having survived.

Children who suddenly found themselves alone in the world,
and were not lucky enough to be looked after by a family like
the Delores or the Gaillards, and had not been rescued by one
of the organizations mentioned above, fell to the care of the
UGIF if they were not picked up first by the Germans or the
Vichy police. They imagined that they would be safe with their
fellow Jews, and no doubt the members of the UGIF too were
under the same impression.

Roger Boussinot told us of a young Jewish girl whom he rescued on the day of the roundup. As she said goodbye and thanked him,

> she handed me a piece of yellow paper with some sort of notice printed on it. At the same time she took out the yellow star of David that we had removed from her clothes in a dry-cleaner's shop, and a safety pin. The message on the piece of paper read: "Israelites, in these difficult times there is at least one organization you can trust your children with, the UGIF, the only Jewish association recognized by the occupation forces." Then there was an address.

At the homes run by the UGIF, the children immediately found food and shelter. What is more, they were among highly devoted people who, while making sure that these new orphans were given all the necessary material comforts, also did their best to provide affection and moral guidance, which were just as urgently needed.

But we know now, as many must have known at the time, that these homes were what Pastor Vergara called "infamous traps." As far as Darquier de Pellepoix was concerned, they were convenient prisons where children who had escaped the roundup would be trapped and could be held until it was time for their deportation. Every child staying at a UGIF home was, in fact, deported—even those who had been farmed out with families. The Rozen children, who had been placed with the Delore family, escaped only because the Delores sent them away to a safe refuge before they were due back at the Jewish center.

Berthe Libers, who was astonished by the work given her by the UGIF on July 15 (that of preparing labels), later was given another task:

> We were to look for all Jewish children who had left Paris for the suburbs or had gone further afield into the country, and bring them back to the Lamarck Center, ostensibly so that they might be looked after. The Lamarck Center had been founded for the shelter of Jewish children whose parents had been deported. We

later discovered that from Lamarck children were sent directly to Drancy.

Berthe Libers refused to comply with the order to look for Jewish children, and she was later arrested and deported to Auschwitz. She was one of the very few people to escape from Auschwitz. In 1947, while listening to the trial of Xavier Vallat, she heard the directors of the UGIF testify in his favor. Indignantly she applied for permission to give evidence and the passage above comes from her statement made on February 9, 1947. As proof, she had with her one of the orders issued to her:

> By order of the SS Obersturmfuehrer, Miss Libers is to go to Championnet to fetch two children, Ida and Georgette Moskovitch, and bring them to the Lamarck Center.
>
> If for any reason she is unable to take the children, she is to bring a statement from the local authorities, either the police or the town hall, to that effect.
>
> On her return, Miss Libers is to write a report on her mission. The pass issued with this order is to be brought back at the same time as the report on the mission.

Chapter 10

From Drancy to Auschwitz

On Sunday, July 19, the Germans and the French authorities began to shuttle their prisoners from one camp to another: from the Vel d'Hiv they would be taken to Drancy, and from Drancy to Loiret, and then back to Drancy. A sinister and seemingly pointless activity, which made the police seem like a murderer who is jumpy because he does not know where to bury his victim.

The first departure from the Vel d'Hiv to the Loiret took place on Sunday morning. Mrs. Dorag, who was there, remembers: "During the night of July 18–19 the first batch of prisoners, a thousand people chosen at random, were taken away. They were herded out like cattle, and we could hear their weeping and their cries in the night." From Sunday through Thursday the great track was slowly cleared. The prisoners were taken away in the same buses that had brought them and were jostled by the same guards. They were driven to Austerlitz station, where the guards on duty were rough with them as they alighted, dragging their belongings and their children behind them.

According to Mr. Sienicki: "They were not at all kind. On the contrary, I would call their treatment brutal. They spoke to us only to threaten and intimidate us. They were above all worried about our trying to escape, and all we heard from them were insults and threats." Another eyewitness, Louis Pitkowicz, gives a similar description of police behavior at that time:

People have often asked me whether I noticed any signs of sympathy in the attitude of the police who were keeping guard over us. To be truthful, I must admit that I did not with my own eyes see them use their truncheons, as I had on other occasions. Some of them managed to remain human and even allowed whole families to escape being rounded up, but in my experience there was no attenuating circumstance to excuse the mobile guards or the French police who arrested us and kept guard over us. They proved themselves to be very efficient at a job which made them directly responsible for the death of tens of thousands of their fellow human beings.

In his *Cahier Noir*, which was published secretly by the *Editions de Minuit*, François Mauriac, under the pseudonym of Forez, recorded his wife's impressions of a departure of Jewish prisoners which she saw at Austerlitz station: "At what other time in history have children been snatched away from their mothers and piled into cattle cars, as I saw them on a gray morning at Austerlitz station?"

For most of the new arrivals, Drancy was just a temporary halt on their journey, but evidently horrific enough to leave an unforgettable memory. Mr. Falkenstein described those July days at Drancy as follows:

Those first days are indescribable. The women, and the newcomers generally, were dumped in some of the staircases and strictly forbidden to move. Except for a few people attached to the kitchens or in charge of provisions, who had passes, like myself, no one was allowed into the staircases. The sanitary problem posed by the women, many of them pregnant or menstruating, with no water and forbidden to go out into the courtyard where the latrines were, is difficult to imagine. There were cases of hysteria, there were attempted suicides, and countless successful suicides. I particularly remember one day at the end of July, coming out of the kitchen where I slept, and seeing three bodies fall from some upper windows, all in the space of a few seconds, and land with a dull sound on the cornice over the ground-floor quarters.

After July 19, children came to add to the confusion and
general feeling of despair. The nineteenth was also the date of
the first convoy of Jews arrested on Black Thursday to be
shipped to Auschwitz. In the words of Georges Wellers, who
was there at the departure:

> On July 19, a thousand prisoners were picked from the
> overcrowded camp, most of them men. Whole staircases
> were emptied. Around 7 A.M. they were collected in the
> middle of the yard inside some barbed wire. From every
> window, thousands of prisoners looked on. In the
> women's quarters there was silent weeping as husbands,
> brothers, fathers, or sons were recognized among the
> crowd in the yard. Completely isolated from the men, the
> women found out about the deportation of their relatives
> directly, like this. A roll call was taken quickly. Then
> three German officers arrived, and the first deportees
> began to walk toward the exit, passing by the east wing
> of the camp as they did so. Suddenly the windows of the
> women's quarters opened, and bread rained down on the
> column of departing prisoners. In a gesture of pity and
> sympathy, the women threw down their own rations. At
> the same time, they shouted words of farewell and
> encouragement to the slow-moving procession. But as
> soon as the last of them had left the camp, the silent
> weeping became loud sobbing, and within a quarter of
> an hour the women's quarters resembled a madhouse.
> Frustrated and powerless, they cried, some rolled on the
> ground, some fainted or tried to throw themselves from
> the windows, or banged their heads against the walls. The
> few women who managed to retain some degree of calm
> helped the heads of staircases to prevent the others from
> harming themselves and to soothe them. After an hour
> the reaction to all this excitement set in in the form of a
> mournful despondency, which lasted until the women
> themselves were deported.

That first convoy arrived at Auschwitz on July 21. Of the 879
men and 121 women, 375 men were taken to the gas chambers
immediately after their arrival. Other convoys followed soon
after. On the morning of July 22 there was another train from
Drancy, the director's office at Auschwitz receiving notice of the
departure at 8:35 of the same day. That convoy duly arrived

at the Nazi extermination camp on July 24 at the same time as the next train was leaving Drancy to arrive at Auschwitz on July 26. The next one left Drancy on the twenty-seventh and arrived at Auschwitz on the twenty-ninth. And so it went on for weeks.

About twelve to sixteen rooms (three or four staircases in Block I) were set aside at Drancy for prisoners about to be deported, and were called the "Departure Staircases." Those intended for Auschwitz usually spent the two or three days between the announcement of their selection and their actual departure in these quarters in the most filthy and uncomfortable conditions, piled seventy to eighty to a room and sleeping on straw or on the bare floor, having first been relieved of all their possessions (personal belongings, as well as valuables) by French members of the Police for Jewish Affairs. They were separated from the rest of the camp, and no other prisoners could come near them, on pain of being included in the convoy. The rules were so strict that the deportees were not allowed to use the "Château Rouge," as the latrines at the end of the courtyard had been called, and two or three buckets were placed on each landing for their use. Ridiculously insufficient—after each departure, the teams of cleaners could not come near the "Departure Staircases" without heavy boots and without the risk of floundering in a mud of filth soaked in urine and excrement.

The convoys always left at dawn. The deportees were out of their quarters by 5 A.M. and gathered inside the barbed wire enclosure in the middle of the courtyard. At six the camp inspectors came and a little later some Germans. At a long table, by the light of a hurricane lamp, the names of the prisoners were called out briskly, each person walking off toward the south gate as soon as he heard his name. There, under the vigilant eyes of policemen, gendarmes, and German soldiers, they waited for the buses. By seven in the morning it was all over; the prison gates were closed, and the "Departure Staircases" were cleaned so that the same evening the deportees for the next convoy would be able to move in.

For the trip between the prison and the railroad station, buses were used and sometimes trucks. In the words of Georges Horeau:

> After each bus had loaded its fifty passengers, it went to Bourget station under an escort of police officers, policemen, and motorcycles. There was a disproportionate number of guards and armed *feldgraus* standing on either side or moving up and down like so many rabid dogs. There would be greetings and congratulations from the satisfied authorities. . . .
>
> At the last minute, on the station platform, men, women, and children would sometimes be separated. Families were broken up by force to the accompaniment of brutal insults. . . .
>
> Then the policemen would push the sliding doors shut, and a railroad employee would put a lead seal on the locks.

The operation had been planned to last two months, at the rate of three convoys of one thousand Jews each per week. But the supply of railroad cars available had been diminished to almost nothing by the demands of the army on the Russian front, and transport became a serious problem. On July 18, Wolf, the inspector of German railroads, had said that he could only supply passenger cars. Ahnert passed the information on to Dannecker, but meantime Dannecker had left. It fell to Roethke to solve the difficulty. On July 20 he cabled Eichmann, asking for freight cars. The reply on July 23 was to make do with what was already available. In the end the Jews were shipped in freight cars, into which they were crowded, ninety or sometimes one hundred twenty people to a car.

Little by little, the public began to be familiar with the Germanic sounding names of Auschwitz, Dachau, Ravensbruck, Bergen-Belsen, Mathausen, but their French counterparts—Orléans, Beaugency, Vendôme, the camps at Pithiviers, Beaune-la-Rolande, Drancy, Le Vernet, Compiègne, Argelès, Rivesaltes, Gurs, Châteaubriant, Noé, Saint-Sulpice, Récébédou, and many others—though in France and run and guarded by the French gendarmerie, were much less well known to the French public than the German camps.

Although there certainly was no comparison between the French camps and the German camps, four hundred thousand people were in fact imprisoned in France in what often were abominable conditions. Furthermore, the French camps acted as a waiting room for the German extermination camps.

All the camps mentioned above served as depots for the Jews arrested during the roundup of July 16, while Drancy was the rail terminal for the trains going east.

As was mentioned earlier, Miss Monod, after seeing conditions in the Vel d'Hiv, guessed that the camps in the Loiret would be just as ill provided for receiving the new prisoners and decided to go to Pithiviers, where she had worked before, and organize some sort of reception. As she had imagined, nothing was ready, and special arrangements were particularly necessary for the children between the ages of two and twelve who were expected. With the inadequate means at her disposal, Miss Monod went to work collecting straw, some blankets, and cutlery and, with the help of the prisoners left in the camp, prepared rudimentary sleeping quarters and dining rooms. (Miss Monod stresses that Mr. Brochard, who was in charge of the camp at Pithiviers at the time, helped her in every way he could, within the limits of his office.) A nearby gingerbread factory at Pithiviers, the Gringoire factory, also proved helpful, providing large quantities of gingerbread without coupons, to be divided among the children. We mention these names because they are part of the history of those days, but also as a token of thanks to those who brought a last bit of sweetness into the lives of the children who were all to die within the next few months.

The first trainloads of Jews were brought from the Vel d'Hiv on July 22 and 23. Families were still allowed to remain together. Mr. Goldenzwag arrived at Pithiviers with his wife and four children, and Albert Tselnick was still with his wife Bella and their three boys: Bernard, aged fifteen and a half; David, fourteen, and Maurice, who was eleven when he was

brought to Pithiviers. Mr. and Mrs. Rosenberg were taken to
Beaune-la-Rolande and had the comfort at least of knowing
that their daughter was in safe hands with the neighbor who
had offered to look after her. But the families were soon broken
up, and Mrs. Rosenberg was transferred to Pithiviers while her
husband stayed on at Beaune-la-Rolande for another six weeks.
On the advice of one of the gendarmes, Mr. Rosenberg wore
the military decoration he had been awarded in 1939, and as a
result gained the privilege of working in the camp kitchen.
After six weeks he was sent to Drancy, where he remained for
eight days before being deported to Auschwitz. While being
transferred from Beaune-la-Rolande to Drancy, the train he
was traveling on stopped at Pithiviers station, which was not
far from the camp itself, and Mr. Rosenberg was able to catch
a glimpse of his wife from a distance. It was the last time he
saw her. She had been kept on at Pithiviers with some others to
look after the children whose parents had been deported. But
women and children alike were all to be sent to Drancy in the
next few days and from there directly to Auschwitz. The
children were arrested with their parents even when they might
have been saved in some cases; it is difficult to imagine greater
heartlessness. But Miss Monod recalled, "I know for a fact that
some children were arrested by the police even though their
parents were not there. I remember two children in the Loiret
camps who had been taken from their homes by the police
while their mother was out buying milk, I think. The
policemen were French. I remember them distinctly, a brother
and a sister, six and eight years old."

Albert Baum was in one of the convoys. He had been
separated from his family, but what he had seen at Pithiviers
was an eye-opener, and he knew that the most important thing
at that stage was to do everything possible to get out of the
situation. He now regretted not having taken advantage of his
freedom of movement in and out of the Vel d'Hiv in the
uniforms he and his friend Bernard Goura had bought from
the members of the French Youth movement. Now, in the
train, they must not miss their chance. In the twilight of the

freight car several of them tore at the barbed wire covering the small window and then jumped.

> We had decided to wait until the train was rounding a corner, because by jumping on the outside of the curve we would be less likely to be spotted. We had already noted that there were gendarmes at the head and the tail of the train only. There were fifteen of us ready to try our luck, and I was the second or third to jump.
> I picked myself up, not much worse for wear after rolling down the embankment. I saw none of my companions, and I don't know what happened to them. As for me, night was falling, and I was near Etampes. I walked all night, all the way to Paris. . . .

All along the route from Pithiviers, the convoy was dropping runaways by the wayside. From Loiret the rail line goes to Etampes, then to Juine, Chamarande, Brétigny, Villemoison, and Juvisy. There, instead of going on to Paris and Austerlitz station, the convoy from which Albert Baum jumped, No. 4040, turned right at Juvisy junction to Gagny and the station of Drancy-Le Bourget. At every curve on the line the train would slow down, and some prisoners would jump off. But at the crossing at Gagny-Neuilly-sur-Marne one of them was seen. Clapping their rifles to their shoulders, the gendarmes shot at the escaping shadow. The sputter of bullets echoed in the night, while the small cones of blue fire looked like miniature fireworks. It was 8:40 P.M. The train stopped and did not move on until 9:30. One of the runaways was caught on the tracks by some Germans on duty to inspect the railroads. The police at Neuilly-sur-Marne and the French gendarmerie carried out widespread searches. In a report to the Germans, Inspector Moreau of the Judiciary Police at Versailles mentioned his anxiety at the number of fugitives who might have escaped. All details of the incident are to be found in a report written by a German named Kluenker, based on information sent by Inspector Moreau. Albert Baum, who told us his experiences on that train, probably does not realize that the events described in the report refer to the very same convoy.

A few days after his escape, Baum was picked up by the

police as he wandered through the city, starved and without
money or papers. He was sent to Drancy.

Mrs. Beckman, who was arrested on the sixteenth and
subsequently ferried from one camp to another, remembers
how she fought with all her strength to save her life and that of
her children.

> I was arrested on the sixteenth with my five-year-old
> boy and my daughter, who was seven. I had an older boy
> of twelve, but he had gone into hiding with his father.

From the Vel d'Hiv they were taken to Beaune-la-Rolande,
where Mrs. Beckman was put to look after the children, with
some other women prisoners.

> It was hard work. The children had no change of
> clothes, and most of them were sick (diarrhea and skin
> trouble) . They were inconsolable, having just been
> parted from their parents, who had been deported. My
> one consolation was that my own children were there
> with me.

From Beaune-la-Rolande Mrs. Beckman and her children were
moved to Drancy:

> We were quite brutally treated by the police as we
> boarded the train. The children were anxious and in
> tears. I was just going to follow my children into the car
> they had been taken to when a policeman stopped me. I
> was not supposed to follow them. I threw myself at his
> feet and begged him to let me pass. I felt ashamed but
> told myself that he was French and would feel sorry for
> me. The next thing I knew, he kicked me in the head.
> One of the social workers helped me up and tried to calm
> me down. She took me back to my place and told me to be
> patient. Eventually she managed to get me into the same
> car as my children, and I found my boy half suffocated
> in the straw underneath the others.

At Drancy Mrs. Beckman was again separated from her
children, and, like the others, she began to realize that ahead
of her was the last deportation, the one to Germany.

> From time to time, I caught sight of my children in the
> yard. Then one day I heard that they were going to be

deported. I rushed out like a madwoman and fell down
the stairs, breaking a leg. I was taken to the infirmary and
given the rudimentary treatment that was available.

Mrs. Beckman still limps today; her leg is weak and deformed
so that it is shorter than the other. That first rumor of the
deportation was merely talk. But three weeks later it turned
out to be true, and she was called to be searched in preparation
for her departure.

I was still limping and in great pain. My son had
caught some kind of influenza or bronchitis and coughed
without a stop. He also had a temperature. I begged an
officer of the gendarmerie to send him to the infirmary,
but he didn't even bother to reply. I dragged along slowly
so that I would be at the very end of the line. Unlike
many of the other prisoners, who seemed more or less
resigned, maybe because I had my son, I was constantly
trying to think of a way out. I don't know whether I
actually moved him to pity or simply wore him out, but
finally I got the gendarme to listen to me.
"My boy has a temperature of 104 degrees, at least," I
said.
"If he turns out to have one degree less, I shall have you
punished," the man replied.

Mrs. Beckman did not know whether that was a threat or a
joke, but the boy was taken to the infirmary with her, and it
turned out that he had a temperature of 105 degrees. The
doctor kept both of them in the sick bay. It was merely a
breathing space, but enough to save their lives. Mr. Beckman,
who had not been arrested, managed to obtain their release
from Drancy. Only the twelve-year-old boy, who was picked up
during a roundup, was deported and never returned.

Four convoys, two from Pithiviers and two from Beaune-la-
Rolande, had left for Germany direct. The first left Pithiviers
on July 31, the second on August 3. Arriving at Auschwitz on
August 2, the first convoy consisted of 593 men and 359 women,
among them Mr. Goldenzwag and Mr. Albert Tselnick, who
were numbers 55293 and 56599 at Auschwitz and still carry the

tattoos on their arms. The second convoy from Pithiviers, arriving at Auschwitz on August 5, brought 1,046 men and women, of whom 482 were taken to the gas chambers on arrival. As far as we can make out, it seems that as early as this, children were included among those who were killed on arrival. The Auschwitz Notebooks, on the subject of the two convoys from Beaune-la-Rolande and the numbers gassed on arrival, mention the presence of children in the convoy. The first convoy from Beaune-la-Rolande, leaving on August 5, arrived at Auschwitz on August 7, bringing 1,014 men, women, and children, of whom 704 were gassed on arrival. Similarly the second convoy, leaving on August 7 and arriving at Auschwitz on August 9, was made up of 197 men, and 871 women and children; 794 persons were gassed on arrival.

Judging from the fact that most of the families arrested during the roundup were large, one could safely presume that most of the fathers and a great proportion of the mothers and the older children were on those four convoys leaving the Loiret camps. That would mean that only nursing mothers remained, about one woman to every fifteen children. If 4,051 children were arrested on July 16 and 17, it is likely that 3,000 to 3,500 children were left on their own when their parents were deported, and of those some 2,000 were infants who did not even know their own names.

Miss Monod has told us that after the departure of the mothers, the authorities spread the rumor that they had been taken to Germany to prepare the camps for their children when they came. They even said that each family would have its own apartment and that the men would work at their trade and the children go to school. But the children themselves did not care about promises of school. More than two thousand were under school age anyway, and they wanted their mothers. Miss Monod was impressed with the sense of responsibility these children had. The older ones, about twelve to fourteen years old, would look after the younger ones and do the chores their fathers used to do around the camp, as if they were grown men.

Miss Monod's description of the children's dormitories—if

you can call rooms with nothing more than some stale straw on the hard floor dormitories—is repelling. The children sleeping on the straw were all covered with sores and impetigo. They were fed on cabbage soup and rutabaga. Every child was suffering from diarrhea but could not have its pants changed because of the shortage of clothes. The social workers and the women prisoners who were left behind to care for the children would quickly wash their one pair of pants, leaving the children bare until their clothes had dried. At night there were other problems. In the two-to-five age group, forty to fifty children would be sleeping in each room. The resulting confusion was unimaginable. They would all have nightmares and call for their mothers in their sleep. If one child woke up crying, the rest would wake up and join in. There were no chamber pots for them to use at night, and they were not allowed out of their dormitories (they would have been too frightened to go out into the night anyway, and there were not enough social workers to help them) ; so biscuit tins were given them, but few of the children dared use them, since they could not sit on the sharp edge without cutting themselves.

Miss Monod has forgotten nothing. She still remembers the tragic case of a mother whose children had been arrested while she for some reason was allowed to go free. Somehow the mother found out that her children were at Pithiviers. Standing outside the barbed wire enclosure, she would beg the guards to arrest her too, so that she could be with them. But the guards had not received instructions to arrest her, and they acted only on instructions.

Miss Monod often went to Paris to report to her office at the Red Cross what was happening and to maintain contact between the prisoners and the various organizations wishing to help them. On one occasion she remembers delivering a letter given her by a seven-year-old:

> Dear Madame la Concierge,
>
> I'm writing to you because I have no one anymore. Last week they deported Daddy; they also deported Mommy. I've lost my pocket book. I have nothing left.

She also remembers two small children, Rosette and Jacquot, a brother and sister, who said that they lived in Paris at number 15A. That is all they knew about their address. But Miss Monod's most heartrending memory is that of the departure early one September morning of a convoy made up almost entirely of little children.

It was beginning to get cold. The kids were half asleep, and it was quite a job to get them down from their dormitories. Most of them sat on the ground, each with his little bundle next to him: just a few clothes tied up in a napkin, sometimes with a doll's head or the wheel of a wooden truck sticking out, their only treasure and perhaps also a symbol of their lost home. The gendarmes tried to get through the roll call, but it was impossible. The children did not respond to the names. Surnames like Rosenthal, Biegelmann, Radekski, etc., meant nothing to them. They didn't understand what was expected of them, and some even wandered off from the group. One tiny boy walked up to a gendarme and started to play with the whistle hanging from the man's belt; a little girl saw some flowers growing on a slope and went off to pick them and make a bouquet. The gendarmes did not know what to do. Finally they were ordered to take the children to the railroad station nearby and not bother with the roll call, as long as the required number of children were put on the train.

We were standing only two hundred yards from the station, but that is a long way for small children hampered by clumsy bundles. I noticed one gendarme take the bundle of a boy of about four or five to help him walk. But he was immediately reprimanded by an adjutant, who told him rudely that a French soldier did not carry the bags of a Jew. Sheepishly the soldier handed the little bundle back to the boy.

I followed the procession of children going to the station, my heart bursting. I could not bear to leave them after having cared for them for so many weeks. I could hardly keep myself from weeping, and I must say that many of the soldiers also found it difficult to mask their emotion. When we got to the platform, I noticed a German soldier standing on an overhead footbridge crossing the tracks, with his machine gun pointing at us. Once we were in the station, the children were loaded onto the trains in a sudden burst of speed. Many of the children were too small to climb into the freight cars without the help of a ladder, so the bigger boys would climb in first and help the younger ones pull themselves up. The gendarmes lifted the babies who were hardly weaned and handed them to the women, nursing mothers, or the children who were already on board.

It was at this point that the children felt frightened. They didn't want to go and started to cry. They would call to the social workers standing on the platform for help, and would sometimes even appeal to the soldiers. Jacquot, a little five-year-old of whom I was particularly fond, started shouting for me: "I want to get down, I want to stay with Mademoiselle. . . ." The door of the car was shut and bolted, but Jacquot pushed his hand through a gap between two planks and continued to call for me, moving his fingers. The adjutant mentioned above hit him on the hand.

All trains leaving Pithiviers and Beaune-la-Rolande at that time went to one of the stations serving Drancy. There the TCRP buses would be waiting to take the prisoners to Drancy camp, which was to be the point of departure for convoys to Germany. So for people who had been transferred from Vel d'Hiv to Pithiviers or Beaune-la-Rolande, Drancy was the third stage on their journey toward death at Auschwitz. Mrs. Goldenzwag, whose husband had been deported with his eldest son on July 31, arrived at Drancy with the three other children, the youngest of whom was five years old. Mr. Tselnick had been deported on July 31 too, but two of his children, Maurice and Bernard, were sent to Drancy. Mrs. Bella Tselnick had been deported to Germany directly from Pithiviers with her son David on the August 3 convoy, as far as can be determined. Mr. Rosenberg too had been brought from Beaune-la-Rolande to Drancy for eight days before being deported to Auschwitz.

At this stage (end of August and beginning of September) the only prisoners brought to Drancy came from Pithiviers and Beaune-la-Rolande, and most of these were children. Hardly any of the victims of July 16 and 17 were left at Drancy.

Coming from Pithiviers and Beaune-la-Rolande, the

children found themselves in a new setting of mad chaos. Georges Wellers told us of this "return" of the thousands of lost children:

> As the children came off the buses, the bigger ones immediately took the smaller ones by the hand and did not let go of them until they reached their dormitories. On the staircases they would carry the younger ones, puffing and panting as they staggered up to the fifth floor. There they huddled together like a flock of frightened sheep, hesitating for a long time before sitting down on the repulsively dirty mattresses. Most of them had lost track of their bundles by now. The few who had remembered to bring them off the bus did not know what to do with their shapeless parcels. Meanwhile the rest of the luggage had been piled up in the prison yard so that as soon as the unloading was finished, the children went down to find their belongings.
>
> The tiny, anonymous bundles were difficult to distinguish one from another, and for a long time small children of four, five, and six went through them, thinking they had found their own things. But after undoing a package and quickly examining its contents, they would find some pants or a small dress which belonged to somebody else and would feel puzzled and discouraged.
>
> In spite of their great distress, however, they would hopefully start all over again. They never quarreled or argued; on the contrary, they were helpful to each other in a thousand different ways, surprising to see in children. After several useless attempts to find their property, they gave up and remained in the courtyard, not knowing what to do. Those who wanted to go up into the bedrooms no longer remembered which dormitory they belonged to. Very politely they would ask somebody to help them: "Sir, I don't know where my little sister is. I think she may be frightened by herself." So one would take the bigger ones by the hand and, carrying the younger ones on one's arm, would wander through the dormitories on the various staircases until the little sister or brother in question was located. They demonstrated such affection as only children in unhappy circumstances can show.

Just as at Pithiviers and Beaune-la-Rolande, the children
were crowded, one hundred to a room, with no provisions for
their needs and comfort. Volunteers among the prisoners tried
to help them, and would get up before the rest in the morning
to clean the babies, wash their clothes, and bring them their
ration of cabbage and turnip soup. Though they were all
condemned to deportation and death, they worked as
devotedly and eagerly as if they were living in normal
conditions. Diarrhea was widespread among the children and
impossible to cure, so they were losing weight visibly. Their
cries and calls and weeping could be heard at night beyond the
limits of the camp.

During the day the older ones would sidle up to the adults
and listen to their talk about the mysterious place where their
parents and friends had gone—a mysterious place about which
people spoke with a mixture of fear and vague hope. Hope,
because most people at Drancy could not visualize conditions
worse than their present ones, where they were suffering
constant indignities in addition to the pain of being parted
from their closest relations. At least they could hope to find the
people they loved at this place they were going to. The
children, hearing conversations about this unknown place in a
country far away, started calling it "Pitchipoi." The nickname
spread throughout the camp and became a common usage.
"We are off to Pitchipoi. . . ." A Yiddish sounding word
which meant nothing and signified the edge of the world, the
unknown.

The children spent only a few days at Drancy before being
deported in groups of seven or eight hundred with about one
hundred fifty to two hundred women, ostensibly to look after
them, but in fact to make sure that the carloads of children
would not get out of hand. Also a few men who were "in
charge"—in keeping with the German method of appointing
someone at the head of a group, whatever its nature. On the
day of their departure, the children were awakened at five in
the morning and dressed in the semidarkness. Drugged with
sleep and cranky from being aroused so brusquely, the youngest

cried and struggled, refusing to allow themselves to be dressed or taken down into the yard. So the soldiers were called in and carried down armloads of children screaming with terror. Then, just as at Pithiviers and Beaune-la-Rolande, a token roll call was taken, the children unable to respond because they did not know their surnames and some not even their names. Here too the main object was to send off the required number.

The night before the departure, the children were searched again, just like the adults on the eve of deportation. Under the direction of Commissioner Bouquin, inspectors from the Police for Jewish Affairs carried out the search. We have an eyewitness account from Georges Wellers:

> Little toddlers of two or three would come into the shed with their minute bundles, which were carefully checked and given back to them all undone. Some volunteers set up a table near the door of the shed to retie the children's parcels as they went out. Brooches, earrings, bracelets were all confiscated by these inspectors. On one occasion a ten-year-old girl came out of the shed with a bleeding ear. The inspector had torn her earring right off when in her terror the girl had fumbled with the clasp.

So not even the trinkets of little children were overlooked as a source of gain. The thousands upon thousands of Jews on their way to extermination left France having been plundered openly and crudely by the last Frenchmen they were to meet. Of the two main inspectors whose duty it was to control the interior of the camp, Koerperich and Thibaudat, Thibaudat was sacked by the administration for underhand deals amounting to twenty thousand dollars. Koerperich was not much better. Only twenty years old, he was both interpreter and advisor and would come to Drancy daily to decide the fate of prisoners whose status was uncertain. His decisions were invariably for deportation. It was a common sight to see him, gay and cheerful, in the company of SS Heinrichsohn (first Dannecker's, then Roethke's aide) . And during the actual deportation process Koerperich demonstrated a zeal painful to watch, often striking prisoners who did not obey his orders with due docility. It is obvious that the Prefecture of Police was able to find inspectors in its ranks who could at any rate equal the Germans at this game.

The soldiers too were often mean and cruel during the execution of their duties. Some were indeed shocked at the prison conditions but carried out their assignments all the same. For the most part, they were indifferent and were roused only by the prospect of making some personal profit on the side. It is enough to quote one survivor's experience: "When we were leaving Pithiviers, the gendarmes, brutes, took our money and our watches, saying as they picked them up that we would have no use for either where we were going."

Another witness, A. Falkenstein, who was arrested on August 20, 1940 (he was then a teacher in Paris), has the following recollection of the gendarmes at Drancy:

> Captain Vieux and his two aides, Lieutenant Barral and Lieutenant Pietri, were especially cruel. One day I saw a little girl of four, who was lost in the middle of the yard, literally stunned by a slap from Barral. As for the gendarmes, there was a difference in their behavior as time went on. When we arrived, they were under the impression that we were common criminals and that there were violent prisoners among us. Little by little, however, they modified their attitude; apart from those who behaved like beasts (and these would have behaved in the same way to any kind of prisoner at their mercy) and others who were involved in a shameless blackmarket racket, selling cigarettes to prisoners at the rate of two dollars each, then snatching back the cigarette as soon as they had pocketed its price, most of the gendarmes ended up being humane and understanding, and I saw some who were as shocked as we were by what was happening.

Georges Horeau's impression was: "There were no disinterested motives. Apart from a few rare exceptions, the gendarmes were not altogether inhuman, and would allow themselves to be lavishly bribed." Another survivor, Théo Bernard, has said:

> Very quickly the gendarmes, at any rate most of them, grasped the fact that they could draw an easy income from the prisoners' need for food, cigarettes, and

communication. And while they were pocketing forty dollars for a packet of Gauloises and ten dollars for smuggling out a letter, their attitude towards their "clients" could hardly be termed anti-Semitic. There was a price on everything, even escape, and the bargaining that took place was purely commercial and untinged by political or racist feelings.

Georges Wellers concludes: "In general, the gendarmes were neither good nor bad. They merely obeyed their superiors blindly and unquestioningly, which puts the burden on the officers, whose responsibility is the greater the higher their rank in the camp."

At that time the man in charge of the directors of the camps was Chasselat, who was their general commander, while general Bailly was inspector general.

The gendarmes' activity, however, was not limited to watching the prison camps, escorting convoys, and carrying babies down into the yard at Drancy and occasionally taking part in a firing squad. In July, 1942, at the height of Operation Spring Wind, the guard, which had become part of the gendarmerie in 1941, at the orders of Colonel Martin, lent its cavalry to Delannoy, the film producer, for his film *Pontcarral*.

Then there was the corps celebration. On that occasion the guard marched past, to the tune of the *Marseillaise* played by the band. So it is not absolutely accurate to say that during the occupation the only time the *Marseillaise* was heard was when prisoners condemned to death sang it defiantly in their prison cells. Ten years later Colonel Martin remembered the corps celebration and the playing of the *Marseillaise* almost as if it had been a feat of arms:

> Military music had been banned, but I used my own resources and organized a band without asking anyone's permission and put Roch as drum major. The band still exists, by the way, and is stationed at Drancy. In July, 1942, it played the *Marseillaise* in public, and General Bailly, the inspector general of the gendarmerie, told me: "You'll have us all put in jail."

Chapter 11

Auschwitz, Poland

Bernard Epstein, who was arrested with his father on July 16, was deported to Germany from Drancy on July 21.

> There were about ninety of us in each car, and for the whole carload there were two pails, one filled with drinking water, which was very soon used up, and the other to be used as a lavatory. I was fortunate in that I was still with my family—my father, my mother, my sister, and her fiancé, Siegfried Friedman. But my father was sick, and his condition was deteriorating. He could hardly breathe. The heat and the crush of human beings was oppressive, and there was a terrible odor from the lavatory pail, which we were unable to empty. Twice the train stopped. Once, on an unused siding, the doors were opened, and two persons from each car were allowed to go out and get water while an SS aimed a gun at them. The second time we stopped at a station.

The stop at the station made a deep impression on the boy:

> It was a station in a West German town. We had crossed the border a short while before. As far as I could see, it seemed quite a sizable town. Our train had stopped because a brake had jammed and one of the wheels on our car had become red hot and there was a risk of fire. We halted beside a platform. The SS opened the doors of our car and told us to get out so that we could be transferred to other cars. Blinking as we came out of the darkness of our cattle car, we suddenly found ourselves on a platform opposite a crowd of ordinary people waiting for a train. It was evening and the lights were on.

Everything was clean. There were window boxes at each window and a neatly printed sign over each door and arrows pointing out various directions. The platform was crowded with women, children, and a few distinguished looking old men with white hair. One of them struck me particularly because he was wearing a tyrolean hat like the actors in *The White Horse Inn*, which I had seen. There also were soldiers in a whole range of different colored uniforms and a variety of helmets and caps. At one end of the platform, nurses leaned against a cart laden with bottles, glasses, and jugs. As we jumped down from our car, we stopped for a moment, hypnotized by this comfortable and peaceful setting. Our convoy had halted in a dimly lit part of the station, and we were not very visible to those on the parallel platform, who saw just silhouettes and perhaps eyes in the shadows, but soon they made out our six-pointed stars and understood without any doubt who we were. They collected on the edge of their platform, pushing each other and almost falling onto the tracks while those inside the station building came to join them and, straining in our direction, they shouted insults and curses, calling us murderers and thieves, bandits, *Schweinehunde* and dirty Jews. The children in the front line shook their fists and stuck out their tongues at us. I shall never forget the hatred in the eyes of that crowd as they stared.

I understood German and could hear the insults, but I was in no way ashamed. I was seventeen years old and knew perfectly well that I had never done anything evil and had committed no crime, nor had my father or my mother and sister who were with me. I was Jewish, but that did not mean anything special to me. I could not understand how anyone could hate me for something outside my control and which in any case was not something shameful. Until then I had had some hopes for our future, but after seeing this crowd I began to give up.

Albert Tselnick, like all deportees, also has nightmarish memories of the long journey to Poland.

It is difficult for me to find the right words to describe the journey from Drancy to Auschwitz. And yet there have been many descriptions of similar journeys. But even the most horrific accounts only convey a fraction of the

real experience, I think. One cannot understand the word
thirst fully, for example, without having died of thirst
oneself. Then there was the strangling heat; women who
would hide behind a curtain of old clothing to try and
tidy themselves up; there was the lack of ventilation,
which would drive us to the smallest gap between the
planks in the sides of the car to snatch a breath of air;
then there was the smell. We were crowded into the cars,
men, women, and children, for two days without being
allowed out, and there was only one pail in a corner of
the car for all of us to use. The two days we spent saying,
"This can't go on! They will have to stop the train. We
will be allowed into the clean air. Nothing can be worse
than this."

Jostled and jolted in the train for two days, Mr. Tselnick
tried to stop thinking, because he was haunted by the picture
of his wife and three children and was frightened of going mad
like others around him, who would talk to themselves or sit
motionless with wild-looking faces in the half dark of the
carriage.

Mr. Goldenzwag traveled on the same train as Mr. Tselnick
and had the same agonizing experiences except that he at least
had the comfort of his eighteen-year-old son's company (if one
can call it a comfort to know that one's son is sharing one's
fate). Mr. Goldenzwag thinks not—his son never came back.
He remembers that in spite of the thirst, the lack of air, the
stench, and the mournful submission of most people in his
car, there was in everyone's heart a faint hope, a hope which
made them think "this cannot go on, this cannot go on." The
thought repeated itself like a refrain in their heads obsessively
in time to the rhythm of the train. A few people went so far as
to rationalize the discomfort of the journey, saying it was a
result of the shortage of cars.

Before the train reached the Nazi camps, there were
hundreds of miles of traveling inside France. Only when the
train crossed into German territory (and Alsace and Lorraine
were counted as such) did the escort become exclusively
German. The crossing of the border took place at Neuberg
(Novéant) in the Moselle country. At that point the French

gendarmes turned back, having until then provided the main body of the escort. In the meetings between the French and the Germans mentioned earlier, it had been agreed that each train would be escorted by thirty French gendarmes and their officer under a squad of German gendarmes.

Thanks to a report written by a Major Serignan, we have precise information on how things went. While the train was in motion, the Germans controlled the brakes. At every stop the gendarmes would get off the train as quickly as they could and form a cordon around the convoy. In order to speed up the formation of the cordon, the men (thirty-three without counting their officer) were divided into three groups and traveled in three passenger cars which were placed at the head, in the middle, and at the end of the train. Things were so well organized that the chances of escaping in French territory were slim.

Serignan's report, which bears the number 1447, is full of information. Had it not been for Commander Sauts, who, in his anxiety to please, had sent a copy to Roethke, later found in the archives of the Avenue Foch, it might never have survived. The report tells of the escape of eleven Jews from a convoy of one thousand deportees. Ten of the runaways were caught (eight by the escort of gendarmes and two by the brigade at Châlons-sur-Marne, which had been alerted by telephone). In Serignan's words:

> Even though they were not responsible for guarding the train while it was in motion, it was the French gendarmes who raised the alarm and who without help from the Germans recaptured almost all the runaways. In the circumstances, not only is there no criticism to be brought against the officers and gendarmes, but they are to be congratulated on their vigilance and their agility. The German sublieutenant himself (Nowak) * appreciated their action and thought fit to congratulate the gendarmes of the detachment several times and with great warmth.

* Probably the Lieutenant Nowak mentioned earlier, who was responsible for the transportation of deportees. In 1966 he was acquitted at Vienna.

As soon as they arrived at Auschwitz, Goldenzwag and
Tselnick were registered under the numbers 55293 and 56599
respectively. Mr. Tselnick described the arrival:

> It was a great relief when the train finally stopped and
> the doors of the car were opened, and all the more so
> because that day the SS did not seem to want to hurry us
> with blows of their truncheons, nor were there any dogs
> to bite our legs. On the contrary, the people there seemed
> to want to calm and reassure us rather than terrorize us.
> We alighted from the train onto the platform, or rather
> ground on either side of the tracks, which we later
> called the "ramp." The camp was not very far, and
> we could see the buildings from where we were. A
> loudspeaker told us to remain calm and to get into a line.
> We then moved forward to a group of officers, who
> questioned us briefly, mainly asking us our age. There
> were some older people near me, sixty, sixty-three and
> sixty-eight years old, and the SS made them form a
> separate group near some trucks that were waiting. The
> younger people like myself—I was thirty-two years old at
> that time—were put into a different group, except for one
> young man who was obviously sick and three pregnant
> young women who were placed with the old people. Then
> the old people and the sick young man and the pregnant
> women climbed into the truck and were driven off in the
> direction of the camp. The rest of us followed on foot.
> For a moment I must admit that I wished I looked sick
> because my legs were stiff with cramp and I could hardly
> walk. I would have much preferred a ride in a truck. Of
> course, at the time I didn't know that the trucks were
> taking those people straight to the gas chambers.

Goldenzwag and his son were also classed among the young
people. And two months later Rosenberg, whose military cross
could not protect him indefinitely, took the same journey
except that by that time the nights were beginning to be icy
cold, in spite of the crowding of the cars. Rosenberg never got
as far as Auschwitz; his train stopped a few dozen miles earlier
at Cazel, where there was another prison camp, an annex to
Auschwitz, and a few of the prisoners who were judged
particularly strong and fit were unloaded. Rosenberg never
got nearer than smelling Auschwitz when the wind spread the

acrid odor of burning bones over the whole countryside. The more he found out about Auschwitz, the less credible it seemed. Only during the winter of 1942, while he was working in a timber yard near a railroad line, did he become convinced that the rumors were possibly true. As he watched, a train stopped and some prisoners alighted, among them a woman carrying a baby in her arms. An SS snatched the baby, put it in a sack, and, swinging with all his might, smashed it against the side of the train. Mad with horror, the mother flung herself at the SS, who shot her pointblank.

André Montagne was already at Auschwitz when the victims of the Paris raids of July 16 and 17 arrived. He had been there since July 8, when he was brought in a convoy of 1,170 deportees from Paris, almost all of them collected from prison camps where they had been held as hostages after a series of incidents organized by the Resistance. He was then eighteen years old. To quote him:

> I have spent time in several concentration camps in Germany, and I ended my prison career at Mauthausen in Austria, which was thought of as one of the worst in the world of Nazi concentration camps. It had been classed as a third category prison by SS Pohl in 1942, which in Nazi terminology meant "prison reserved for inveterate and hopeless criminals." But none can be compared to Auschwitz, especially as it was during the summer of 1942. There are no words to describe the horror of Auschwitz at that time. One can say: "Auschwitz was Hell." But who can imagine Hell without having been there?
>
> In July, 1942, the camp of Auschwitz-Birkenau was not yet sufficiently well equipped to satisfy the murderous needs of the Nazis. There was only one small crematorium, and it was too small to burn the bodies of the new arrivals, who were being killed by the thousands. The poor Jews who had been judged unfit on arrival, and were destined for the gas chambers, would be sent to Birkenau, half a mile from Auschwitz, where they were taken to a birch wood at the end of the camp. (The name Birkenau is derived from the German word *Birken,* which means birch.) There was at that time a group of sheds in

the birch wood, built as vast airtight halls with
ventilation shafts. From a distance they looked like a
bathing establishment, which misled the victims and
made them easier to handle.

The selected prisoners would be taken to the birch
wood in convoys of eight to ten trucks filled to capacity,
and accompanying each convoy there would be one of the
camp doctors in a private car, who had to be present at
the execution. The sheds in the birch wood were fenced
off by a double roll of barbed wire. The prisoners were
brought inside the barbed wire enclosure and unloaded,
and men, women, and children were told to undress
completely. Then, to maintain the illusion and to avoid
panic, the SS distributed a towel and a cake of soap to
each prisoner. They were then led into the sheds, which,
once they were full, were sealed hermetically. Specially
trained members of the SS next threw containers of
Cyklon B gas through the ventilation shafts. After ten to
fifteen minutes the doors were opened again and a special
unit made up entirely of Jews went in to remove the
bodies. (These Jews were gassed in their turn a few weeks
later to eliminate witnesses to the executions.) The place
was then cleared for the next convoy. The towels and
pieces of soap were carefully collected for redistribution
among the next batch of prisoners, and so on. Gold teeth
were torn from the jaws of the dead in the same spirit of
economy, and the women's hair was shaven and their
rings and earrings removed if they still had some left.

We know that the first convoy of prisoners arrested in Paris
on July 16 and 17 left Drancy on July 19. The Auschwitz
Notebooks mention its arrival on the twenty-first, detailing
that it was composed of 879 men and 121 women and
emphasizing that of these, 375 had been taken to the gas
chambers immediately on arrival. The second convoy arrived
on July 24 with 615 men and 385 women, of whom 569 were of
Polish origin, according to the Notebooks. On July 26
another thousand Jews arrived from Drancy; 370 men and 630
women. On July 29 there was another convoy of 990 Jews, 248
men and 742 women. We have Bernard Epstein's account:

> We arrived at Birkenau on July 24 in the evening. The
> train came to a halt alongside the famous "ramp." The

doors of the cars were opened, and the SS made everyone
get out. We were half dead with exhaustion, but luckily
for my father for some reason there was no separation of
the fit from the unfit that day. My father was finding it
difficult to drag himself along. My sister's fiancé and I
held him up between us so that he stood on his feet more
or less. At this point there was an unexpected disturbance.
A prisoner who had gone mad after the departure from
Drancy began running all over the place, completely out
of his mind. The SS went after him. It did not take them
long to catch up with him, and they set upon him, beating
him with incredible savagery. In a few seconds the poor
man collapsed, dead, and was taken away on a stretcher.

I had begun to give up hope after seeing the hatred of
the crowd at the station in Germany, and now I was not
able to hide my despair. Perhaps because I was still young,
I had to share my feelings of foreboding, and I turned to
my mother and said, "This is the last time we shall be
seeing each other." She flung herself into my arms, and so
did my sister. My father and my sister's fiancé were with
us, and we stood for a few seconds embracing each other.
Then we were separated, women on one side and men on
the other, and were led separately to the women's camp
and the men's camp. I never saw my mother or my sister
again. I was still holding up my father with the help of
my sister's fiancé and making him walk. It was dark by
now. By the light of the projectors I could see in the
distance, near the huts, what looked like enormous
stacks of neatly piled logs. I could not make out what they
were exactly. Next day at dawn I found out what they
were. For the first time in my life I saw thousands of
human corpses.

Not all the trains traveling to Auschwitz during July and
August, 1942 (the first months during which the Final Solution
was being applied seriously) came from France. Once the
border was crossed, the old patched-up cars, carefully padlocked
to hold in the flood of misery inside them, were hooked onto
locomotives decorated with the words painted on all
locomotives used in the Third Reich, the arrogant Nazi motto:
"Our wheels are rolling on to Victory." They collected their
cargo from all the countries of occupied Europe: Poland,
Belgium, Holland, Denmark, and Russia. On August 2 one
thousand Jews arrived from Golojow; on August 4 there came

1,013 from Westerbork, the Dutch equivalent of Drancy; on August 5 some 744 deportees came from the camp at Malines. At the same time there were the convoys from Pithiviers on August 2 and 5, as mentioned above, the second of which numbered 1,046 Jews, of whom 482 were killed immediately.

From August 5 onwards, the sinister words *wurden vergast,* which until that time had only appeared in the Auschwitz Notebooks intermittently, became a regular part of the registration of the arrival of each convoy. On August 7, for instance, 1,404 Jews arrived from Beaune-la-Rolande, and for the first time children were mentioned by the Auschwitz Notebooks. The 204 men and 496 women were registered; the rest, 704 persons, *wurden vergast*—which means all the children. Two days later, on August 9, a convoy from Beaune-la-Rolande and Pithiviers arrived with 197 men and 871 women and children; only 63 men and 211 women were registered. The remaining 794, including all the children, *wurden vergast.* On August 12 another 1,006 men, women, and children arrived from Drancy; 140 men and 100 women were registered, 766 *wurden vergast.* On August 14, from Drancy, 1,162 more Jews arrived at Auschwitz; 877 *wurden vergast.* On August 16, still from Drancy, there was a convoy of 991 people; of these 876 *wurden vergast.* August 21—997 Jews arrived; 814 were gassed. August 23—973 Jews came; 865 were gassed. August 26—1,057, of whom 965 were gassed. August 28—948 Jews arrived, and 885 were gassed.

During August and September, 1942, the convoys of Jews arriving from every part of Europe, and especially from France, were so numerous that the arrangements for killing prisoners by gas at Birkenau proved insufficient. Consequently whole convoys of Jews were shot dead instead. We have an eyewitness account from Nathan Sienicki, who was arrested on Black Thursday by the Paris police and like Goldenzwag and Tselnick was brought to Auschwitz from Pithiviers in the convoy of August 2, 1942. His wife and daughter Régine, who was still recovering from an operation, were also on that train, but they never came back. Mr. Sienicki's brother and sister-in-law, together with their eight children, were on that train too and were all killed. Mr. Sienicki's description of the first weeks of his stay at Auschwitz follows:

> As soon as we arrived, we were taken to Birkenau. I never saw my wife or my daughter again. Once I saw two of my nieces from a distance. I was too far off for us to be able to speak to each other, so they simply made a gesture of despair with their hands. But for a few days I worked with my brother in the same unit. Our job was to carry planks and panels of wood for the construction of new huts. Our boss was a Polish "kapo" called René, whose number was "25." He was a common criminal and wore the letter *M* on his chest, which distinguished him as a murderer. He had come to the camp the day it was opened on July 14, 1940. His cruelty was unbelievable. He would beat us without stopping and force us to run on the job. Every morning we started out with 120 people in his group, but more than half would be dead before the day was over. An average of seventy people a day. I stayed in his squad until the end of August, 1942, when I was transferred to Golojow, an annex to Auschwitz where there was a stone quarry. I had to say goodbye to my brother, who was worn out and can't have survived very long after my departure.
>
> But before being transferred, around August 10, I was chosen to join a *sonderkommando*, a special unit whose job it was to dig huge trenches at the edge of the Birkenau camp near the part called "the Birch Wood," which was not far from the huts used as gas chambers. The trenches were approximately eight feet wide and eight feet deep. When they were dug, the SS made us stand to one side and then led women, old people, and children to the edge of the trenches, shooting them down with machine guns so that they would topple into the trenches. We then had to cover the bodies with earth, but the victims were so many and the layer of soil covering them so thin that blood seeped out of the earth as if it were a sponge.
>
> Fortunately I only stayed two days on this horrible job. I was lucky not only because René's team, to which I returned, was comparatively less terrible, but because every man who worked on the trenches was later executed.

Simon Gotland is a valuable witness, being one of the very few survivors from Auschwitz. The statements he made at the

Auschwitz trial at Frankfort were collected in a book entitled
The SS Executioners and Their Victims, published in Vienna.
He was very helpful and told us what he saw of the fate of the
Jews arrested in Paris on Black Thursday. He had seen their
arrival at Drancy and later the arrival of the children from
Pithiviers and Beaune-la-Rolande. He himself was on the
convoy which left Drancy on July 26 and arrived at Auschwitz
on July 29. His registration number was 53908. During the
summer of 1942 he spent several weeks digging long ditches,
mass graves for the corpses of the Jews who had been gassed,
and sprinkling the bodies with quicklime before covering over
the graves, which were 35 feet long and 25 feet wide. He was
witness to many scenes of atrocity, which he has survived to tell
about.*

But there was other evidence—the SS themselves. The diary
of Obersturmfuehrer Johann Kremer, an SS doctor, has been
found which records the events at Auschwitz at this time.
Professor of anatomy at the University of Munich before the
war, he was appointed to Auschwitz on August 30, 1942, as a
replacement for a doctor who was sick. His arrival is mentioned
in the Auschwitz Notebooks. On September 2 at 3 P.M. he was
present at an execution by gas for the first time. The victims
were Jews who had come from France, a convoy numbering 957
people from Drancy, of whom only 12 men and 27 women were
registered while the 918 who were left were executed. The
people on this convoy had all been arrested on July 16 in Paris.

In his diary Johann Kremer wrote: "After what I have seen
today, Dante's Inferno seems a farce."

On September 5 he was present at the extermination of eight
hundred sick women taken from the hospital in the women's
camp.

---

* Simon Gotland was one of the members of the Resistance Committee
at Auschwitz. There were organized escapes from the camp and a
rebellion during which the prisoners blew up one of the gas chambers.
Among the members of the Resistance Committee were Cyrankiewicz,
Prime Minister of Poland, and David Smulewicz, who was able to take
a photograph of a cremation and smuggle the picture out in 1943.

This is the extreme of horror and terror. Thilo was right when he told me that here we were in "the world's anus."

And yet Johann Kremer did not forget to add to his journal for that same day:

Because of the exhausting work they had had to do, the SS who took part in this operation were issued with supplementary rations of $\frac{1}{5}$ of a quart of alcohol, 5 cigarettes, $\frac{1}{5}$ of a pound of sausage, and one extra ration of bread.

Next day, September 6, which was a Sunday, Johann Kremer mentions: "We had an excellent lunch today—tomato soup, $\frac{1}{2}$ chicken and roast potatoes, cake and vanilla ice cream."

The professor of anatomy had a sturdy stomach. All the same, in the entry for October 18 he seems to feel some emotion:

Today, Sunday morning, although the weather was icy, we had the eleventh *Sonderaktion* (Dutch). A terrible scene—three naked women begging for mercy.

Though young Bernard Epstein was at Birkenau with his sister's fiancé, they did not work together. Meanwhile his father, who was dying, had been transferred to the infirmary. By some miracle the old man had not been taken to the gas chambers. The huts of the infirmary were full, and hundreds of sick people were lying outside, half naked, on the bare ground day and night. Bernard's father was one of these. Risking execution, Bernard went to see him but his father no longer recognized him. As a last gesture of filial affection, Bernard was able to slip a stone under his father's head for a pillow. Here are his recollections:

At Birkenau I found my uncle, who had been arrested at Lunéville at the end of July, 1942, with his wife and two sons. My uncle was the only one of the family to survive. When he returned home, he found out that his eldest son, who was eighteen, had been killed while fighting in the Resistance near Tarbes. The boy's grave is there today.

I was lucky because I was young and strong and was fluent in German. It was my mother tongue, since my family had fled to France from Germany. The commander of the camp asked for fifteen young men, aged sixteen years, who apparently were needed as overseers to inspect the work on the mines where in the future slaves from all over Europe would work. But meanwhile I caught typhus and had to go to the infirmary. There again I was lucky. When the SS came to give the typhoid cases injections of gasoline that would kill them off, a German male nurse, also a deportee, warned me and hid me in the "Cave of the Dead," where the dead were laid out for cremation or burial. I laid myself down among them, stark naked, until the SS had gone away. I don't know how I managed both to survive the disease and escape the injection. It was a miracle. My sister's fiancé was less lucky. He too caught typhus but was killed by an injection at the end of 1942. I was the only one of my family to survive.

The Final Solution had been launched, and the death factory of the Nazis had been put to work and exceeded all expectations. Though the Nazi imagination had thought up the crime, it had not gone beyond that. The existing arrangements for execution could not handle the flood of incoming material. As late as July, 1942, there was only one small oven for cremations at Auschwitz, and the construction of the giant crematoria at Birkenau was begun only then. In spite of the speed with which the construction work was managed, the new ovens were not ready until November, 1942. Which means that while the deportations continued from the end of July through August, September, and October, there were no facilities for burning the bodies of the Jews who had been gassed or shot.

Numerous mass graves were dug, identical with the ditches described by Gotland and Sienicki. But soon there was a new problem: the lack of space for digging ditches. So the corpses were spread in the surrounding fields, layer upon layer hidden only with a thin covering of earth. The summer in Poland that year was very hot. The smell from this charnel house soon spread throughout the region and made it quite unbearable.

The men whose work it was to bury the corpses were locked up apart from the rest, because they were impregnated with the pestilential smell. They could not wash themselves, because water was beginning to run short. Typhoid broke out and spread throughout the camp. The first cases were noted on July 13. The Auschwitz Notebooks say that the infirmary register recorded numerous cases of typhoid, and prisoners in crowds came to the infirmary only to die there.

There was, of course, no pretense of treating the sick. They were killed by injecting phenol directly into their hearts. On August 8, for instance, forty patients were given phenol injections:

> An SS doctor went through the prisoners in the infirmary in block 20 and chose forty among them. That same day these were all killed by an injection of phenol in the heart.

On August 10, fifty-five of the sick were given the same treatment. On August 11, seventy; on August 12, thirty-seven; on August 13, sixty; on August 14, fifty-eight; on August 15, thirty-eight; on August 18, eighty-two; on August 19, sixty-seven; on August 20, fifty-nine; on August 22, ninety-two; on August 24, thirty-three; on August 25, eighty. . . . On August 20 the Auschwitz Notebooks mention a supplementary operation:

> With the excuse of fighting the typhus epidemic, the directors of the camp decided to exterminate the sick as well as their lice, which were spreading the disease. So 746 sick people and convalescents were chosen from Block 20, where the infectious diseases are treated, and taken to the gas chambers at Birkenau. Some of the prisoners, however, succeeded in hiding in a drainage pipe in the courtyard. This operation was conducted by the chief physician of the camp, SS Obersturmfuehrer doctor Friedrich Entress, assisted by S.D.G. Joseph Klehr.

Many of these patients must have been victims of the Black Thursday roundup.

The mass execution of patients in the infirmary can hardly

have contributed to the fight against the epidemic; it contributed rather to the catalogue of atrocities, inspiring the authorities to execute all the sick in relays, just as those who were unfit on arrival were disposed of in the gas chambers. At the same time, the phenol injections continued: twelve on September 2, eight on September 6, thirty-three on September 7, twenty-three on September 16, ninety-eight on September 17, thirty-one on September 19, twenty-four on September 22, etc. The accumulation of corpses was such that new methods of disposing of the bodies had to be thought up. On September 16, Rudolf Hoess, the commander of the camp, who had been promoted to the rank of Obersturmfuehrer by Himmler during his July 17 visit, went to the nearby town of Chelmno, where there was another concentration camp. Here hundreds of thousands of Polish Jews had already been executed and there had been the same problems. The object of Rudolf Hoess's trip was to find a way of clearing the corpses from the trenches without stopping the mass executions, whether by gas or shooting. On this journey Hoess was accompanied by SS Untersturmfuehrer Hoessler and SS Untersturmfuehrer Déjaco, as well as SS Standartenfuehrer Blodel.

As a result of this trip, which was reported in the Auschwitz Notebooks, starting on September 20, they began to burn the corpses in the open air in heaps of two thousand. The bodies were not only those of newly executed Jews but also corpses disinterred from the mass graves. The bodies were interspersed with logs of wood or branches and the whole pile would be soaked in gasoline and then with methanol (methilic alcohol) . The vast quantities of human ashes that were collected after these open air cremations were loaded onto trucks and spread over the nearby fields. This went on from September 20 to November 30, when the Auschwitz Notebooks say:

> The destruction of the corpses buried in the mass graves is now complete. The number of corpses burned was 107,000 and were the bodies of Jews recently brought from abroad as well as prisoners who died at Auschwitz during the winter of 1941–1942, when the No. 1 oven was

not yet working. The total also includes all corpses from Birkenau.

Three days later, on December 3, the Notebooks go on to say:

> The three hundred prisoners working in the *Sonderkommando,* whose task it was to destroy the corpses, have been taken from Birkenau to Auschwitz and killed by gas in the cremation chamber of the No. 1 oven. Thus the witnesses to the destruction of 107,000 corpses have been liquidated.

One hundred and seven thousand bodies. However shocking the number, there was still a long way to go: millions of victims were still to meet their death at Auschwitz-Birkenau in the next two years, until January, 1945, when the Red Army entered the camp.* Among these 107,000 corpses were nearly all the 13,000 Jews rounded up in Paris on July 16–17, and at any rate all the children who had not originally been intended for arrest by Théo Dannecker but who were eventually included in the raids when Pierre Laval, head of the Vichy government, had suggested that they should go too.

We have traced their journey to its end from that early morning of Black Thursday, July 16, 1942, when French policemen came for them just as a sunny day was breaking over Paris.

---

* Of the 4,400,000 victims deported to Auschwitz and its annexes, only sixty thousand were still living in January, 1945; which means that 98.5 per cent of the victims were murdered. This figure was cited at the Auschwitz Trial, which took place in Frankfort between December 20, 1963, and August 18, 1965.

Chapter 12

Letting the World Know

The first reaction of those who, despairing and powerless, witnessed the crimes of July 16, 1942, was a desire to publicize them. The people had to know, and the facts must not be suppressed. The public must be told at once.

During the night of July 16–17, Myriam Novitch wrote a pamphlet in which she described all she had seen. An Armenian friend of hers printed it, and the next day she was able to distribute it.

As soon as the first details were collected—mainly from the account of the Cathala sisters who had gone into the Vel d'Hiv on the first day, from the evidence of a social worker who wrote to her father, and from the descriptions of the few Jews who had been released—the leftist organizations produced a special issue of *Notre Voix*.

It is hardly possible for us now to imagine the difficulties that surrounded the publication and distribution of such a paper in France at that time. Distribution was immediately guaranteed by the members of *Solidarité*, and they reached a wide audience of Jewish and non-Jewish elements. Members of *Solidarité* had the satisfaction of being able to say that as soon as they knew about the impending roundup, and as soon as the few conscious indiscretions on the part of the police reached them, they had warned the intended victims. Unfortunately in a number of cases their warnings had been useless.

Other pamphlets and newspapers also did their best to spread the news. All of them seem to have felt the urgent need to publicize the facts; the communication of this information seemed as important as rallying the readers to support the persecuted and join in resisting the enemy. The motives for publishing the facts were twofold: the first and more immediate one being to rouse the public and the second, long-term motive, to record the facts for the future.

Among the papers of the Gestapo was found a letter quoting one of these pamphlets. The text mentions the suicides of July 16 and 17 and places the number of women who had killed themselves at three hundred. At the bottom of the letter, Roethke, who had a habit of commenting on everything, wrote "Unfortunately, no." In his way he too was giving evidence without knowing it.

The clandestine press of the Resistance made every effort to present a true picture of the events. Not only did it report what took place, but it also recorded the indignation and protest expressed by the various movements. In the *Lettres Françaises,* which she had just begun (the second one of the series, to be precise) , Edith Thomas wrote:

> I saw a train go by. In the first car were French and German soldiers. Next came cattle cars sealed with lead. Thin arms of children hugged the bars. A hand fluttered outside the truck like a leaf in a storm. As the train slowed down, voices called out "Mother." There was no reply except the screech of brakes. The truth: people are made to wear yellow stars; children are torn from their mother's arms; every day men are shot; the methodical degradation of a whole people is going on. The truth is banned. It must be shouted from the rooftops.

In a special edition of the *Franc-Tireur* with a September, 1942, date, there was the following:

> Since August 26 the horrors which happened in this part of the country are spreading into the area called the free zone. In Lyon, Toulouse, Marseilles, Nice and Montélimar, in the cities and villages in every part of France, French people have been the indignant witnesses to unspeakable and heartrending sights. The poor Jewish refugees are being tracked down by the Vichy government

and handed over to their Nazi executioners. Old men of sixty, women, and children, unhappy children, are being piled into trains with the adults and sent to Germany to die. This is happening in our country. The Vichy government seems to have set its heart on dishonoring France.

This wasn't the first time that the Resistance took a stand on the question of the persecution of the Jews. Already on May 4, 1942, a report of the prefecture of police notes bitterly: "The communists are assuring the Jews that they have captured the sympathy of the French people and that the French are aware of the sacrifice of the Jewish hostages who were shot."

As early as its April issue, which appeared in May, the *Cahiers du Témoignage Chrétien* had expressed its feelings clearly:

> The anti-Semites interpret the forced silence of the nation as acquiescence. Fellow Frenchmen and Christians, we want to break that silence. If it is prolonged further, this silence will lie heavy on your consciences and will indict France and especially the Christians in France as accomplices before the astonished eyes of the world. In short, France wants no part in this!

After the tragic events, the need was unanimously felt for the establishment of an organized resistance against racism, later to become part of the CNR. News of the events spread rapidly. Someone would read a pamphlet, an eyewitness account would be heard on the BBC, and from mouth to mouth the story traveled. Sometimes it was exaggerated or untrue, there were omissions and alterations, but the essence of the facts of the Paris pogrom and its results reached every French household within a month at most. Few people could pretend that they knew nothing.

Inevitably mention must be made of the BBC. The daily transmission of "Frenchmen Speak to Frenchmen," with its unforgettable signature tune, was heard in millions of homes at 9:15 each night, against a background of heavy disturbances.

How was it that London was so well informed? We know that

when Mrs. Errazuriz asked Dr. Didier-Hesse for information
for transmission on the radio, he told her what he knew. Was
that the method? In 1945, during a commission of inquiry, Mr.
Edinger said that it was the doctors' reports that had been
broadcast, but when asked about it again in 1966, he no longer
remembered how the information was passed on.

Whatever actually happened, on August 3, 1942, the BBC
dedicated a program to the subject of anti-Semitism for the first
time. On August 5 the subject was again touched on in a
program called "The German Plan for the Degradation of
France." The words were by Brunius and ended with the
following appeal:

> As in Germany, in Czechoslovakia, in Austria, in
> Poland and everywhere, the persecution of the Jews is
> but a prelude, a preliminary step toward the enslavement
> of the whole of the French nation.
> The only way to stop this is by supporting and standing
> by the persecuted, supporting all victims and all
> threatened people. Every Frenchman who has a bed or
> some food, however simple, should shelter, feed, and
> protect a Jew or a tramp.

On August 8 the following text, written by Vachet, was read
on the BBC evening program in French:

> We know today that they have introduced their
> pogroms into France, the classical land of liberty, the
> country famous for its tradition of human dignity and
> generosity. Who has not heard of the concentration camps
> of Drancy, Compiègne, and the Vélodrome d'Hiver, and
> their sinister reputations? It is to these places that the
> Germans have been sending Jews for months after making
> arbitrary arrests of individuals. But they are improving
> their methods and no longer arrest the Jews one by one
> but round them up en masse. Women and children have
> been shut into the Vel d'Hiv. Men have been taken from
> their families without feeling and sent to concentration
> camps, from which they are deported into exile in Poland
> or Russia.

Abroad the events taking place in France prompted loud
protest. Above all, the cooperation of the French police and

the government of Marshal Pétain roused general indignation
and anger. The world knew what to expect from the Germans;
it was now shocked by the attitude of the French. The Mexican
government filed an official protest with President Laval
against the handing over of Jews and Spanish republicans.

During the last days of August, 1942, the American chargé
d'affaires, Mr. Tuck, protested to Laval against the betrayal of
Jews to the Germans. Laval in reply asked ironically whether
America would be ready to take the Jews. Tuck did not answer.
At a demonstration at Vichy on September 19, Laval explained
that the men, women, and children delivered to the Germans
were "undesirable elements involved in the black market and
in Gaullist and communist propaganda." He made sarcastic
references to those who would like to tell him what to do but
were unwilling to look after the Jews themselves. He omitted
to mention that Tuck had brought the matter up once more,
insisting that Laval make an official offer to the United States
government, and that he had refused.

On July 14 the Hungarian consulate made a protest against
the deportation of Hungarian Jews.

That summer of 1942 a group of Catholic clergy took a firm
position on the question of the persecution of the Jews. Six
days after the roundup, on July 22, the annual assembly of
cardinals and archbishops was held in Paris. Cardinal Suhard
was elected to present the following resolution to Marshal
Pétain:

> We cannot smother the voice of our conscience. We
> therefore ask that you bear this fact in mind and see that
> the demands of Justice and the rights of charity are
> respected.

Already on June 19, 1942, at Vichy itself, Reverend Victor
Dillard,* preaching in the Church of Saint-Louis de Vichy in
front of a congregation that included some of the highest

---

* Reverend Dillard had to leave Vichy soon after. A forerunner of the
working priesthood, he went to Germany to bring the comforts of religion
to those who had been requisitioned for forced labor. He was arrested
by the Gestapo and died at Dachau on January 12, 1945.

ranking officials of the Pétain government, invited the faithful
to pray not only for the prisoners of war, but also for the eighty
thousand Frenchmen who were being mocked and made to
wear a yellow star.

On August 20, Msgr. Saliège, the archbishop of Toulouse,
happened to be at the training college on the occasion of
sacerdotal retreat. Also there was Miss Thérèse Dauty, who had
witnessed deportations at the camps of Noé and Récébédou on
August 8 and described what she had seen to Msgr. Saliège,
deeply disturbing him with her account. As soon as he returned
to his residence, still under the impact of his emotion, he
dictated to his secretary a pastoral letter, written in the
strongest terms, which is one of the most beautiful
condemnations of racism ever made. His instructions on the
letter were: "To be read next Sunday without comment."

The following Sunday was August 30. Meantime the regional
prefect was told of the pastoral letter by informers, and he
summoned the auxiliary bishop, Msgr. Courrèges, to his office
on the morning of the twenty-ninth. Msgr. Courrèges described
the interview:

> The prefect said: "It is about the Archbishop's pastoral
> letter. We cannot allow it; it is unjust. While it is true
> that many Jews have been deported, it is not true that
> there have been terrible and shocking scenes."
> I argued. "The archbishop has already decided to read
> the letter and will not change his mind."
> "In that case I will have to seize the letter."*

At Montauban Msgr. Théas had also composed a letter of
protest. He told the prefect, Mr. Martin, after giving him a
copy, that it "would be read during the services to be held in
the whole of the diocese."

Prefect Martin immediately "worded" (his own expression)
a telegram to the regional prefect, Cheyneau de Leyritz, at
Toulouse (who already had the problem of Msgr. Saliège on
his hands!) and to the government. The text follows:

* Quoted in *Juifs mes frères* by Jean Toulard (Editions Guy Victor).

All information received confirms that operations
planned against Jews are known to the interested parties.

He was referring to the roundups which were taking place in
the free zone of France according to plan. Mr. Martin's
telegram continues:

I fear painful incidents or perhaps suicides. Several
groups, especially religious groups, demonstrate real
emotion in spite of marked hostility toward Jews till now.
Public opinion will doubtless be very troubled.*

Then, having warned his superiors, Mr. Martin summoned the
archbishop himself. They had a polite discussion at the end of
which Mr. Martin did not press his opposition to the reading
of the letter in the churches but asked that it be omitted in the
"Legion" mass, which government representatives would
attend.

Laval had been warned by the prefects and was furious. He
not only called Msgr. Rocco, who was replacing the absent
nuncio, to tell him bluntly to inform the Pope and the
Secretary of State, Cardinal Maglione, that the French
government would never allow "such interference of the
Church in affairs of state," but he also hastened to inform the
Germans in the person of Ambassador Otto Abetz, from whom
we heard the details of the story.

Meanwhile the parish priests in the Toulouse region had
received copies of Msgr. Saliège's pastoral letter. Cheyenne de
Leyritz had also prepared his move. On Saturday policemen
and gendarmes called on the priests to inform them that the
prefecture was banning the pastoral letter. With so little time
before the service next day, many priests spent the night
traveling long distances to knock at the door of the archbishop
and ask for final instructions.

"They are to read it! They are to read it!" exclaimed Msgr.
Saliège, who had been roused from his sleep.

The eighty-one-year-old curé of Beauchalot, Father Ratio,
had not been told of the ban when he got ready to read the

* *La vie de la France sous l'occupation* (Hoover Institute), I, 447.

letter on Sunday, only to discover that he had forgotten his glasses.

"Never mind," he said, "we'll read it next Sunday."

At that moment a gendarme came forward to inform him of the prefectorial ban. Immediately the priest sent someone to fetch his pince-nez and, after reading the prefect's message, went on to read the pastoral letter:

> BRETHREN:
>
> There is a Christian morality and a human ethic which imposes duties and recognizes rights. Both rights and duties are parts of human nature.
>
> They were sent by God. They can be violated. But no mortal can suppress them. The treatment of children, women, fathers, and mothers like a base herd of cattle, the separation of members of a family from one another and their deportation to unknown destinations, are sad spectacles which have been reserved for us to witness in our times. Why does the right of asylum of the church no longer exist? Why are we defeated? Lord, have mercy on us. Our Lady, pray for France. In our own diocese, in the camps of Noé and Récébédou, scenes of horror have taken place. Jews are men and women. Foreigners are men and women. It is just as criminal to use violence against these men and women, these fathers and mothers with families, as it is against anyone else. They too are members of the human race. They are our brothers like so many others. A Christian cannot forget that. France, our beloved country; France, known to all your children for a tradition of respect for human life; chivalrous, generous France, I trust in you and do not believe that you are responsible for these horrors.
>
> > With my affectionate devotion,
> > JULES-GÉRARD SALIÈGE
> > Archbishop of Toulouse

In nearly half the churches of the Diocese of Toulouse, the archbishop's pastoral letter was read, while in every church in the diocese of Montauban the words of Msgr. Théas' protest were also read that Sunday:

> I wish to voice the indignant protest of the Christian conscience, and proclaim that all men and women, Aryan

and non-Aryan, were created by God and are therefore
brothers. All men, whatever their race or religion, have a
right to the respect of their fellow citizens and their state.
The current anti-Semitic measures are in contempt of
human dignity and violate the most sacred rights of
individuals and families.

Msgr. Théas had already written a letter to the rabbi in his
town in December, 1941, saying:

> The harassment and the brutal persecution of the Jews
> has roused protests from the Christian conscience and all
> that is honest in humanity. I wish to express my deep
> sympathy and assure you of our prayers on your behalf.
> The hour of divine justice will come. Let us have faith.

Other members of the Church too reacted as energetically:
the archbishops of Paris, Albi, Marseilles, and Lyon took the
initiative and protested, thus giving a number of priests in their
dioceses the moral freedom to voice an indignation which had
long been pent up and was pronounced all the more
vehemently from the pulpit for its long suppression. This was
particularly true of the curés of Saint-Lambert, Saint-Etienne-
du-Mont, and Saint-Pierre-du-Gros-Caillou, in the Paris region.
The latter interrupted a sermon briefly but vigorously with the
words:

> You ask about the attitude of Catholics? We have been
> doing everything within our power to weaken the
> original plans.
> My sermon shall be short. I know it may earn me
> imprisonment in a concentration camp, but it is my duty
> to repeat: Pope Pius XI has condemned racism. Amen.

In the temple at Chambon-sur-Lignon, where a few Jewish
refugees were attending the service, Pastor Trocme condemned
the persecution of the Jews in his sermon. He was only
demonstrating the attitude taken by the Protestant church
from the beginning of the German occupation.

During the summer of 1942, the Reformed Church made
loud protests. In many churches sermons similar to that of
Pastor Trocme at Chambon-sur-Lignon were delivered. On
September 9, Pastor Boegner asked for an audience with Laval

and was received. During the interview he expressed
indignation at what was happening, in the name of the
Protestant Federation of France.

The Reformed Church had already made solemn protests in
both the free and the occupied zones of France. It was the first
to voice officially its support of the Jews who were being
persecuted by anti-Semitic German statutes and the Vichy racist
laws. In May, 1941, the National Council of the Reformed
Church of France appointed Pastor Marc Boegner to convey
the following message to the Grand Rabbi of France, Isaiah
Schwartz:

> We wish to express the pain we all feel at the racist laws
> introduced in our country and the suffering and injustice
> these laws are inflicting on the Jews of France.
> Those among us who think that the state has been
> faced by a serious problem in the form of the mass
> immigration of large numbers of Jewish and non-Jewish
> aliens into France have always expressed a belief that the
> solution should not violate the respect for human life,
> that it should honor the undertakings of the state, that it
> should fall within the demands of Justice, of which
> France has always been a champion. They are all the more
> saddened by the vigorous enforcement of a law which is
> being aimed at the Jews alone, affecting both French Jews
> who have lived in France for many generations and often
> for centuries, and the recently naturalized Jews.

It is perhaps necessary to explain that this letter was written
during a time of repression and to underline that it was sent
twelve days after a roundup which took place in Paris at the
orders of Commissioner François and filled the Loiret camps
at Pithiviers and Beaune-la-Rolande with Jewish prisoners. It
is clear that the French police no less than the Germans kept
quiet about this kind of exercise, and the press was silenced by
the occupation forces. So that, as yet, no one was aware of the
tragic truth, Pastor Marc Boegner no more than any one else.
One should also note that though the letter was mainly
concerned with the Jews of France, it does not omit to mention
the recent immigrants and state that the problem they raise
must be solved within the bounds of respect for human life.

Also noteworthy is the fact that during the National Council of the Reformed Church of France, which took place before the letter was written, mention was made of the help that had been brought to many Jews by several pastors, especially the one at Colombes, who had not hesitated to supply the Jews with fake baptismal certificates.

Until the moment the violence of the persecution came to light during the summer of 1942, the attitude of the Catholic hierarchy toward the problem of racial discrimination tended toward acquiescence if not outright approval, in contrast to the Protestant church. Pastor A. N. Bertrand had several times suggested to the Catholics the need for a protest to the Germans:

> Each time I was invariably received with the utmost courtesy and kindness by the prelates, but just as invariably they refused to make any gesture of opposition to the governing body of the time.

So it was not entirely without foundation that Mr. Martin, in the telegram already quoted which he sent to Cheyneau de Leyritz and Vichy, said that the religious groups were moved "in spite of open hostility to the Jews till now."

At the time of the drafting of the statutes against the Jews, Xavier Vallat had sent representatives to the bishops of the free zone to ask their opinion. Msgr. Saliège himself had declared at the time: "As far as the Church is concerned, Mr. Xavier Vallat's position is unassailable." During his trial Xavier Vallat could say with justice:

> Had I received some intimation, not necessarily from the Vatican but from some official representative of the Catholic hierarchy in France, telling me that such a point in the law was contrary to Catholic doctrine with regard to the recognition of civil law, I could have modified the point in question or, failing that, I could have resigned.

The Vatican was and continued to remain silent, a silence that lay heavy over the whole of Europe.

When the "Statute of the Jews" was put into effect, Pétain,

who was perfectly aware of what was being done during his term of office, under his name, and under the cover of his prestige, asked his ambassador to the Vatican, Léon Bérard, to find out what the reactions to the French anti-Semitic legislation were in the Vatican. On September 2, the ambassador sent a report in which he declared:

> Nothing was ever said at the Vatican which might suggest that the Holy See felt any criticism or disapproval of the laws and regulations in question.

The letter ended: "I have it from a reliable source that the Vatican will pick no quarrel with you over the statute of the Jews."

The German Ambassador in France, Bergen, reporting to his superiors in Berlin on the repercussions in France after Operation Spring Wind, was able to write:

> These measures have been criticized by the leaders of the Church, especially the way they were put into force. The Archbishops of Paris and Lyon and several other bishops have protested, and their protests have been made public as far as possible. *But they are not motivated by instructions from the Vatican."* *

Certainly surprise was expressed in Rome that such things could happen in France, but not the least protest was made. One year later, on July 16, 1943, Father Marie-Benoît was told by the Pope: "Who would have expected this of France?"

Mr. Gillouin, having asked for an audience with the nuncio, was received by Mr. Bartoli, the first counsellor at the nunciature, who explained how the Italian government had resisted German pressure to introduce racial legislation. The whole object of Mr. Gillouin's visit had been to obtain this information and suggest the procedure to Pétain. He had in fact given up hope of action or resolution on the Marshal's part. Bartoli also told Gillouin:

> I imagine that it is out of consideration for the difficulties France is currently experiencing that the Pope

* The italics are those of the authors.

has not yet taken a stand against your anti-Semitic
legislation. But he will certainly do so at the first
favorable opportunity.*

The favorable occasion took time in coming.

Pope Pius XII remained silent. Unfortunately, this cannot
be denied. His attitude was dictated by "the doctrine of
contempt." Analyzing the resolution of the assembly of
cardinals and archbishops taken on July 22, 1942, some scholars
like Rabi read the following nuances into it: While we rise
against the deportations in the name of the laws of charity, as
far as the demands of the law are concerned, we are in no way
opposed to the statute.

In the diocese of Toulouse, half the priests were intimidated
by the prefect's ban and did not read the pastoral letter of
Msgr. Salièges. But worse than that, many of them turned
informer, bringing the prefect's attention to the subversive
plans of the archbishop. The bishops of Fréjus and Monaco, as
well as the abbots of Leyrins and Frigolet, took the opportunity
of this open crisis within the Church to write a joint message to
Marshal Pétain, reaffirming their loyalty to the government and
disassociating themselves from the "unpatriotic Christians."

In October, during an evening organized by the
"Collaboration" group of upper Languedoc, Father Sorel was
not at all embarrassed to "protest against the excessive noise
that has been made about the so-called inhuman measures
supposed to be taken against the Jews in France," and further
to call for proper measures to bring about a solution of the
"Jewish problem."**

Even if half the priests in the Toulouse diocese, some of
whom went so far as to become police spies, disobeyed Msgr.
Salièges' instructions, one must remember that the other half

* René Gillouin: *J'etais l'ami du Maréchal Pétain* (Edition Plon).
** Father Sorel, a loyal partisan of the Vichy government and a leader
of the "Collaboration," made several appeals for violence against the
Resistance and the Jews. For a long time the Resistance hesitated to
strike a priest, for fear that the action might be misunderstood. But he
was well known and there was no such misunderstanding when he was
executed by the Resistance in the autumn of 1943.

did support him in this and that other high dignitaries of the
Church in Paris, Lyon, Marseilles, and Montauban spoke out,
and encouraged the priests who had until then used their own
judgment in extending help to the Jews.

This stand, representing the feelings of many, though it was
taken late and though it was not unanimous, had wide
repercussions. The two girls mentioned earlier as having kept
a diary that summer, Benoîte and Flora Groult, comment on
this. In her entry for October 20, 1942, one of them wrote:

> The Germans have blamed Cardinal Gerlier and the
> French priests for defending the Jews in their sermons.
> But if the Church had risen in one body like one man,
> like one Christ, and had defended the race among whom
> God appeared in the flesh, what would have happened?
> The duty of Christians would have been clear, and the
> Church would have been all the greater for its act. What
> it comes to is that the Church has used violence only in
> its religious wars and has burned only heretics instead of
> these dirty bastards. . . .

But there was no doubt or hesitation on the part of the Free
French. On August 22, 1940, General de Gaulle wrote a letter
of comfort and support from London to Mr. Albert Cohen, the
political adviser at the Jewish World Congress in New York. It
will suffice to quote the following passages:

> On the day of victory, in which I firmly believe,
> liberated France will not fail to make it her duty to see
> that justice is done for the wrongs suffered by all victims
> of Nazi domination, and among the rest, the Jewish
> communities who are currently the objects of intolerance
> and persecution in the German-occupied countries. I
> firmly believe that as soon as France is again free, and its
> traditionally democratic institutions are liberated, every
> French citizen, whatever his beliefs, will be able to enjoy
> his right to justice and equality.

What about the Jews? How did they react? It might sound
like a strange question, but it was being asked daily after these
events. After Thursday, July 16, and after the summer of 1942,

no doubts remained as to the German intention to deport all
Jews living in France, nor was there any doubt of the
complicity of the Vichy government. Until then there had been
hope, especially in certain French-Jewish circles where the
illusion persisted that their nationality would protect them,
and there was a feeling, shared by many of those who had
chosen France as their adopted country, that certain things
were inconceivable in this civilized country. The tragic events
of the summer of 1942 strengthened the bonds between the
French Jews and the immigrant Jews and drove large numbers
of them to join the Resistance, just as a year later the slave
labor camps were to make young Frenchmen of every creed
and sentiment join the *maquis.*

After July 16, thousands of boys and girls between eleven
and eighteen, who had escaped the roundup, found themselves
outlaws and outcasts overnight, without a penny to their name
and no idea where they could find food or a bed. These
youngsters joined the Resistance, not only because of the
opportunities it offered, but because by joining its forces they
could identify with the concept of resistance and so, in a
struggle which was comparable in intensity to their own
personal confusion, they could avenge their families and regain
their own liberty and sense of dignity.

We mentioned earlier that while the Goldberg and
Fingercwajg families were being arrested, their two teenaged
sons escaped and joined the Resistance. They joined the ranks
of the FTP and after a number of successful missions, a list of
which was one day to be proudly displayed under their photos
on the walls of Paris, they were arrested by the Germans in
November, 1943. Condemned to death during the Manouchian-
Boczov group trial (the case of the "Red Notice"), they were
shot on February 21, 1944.*

* There is a street in the XX Arrondissement which is named after the
Manouchian Group. On the occasion of the opening of the street,
Aragon wrote a poem, *"l'Affiche Rouge,"* which was later set to music and
sung by Léo Ferré. A film on the subject is currently (1967) being made
by A. Gatti.

We mention these two young men because we want to quote their last words. They were seventeen and nineteen years old, and were condemned to death with twenty-three of their comrades (one Rumanian girl, one Spaniard, two Armenians, three Frenchmen, three Hungarians, five Italians, and eight Poles). Each of them wrote a farewell letter to his family, his parents, or his wife.

But in the case of young Goldberg and Fingercwajg, their families had been arrested on July 16. Fingercwajg had one single distant relative left to write to, and so he wrote:

Paris, 2/21/1944

Madame:

I am addressing to you the last words I shall ever write, in order to say my last farewell to a life that I wish had been better.

If my parents and brothers are fortunate enough to come back alive from their tortures, tell them that I died bravely, thinking of them. I am also sending you some clothes to give to my parents if they should come back.

Léon Goldberg wrote:

Dear Parents:

If you come back (and I think you will), don't mourn for me. I did my duty, fighting as hard as I could. I fought so that you, Henri and Max, my dear brothers, might have a better life if you come back.

With all my soul, I embrace you, dear parents and dear brothers Henri and Max. Your son, Léon. Vive la France.*

Fingercwajg's parents and brothers did not return. His youngest brother, eight years old, was given the clothes left by Maurice. Nor did Goldberg's parents or his brothers Henri and Max return. They were condemned to death the day they were arrested, on July 16, 1942, at dawn.

Louis Pitkowicz had escaped from the Vel d'Hiv and gone to stay with the Haut family. He was fourteen years old. Some

* From *Lettres de Fusillés* (Editions France d'Abord).

months later, while he was staying with Etienne Moulin in
Lyon, the latter was arrested and Louis joined the Resistance
as a liaison agent for the MLN (Mouvement de Libération
Nationale). On June 22, 1943, he was arrested by the Gestapo.
He was then fifteen years old. After being beaten and tortured,
he escaped while leading some Nazi policemen to a false
rendezvous. They shot at him, but he escaped. Picking up his
contact with the Resistance, he was sent to Paris, where again
he worked as liaison agent. In December, 1943, he was arrested
by the militia in a trap set at the Porte Dorée. Some time later,
on July 14, 1944, while being transferred, he escaped from the
train at Lyon station and returned to stay with the Haut
family.

After crossing the demarcation line, Nat Linen joined the
FTP at Grenoble. He was arrested in 1944 and deported, and
had after all to make the journey which had been planned for
him in 1942. At least he had the consolation of knowing that he
had spent the time in between working with the Resistance.
To this day Nat Linen has two registration numbers tattooed
on his arm: 9685 B and 193136. He was on the only convoy to
be registered twice, once as a Jew and again as a political
prisoner.

In Grenoble, Mrs. Rado fought in the ranks of the UJRE,
distributing pamphlets and establishing contacts. In Toulouse,
Paulette Rotblit, who was arrested and condemned to death in
1944 by the militia, was saved by the liberation of the city.

This Jewish movement to join the Resistance was not new.
Having been proclaimed enemies by the Nazis, they had an
extra reason for wanting to engage in the fight, each joining
the group most suitable to him according to his possibilities
and his aspirations.

As in the French resistance in general, here too there were
great political families and sometimes families divided by
politics. The important thing is that there were Jews who
wanted to fight and to resist, and there were whole formations
of Jewish *maquis*.

There were other formations within the Resistance organized by the communists that were also wholly Jewish. The reason was less religious than of a practical nature—namely, a linguistic grouping.

In conclusion, it is true to say that many Jews fought in the ranks of the FFL and in the various Resistance movements, side by side with comrades from every kind of background, creed, and political leaning. In this struggle, as in 1939, the immigrants found a way of demonstrating loyalty to their adopted country. Like most resistants, their aims were to liberate France and establish a better society. It is difficult to trace the part played by the Jews in the fight against the Germans, a difficulty compounded by the fact that the majority of Jews did not want to be distinguished from other Resistance fighters.*

* All the same, there are books reporting the Jewish contribution, notably David Knout's *La Résistance juive en France 1940–44*, written in 1946 and not without errors. See also David Diamant's *Héros juifs de la Résistance Française* (Editions Renouveau) .

Chapter 13

Collaboration

The size of the roundups of July 16 and 17 and the later raids which followed in the free zone, as well as the shocking incidents resulting, had caught public attention. As we have just seen, a significant part of the Catholic Church had finally had the courage to take a stand openly and so joined the Protestant Church in feeling. But the events had been too disturbing for people to keep silent. Their consciences were affected.

The very scale of the operation meant that there were inevitably many witnesses to the events. The reports of these witnesses, added to those of runaways and fugitives, the broadcasts of the BBC, and the secret newspapers and pamphlets, as well as the appeals and protests, were the main sources of information which contributed to the publication of the truth and the rousing of public opinion.

After Black Thursday the journalists in Paris had asked for details. The German propaganda service, which controlled the distribution of news, had been instructed by the IV J section "not to publish anything in the interval before the next raids." And in general a certain number of suggestions had been formulated with regard to the contents of the articles which would eventually be permitted for publication. The tens of thousands of victims were to be made to appear as criminals (this included the children), lawbreakers, and bandits involved in the black markets. The roundups were to be presented as salutary police measures. Precise instructions were dictated:

In these articles it would be suitable to bring to the reader's attention the fact that the Jews had, as is their habit, behaved with such impertinence that the severe measures had been deemed necessary. Most of the Jews arrested were those who would have continued to operate the black market, forge documents, spread corruption, and generally break the law. As a result the safety of the occupation forces demanded severe reprisals against the Jews, who openly and daily violated the orders of the Militaerbefehlshaber, the Head of the SS, and the laws of France.

While the German censorship did not forbid the mention of the roundups, the collaboration press published what the Germans wanted to hear: already in May, 1941, after the first arrests, the collaboration press reported the events as follows:

A few cases of hysteria, a few noisy demonstrations, and then everything returned to normal. Flanked by policemen and republican guards, the Jews climbed into the buses and trucks of the Emergency Police.

Five thousand Jews have left; five thousand alien Jews have spent their first night in a concentration camp. Five thousand parasites less in Paris, which was suffering from their presence as from a chronic disease. The first step has been taken, and there will be others.

How many others!

After the raids of the summer of 1942 the collaboration press zealously applied the suggestions of the IV J office when composing their reports. All the articles, from those appearing in the *Petit Parisien* to those published by *Je suis partout,* were in the same vein—namely, that everyone arrested had been involved in the black market or was otherwise criminal.

But these were nothing compared to the fantasy published in the weekly *Le Pilori* on July 23, 1942. It was an essay anticipating the death of the last Jew and signed Jacques Boureau. It appeared one week after the roundup, when the first convoy of prisoners was making its way to Auschwitz.

The author quoted an extract from the diary of an "average Frenchman" living in the Year of our Lord 2142, two centuries after these events. A decree dating from July 25, 1942, had ordered the sterilization of all Jews except for three couples to

be kept at the Vincennes Zoo. The children of the three couples
were to be sterilized in their turn except for the oldest boy.
This is what the diary signed Jacques Boureau says in the entry
for July 14, 2142:

> July 14, 2142. There is wonderful news in Paris today.
> The national radio and television newscasts have just
> informed us that the last Jew has died. We have at last
> finished with this abject race whose last representative has
> lived in the old zoo in the Vincennes woods since birth,
> in a special cage, where our children could watch him
> move around in simulated freedom, not so much for
> entertainment as for moral edification. He is dead. It is
> just as well. I personally have always been worried that he
> might escape, and God knows what damage a Jew can do
> when he is set loose. For ten years now he had been living
> alone, since the death of his mate, who luckily was sterile.
> But one can never be sure with this species. I think I
> shall have to go to the zoo to make absolutely sure that
> the news is true.

What comment can one make?
In view of public feeling, the Pétain government was forced
to hold a "press conference." It was held on September 9, in the
presence of French and foreign journalists. The representative
of the Ministry of Information appeared, elegantly dressed and
very relaxed, and read out a declaration which sounded like a
credo:

> The government cannot keep count of the protests
> which have been addressed to it from various sources.
> While the protests represent ideal, religious theses, which
> those who sent them are free to have, the government has
> to act in accordance with the highest interests of the state.
> A cloud of rumor has formed around this affair which has
> been difficult to control. While the government is aware
> that the measures have their painful side, the misleading
> reports are a result of unfounded word-of-mouth
> descriptions. . . .

The collaboration press printed a few short items of news,
slanted according to the wishes of the *Propagandastaffel* and
the Pétain government.
René Gillouin, who was a Vichy supporter by conviction but

at the same time consistently disapproved of the anti-Semitic measures, held the position of "royal counsellor" to Pétain until 1942. Like many others, he witnessed deportations.

> Some months later I retired to Vaison-la-Romaine, and there I was present at a roundup of Jews conducted in such revolting conditions (children snatched from their mothers, women from their husbands, and all driven into cattle cars under the blows of policemen's truncheons) that I wrote to Marshal Pétain in a burst of indignation. . . .

In his letter to the Marshal he wrote:

> The government has taken yet another shameful step. Not content with persecuting men beyond the limits of humanity, it has consented to become the executioner of women and the torturer of children. It is too much. The national conscience is rebelling: through priests and ministers, by resisting the accomplishment of atrocious missions, it is signaling to your government that it has surpassed the bounds of its powers and has failed in its duty.

He called on the Marshal "to extinguish the unspeakable crimes committed in your name." But all this produced no results. One day, talking of Mr. Gillouin, Marshal Pétain asked in surprise: "But why on earth is Gillouin siding with the Jews?" On June 12, 1942, pleading on behalf of some protégés of his, Jewish wives of prominent members of society, Pétain wrote to Ambassador De Brinon without a trace of shame: "In order that the just measures taken against the Jews be understood and accepted by the French, it is necessary that the Germans consent to a small number of exceptions." Which says a lot for his feelings on the subject.

We have already seen how much faith was put in the hero of Verdun's promise that Jewish veterans, the war wounded, and those awarded the military cross or the Legion of Honor for bravery in battle would be protected. Rosenberg, Faynzilber, and many others went to hide with the wives of prisoners of war and trusted in their medals. They would soon have been disillusioned had they read the correspondence between Pétain,

the lawyer Pierre Massé and others in 1941. These documents
are often quoted but are indispensable in presenting evidence
of the nature of relations between Vichy and the persecuted
Jews. Pétain did not even bother to reply to the following
letter sent by Pierre Massé, who wrote:*

> MONSIEUR LE MARÉCHAL:
>
> I have read the decree which declares that no Jew can
> become an officer, not even those who are descended from
> strictly French ancestors.
> I would be very much obliged if you could let me know
> whether I should remove the insignia of my brother, a
> sublieutenant of the 36th Regiment of the infantry who
> was killed at Douaumont in April, 1916; my son-in-law,
> sublieutenant of the 14th Regiment of the dragoons, who
> was killed in Belgium in May, 1940; my nephew, a
> lieutenant of the 23rd Colonials, killed at Rethel in May,
> 1940.
> Can I leave the military medal my brother earned at
> Neuville-Saint-Vaast and which is buried with him? Can
> my son Jacques, sublieutenant of the 62nd battalion of
> Chasseurs Alpins, who was wounded at Soupir in June,
> 1940, keep his rank?
> I wish to obey the laws of my country even when they
> are dictated by the invader.
> With the assurances of my deepest respect,
>
> PIERRE MASSÉ

On the other hand, the Marshal answered the following
letter sent by a woman:

January 27, 1941

> MONSIEUR LE MARÉCHAL PÉTAIN:
>
> I have read in our local newspaper that "in accordance
> with the law of December 3, 1940, Mr. Peyrouton has,
> among other names, revoked Cahen's appointment as
> Chef de Cabinet in the Prefecture of the Côte-d'Or.
> Mr. Peyrouton should have informed himself better
> before taking this measure; he would have found that
> the applicant, Jacques Cahen, was killed on May 20 and

* Quoted from *Homage to Pierre Massé* (Edition Calmann-Lévy, Paris,
1948).

buried at Abbeville. He followed in the glorious tradition of his cousins, who died for their country in 1914–1918, aged twenty-four and twenty-five. They were our only sons and would have been horrified at such treatment.

Yours, etc.,
MRS. NERSON

Here is the reply:

Vichy, January 31
Marshal Pétain's Office

MADAME:

The Marshal has read the letter you wrote him about your nephew.

He was especially moved, for one of his aides was with M. J. Cahen on May 20, 1940, just a few hours before he fell.

The Marshal will ask the Minister of the Interior to reconsider the measure taken with regard to your nephew.

With my sympathy and respect,

Yours, etc.

Laval, whose idea it had been to include the children among the deportees, was angered by the attempts to oppose his decision. In an interview with Msgr. Rocco, during which he expressed his displeasure at Msgr. Saliège's letter, he declared that "if the clergy were going to shelter Jewish children wanted for deportation, he would not hesitate to get them with the help of the police."*

No, he would not hesitate. On September 9 he told Pastor Boegner, who had come to complain, that he was taking preventive measures and that he would not allow alien Jews to remain in the country, not even the children. "I persisted," says Pastor Boegner, "and tried to get him to agree to entrust the children to institutions qualified to look after them. But he wanted them to go."**

Surely in the higher circles at Vichy they were aware of the destination and fate of the children and other deportees. How

---

* Reported by Abetz.
** Reported by Pastor Boegner.

else can one explain why, during a meeting on September 2, 1942, of which we have the minutes, Oberg and Laval thought it would be useful in the future to *announce officially* that deported Jews were taken to labor camps in Poland? On the same occasion Laval complained of the difficulties he had had, especially with Cardinal Gerlier. Handing over the Jews was not as simple as delivering goods from Woolworth, but he would do his best.

On July 19 or 20 a policeman was killed in the XVIII Arrondissement. Was that a warning? The next day Bussière, the Prefect of Police, accompanied by the head of his office, Brissot, and by Hennequin, Leguay, and Ingrand, the representative of the Minister of State for the Interior, came to pay their last respects to the body. Until today the circumstances of the murder are unknown. Could it have been a gesture carried out by one of the witnesses to the arrests on July 16 who wanted to punish the Paris police?

One must remember that for two days policemen, guards, and gendarmes had been seen at work, and the painful scenes resulting had roused the feelings of the public. There was a feeling of disapproval, contempt, and even hate for the police at that time. Not only had they accepted a task unworthy of them, but in doing it they had brought dishonor to the uniform of the French police. At the Nuremberg trials, the German Knochen was able to say:

> There was the French police, which carried out the anti-Semitic measures with its special police for Jewish affairs (an institution of the Commission for Jewish Affairs), and on the whole the French police played a much more important role than the German organization.
> The Germans established contact with the French police and did what Dannecker needed to have done, but it was the French police who carried out the operation.

Special praise must be given to those who refused to take part and resisted the inhuman measures, and all the more because they seem to have been rare exceptions. In his history

Rabi writes: "Not once did the police refuse to proceed with the arrests they had been made responsible for, the only exceptions being the very rare occasions when they overlooked an escape."

The writer Serge Groussard says the same thing:

> Not one of the 13,000 arrests was made by the Germans. The French police took care of everything. It chills my blood to write this, but it is the truth. One must add that Roethke's report emphasizes that there was a lack of enthusiasm among a large proportion of inspectors and officers who were appointed to this mission. But except for a few isolated instances, this did not stop them from obeying their orders.

There were leaks from the Prefecture which put a considerable number of people on their guard and so saved them. All the officials at the Prefecture of Police knew, in more or less detail, that preparations were being made for a roundup. It is difficult to establish how many of these felt it their duty to warn the intended victims of the raids, though it is certain that a number of them did so. Mostly they passed on to their acquaintances information which they knew would travel further.

And when a few policemen gave their victims a chance, did they realize how faint that chance was? That was the only undertaking on the executive level on behalf of the Jews. Not one of the high officials at Vichy can boast of having done as much. Only Mr. Benoist-Méchin, who attended the Council of Ministers on July 2, had on July 13 warned one family.

After the roundup, some policemen resigned. A contemporary pamphlet speaks of "hundreds of resignations," but that is an exaggeration. We can trace only two resignations, one of them that of the policeman who helped arrest the Rozen family at Nogent-sur-Marne. One report mentions two gendarmes at Choisy who refused to take part in the arrests.

In August at Lyon, General de Saint-Vincent refused to let his troops or officers take part. As a result, General de Saint-Vincent was retired early on the orders of General Bridoux, the

War Minister at Vichy. Saint-Vincent was replaced by General Maire on September 1.

Although the Italians were allied with the Germans, an officer of the Italian army declared: "The Italian army must not soil its hands in this business. [He was referring to the demands of the German army in Croatia.] It is bad enough for the army of a great country to have to permit such crimes or to stand by and watch them. . . ."

Even in France the Italian army opposed the Nazis, the police, and the gendarmerie and resisted the racial measures. The Italian general stationed in Grenoble demanded that the French police cancel the arrest of three hundred Jews who had been required as hostages by the Germans. Similarly at Annecy, when the Jews were arrested by the French gendarmerie, the Italian army took over the gendarmes' barracks in order to free them.

There was resistance in Finland too, another ally of the Germans in the war against the Soviet Union. Although the head of state, Marshal Carl Gustaf Mannerheim, had been asked several times by Ribbentrop to solve "the Jewish problem," he had always firmly refused. He would declare that in his eyes there were only Finnish citizens; he recognized no distinction of race or religion and felt responsible for them all. When the same suggestions were made to the Foreign Minister, Witting, he repeated: "Finland is an honest nation. We prefer to die with the Jews; we shall never betray them." As a result of this courageous policy, no Jew ever was anxious for his safety in Finland, and there were Jewish officers in the Finnish army who ironically were saluted by the German soldiers by virtue of the agreement between the two countries.

When the German troops occupied Denmark and King Christian was asked to enforce the wearing of yellow stars by the Jews, the King was able to parry the German order by proclaiming that he himself would wear a yellow star. While the roundup of Jews was being prepared for in July, 1942, in France, no measures were taken against the Danish Jews. It was not until August, 1943, that the Nazis decided to use a more forceful method, and only on the night of October 1–2 did the Gestapo by itself proceed to arrest the Jews. There were eight to nine thousand Jews in Denmark at the time, but the Danish government heard of the raid and alerted the whole population, with the result that, of the nine thousand, the Gestapo arrested only 450. The rest were hidden by the Danish people and smuggled by boat to Sweden.

In France the total number of people deported *for racial reasons* was well over one hundred thousand.

Afterword

Most of the surviving deportees were repatriated in April and May, 1945. They arrived at the Gare de l'Est, where an excited crowd was waiting for them, but they hardly seemed aware of what was around them. They were slow-moving, unreachable, as if they had turned inward and retreated inside themselves. Their movements were odd, jerky, almost rude. If anyone came near them, they would hug their small bundles tightly to themselves and take a firm hold of their package of bread, as if they were frightened that it would be taken away from them. From time to time they would suddenly raise a bent arm, as if warding off a blow. They could not move very quickly. One saw them gather in groups of two or three and sit down on the edge of a bench or on some steps, their hands on their knees, not knowing what to do with their long, thin arms. Someone would unpack a little bread, which they shared, and then they would sit chewing it slowly and carefully, as if they were trying to extract every element of nourishment from it.

There were flowers for them, and crowds of kind people who had come to welcome them back. But suddenly the flowers seemed out of place, and the people holding the bouquets felt they could not offer them. Flowers! Nine months earlier there had been flowers all over the country, for the liberation soldiers who had appeared, sunburned and covered with dust, amid the rumbling of half-tracks and tanks in the sputter of the last machine-gun fire. There had been flowers for the Resistance fighters, with their assorted uniforms and guns, unlikely

209

looking and a bit frightening when they came out of their
hiding places in August, 1944. In the general celebration the
police too had received bouquets, and so had the prisoners of
war returning after five years—but somehow flowers seemed
banal for the deportees, these living shadows, walking
skeletons, with lost, faraway expressions in their sunken eyes.
They seemed to come from another world.

Of the two hundred thirty thousand who had been taken
away to Germany in sealed cattle cars, thirty-two thousand
came back. Of the total number of deportees, nearly half—one
hundred ten thousand—had been arrested for racial reasons,
because they were Jewish. The rest had been deported for
political reasons, because they were members of the Resistance,
Gaullists, communists, members of the secret army, or belonged
to the network of Franc-Tireur Partisans, and had acted against
the occupation army. There were also some ten to fifteen
thousand Spaniards handed to the Germans. There were a few
boys who were neither Jewish nor involved in the Resistance
but who had been picked up off the street by the Germans,
perhaps as a preliminary to some other larger plan, and had
wasted their youth in the concentration camps. There was too a
small proportion of common criminals, double agents, and
black market racketeers.

Of the political deportees, some twenty-nine thousand
returned, which is to say about 22 per cent; of the Jewish
deportees, only three thousand came back. That is only 3 per
cent, and these were all adults. Not one of the children
returned.*

Of those arrested on July 16 and 17, 1942, far less than 3 per
cent returned. We have described their arrival at Auschwitz
and how they were put to work in July, August, and September

---

* The figures quoted are generally held to be correct. With regard to
the deportees for racial reasons, the Jews, Hennequin in his deposition
admitted that the French police were responsible for eighty-five thousand
deportations. Taking into account the fact that it was in Hennequin's
interest to make the numbers as small as possible, and also the fact that
there were arrests made directly by the Germans, one can bring the total
of Jewish deportees up from one hundred to one hundred ten thousand.

of that year. All the children, most of the women, and the old
and the sick and the physically weak had been picked out on
arrival and taken to the gas chambers immediately. The
Auschwitz Notebooks record day by day the number of victims
exterminated. Those who were fit enough to be used as
laborers were indeed "worked to death," as the Germans had
decided at the Wannsee conference.

After thirty-four months, when the Red Army freed the
camp, little was left of the 12,884 people arrested on July 16
and 17, 1942 (4,051 children, 5,802 women, and 3,031 men)
except a heap of ashes. There also were some personal
belongings left in the immense stacks of shoes, dolls, clothes,
suitcases, and eyeglasses which the Russians found in the
Canada (warehouse building) and which are now housed in
the Auschwitz museum. Among them you will doubtless find
some spectacle case with the name of a Paris optician on it.
But most of the belongings of the victims of Black Thursday
would have already been distributed among the Germans by
the time the Red Army arrived. While the Germans pretended
for a long time to know nothing about the concentration
camps, they seem not to have been at all puzzled or surprised to
be given second-hand clothes with labels coming from Paris,
Warsaw, Salonica, Amsterdam, Budapest, Belgrade, The
Hague, Lyon, Athens, Marseilles, etc. The gold teeth and
fillings had been melted down and converted into ingots, which
were kept in the safes of the Reichsbank. The women's and
girls' hair was combed and cut and, after being spun into
thread, was used to make industrial felt from which slippers
were made for the sailors in the submarines.

There were also a few survivors. The general figure for
survivors among Jewish deportees is 3 per cent. That would
mean 450 of the 12,884 Jews arrested in Paris on July 16 and 17.
But far fewer than 450 actually came back. We have contacted
Tselnick, Sienicki, Albert Baum, Rozen (Hélène Rozen's
father). We found Rosenberg, Epstein, Goldenzwag, three
others, and that is all. Their children, their husbands, wives,
parents, brothers, and sisters never came back. Of the deportees

repatriated in 1945, only twenty or thirty were survivors of the
Black Thursday roundup, not more. Perhaps not one of the
5,802 women and certainly none of the children came back.
Neither young Régine Sienicki, who was gassed with her
mother, nor the four Goldenzwag children, nor the four
Tselnick children, who died with their mother (as did Thérèse
and Adolphe Barbanel), nor Pitkowicz's sister, nor Epstein's
sister ever came back.

Those who did return came back by train, arriving at the
Gare de l'Est one morning in April, 1945. Disoriented and
unseeing, they were led to the exit by some Red Cross nurses.
Coming out from the twilight of the station into the bright
spring sunlight, they finally were returning to reality.

It must still have seemed like a dream. They found
themselves on TCRP buses: the same buses which had taken
them to the Vel d'Hiv were still driving around the streets of
Paris. At the back of the bus there would be a policeman
wearing the same uniform as the policemen who had knocked
on their doors that morning. Now he was leaning back on the
rear platform of the bus, relaxed and suntanned, with a smile
on his face, but wearing the same uniform! It seemed hardly
possible. The deportee turns back his cuff. There is the
tattooed number, as indelible as the scars on his heart.

Paris was just the same—the same bus routes, the same buses,
the same police uniforms, and only three years had passed.
Three years ago the deportees had their families sitting next
to them when they rode the bus to the Vel d'Hiv. Now there
was no one, and the survivors had no tears left to shed. Their
eyes were dry and their eyelids red and swollen from an
infection caught in prison. The sight of the police uniform
brought back memories of July 16 in the morning, and they
could not think of anything else.

But now they were going to the Hotel Lutétia. People would
stop at street corners, shake them by the hand, and offer them
fruit. The deportees would smile and thank them.

The reception center for returning deportees had been set
up in the Hotel Lutétia after the Germans had moved out. A

newly created Ministry of Prisoners of War, Deportees, and
Repatriates looked after the survivors with the help of social
workers and nurses. There were a few formalities. People had
to be identified and given the necessary papers, sometimes
temporary papers, while details were checked. Identity checks
were necessary because there were attempts made fraudulently
to come back as repatriated deportees by Frenchmen who had
volunteered to go and work in Germany (there were such
volunteers) or had collaborated with the Gestapo and needed a
more respectable identity. But they were easy to spot: they were
too healthy looking and not nearly thin enough. A medical
checkup, an issue of clothes, a meal, and the returning
deportees were ready to resume normal life. They would never
be the same as they had been before, but at least they would
stop being a number in a register and become living human
beings. Even that was difficult to adjust to.

Exhaustion and malnutrition killed many of those who
returned after they came back. Even at the camps there were
survivors so worn down that they were literally shadows,
skeletons moving like human beings, and only in their eyes was
a very small spark of life visible. The doctors in the
repatriation commission did not let them undertake the
journey back. They died very soon after their liberation.
Others died on the return trip.

At the Hotel Lutétia people waited to ask the newly
returned survivors about their own relatives:

"Pierre Lévy, he is twenty-two. He was at Fresnes, then at
Dora."

"Mine was at Ebense; he was alive in January, I know that.
He has a big scar on his face and always hung his head a
little. . . ."

"Two brothers, they were at Montluc and then at Drancy in
July, 1944. . . ."

"A woman and her three children, David, Léon, and Rita,
from Pithiviers. . . ."

They would take hold of the deportees' arms as if they
wanted to hold them back and make them say what they

wanted to hear: "Yes, I know him, I saw him, he is well, he was alive. I'm sure he'll come back. . . ." But the men in the striped uniforms walked on and said nothing.

People would show them photographs; they would look without seeing. Wedding pictures, family groups, snapshots, and passport pictures taken in happier times. But what resemblance could there be between this smiling man wearing a shirt, coat, and tie, and this lady with long and well-kept hair and what they must have looked like at Auschwitz—thin and bent with hollow cheeks and thin necks? And even if a feature or some detail in a photograph awakened a memory, the deportees preferred to remain silent and would pass without saying anything.

Mr. and Mrs. Delore came to the hotel daily, taking shifts. On the notice boards there were lists of people who were definitely freed, short lists with few names. The Delores had looked after the Rozen children since 1942 when they had taken them in and hidden them. Their mother had been transferred from the Rothschild hospital to Drancy and from there to Auschwitz. The father had left from Pithiviers. Now the Delores were waiting for the return of Mr. Rozen and of their son. He had been deported for having evaded the forced labor service, which sent young French men to work in Germany; he was classed as a *réfractaire,* which like *résistant* was a punishable category in occupied France. The boy had tried to join the army in Africa but had been caught on the Spanish border and deported. Since then the Delores had heard nothing about him. But then one day, and miraculously the same day, the Delore boy returned from Buchenwald and Hélène Rozen's father came back from Auschwitz. Mrs. Rozen never came back.

Some people returned and found no one waiting for them. The Spanish exiles had no family in France. Some of the Jews had no family left. Mr. Goldenzwag was given a small suitcase and a repatriation card which served as an identity card (but no cigarettes and no money, because he was a foreigner and was not entitled to the small repatriation fund and the ten

packets of cigarettes that French repatriates received) . He
hesitated for some time as he stood alone in the street, then
decided to go back to his home on the Rue du Pot-au-Fer. The
concierge was there and let him in. Obviously people had lived
in the apartment, and everything had been taken. Later he
would go and lodge a complaint at the Panthéon police station.

For weeks afterwards, Mr. Goldenzwag would go to the Hotel
Lutétia every morning. It became his main activity. But neither
his wife nor any of his children returned. He knew they would
not come, but he continued to go to the Lutétia. It fulfilled a
need; he had nothing else. There were others there like him,
among them an acquaintance, Jules Isaac.

> I had no idea what had happened to my family. I could
> not imagine the horrors they had suffered. People kept
> things from me. I became deaf and could not hear the
> radio. For a long time I used to go to the Hotel Lutétia
> to scan the names of those who had returned. I only
> discovered the terrible truth in 1945. It literally broke me.

There was no one to meet Albert Baum. He was the only one
of his family to return. Louis Pitkowicz, his brother Bernard,
and their sister Rosine, who had all three escaped from German
and French jails, hoped to find their family at the Hotel
Lutétia, but no one returned. Their father, who had given
himself up and come out of the cellar, their mother, and their
little sister Fanny all died in Germany. Nat Linen's mother,
who had thrown a coat over his yellow star outside the Vel
d'Hiv, also never returned. Nat knew that it was useless to
wait. He himself had just come back from Auschwitz with two
numbers tattooed on his arm. He knew how slight the chances
were for her survival. He would never forget her gesture.

Mrs. Lichtein, who had escaped from the Vel d'Hiv but had
been denounced and captured in 1944, did return. So did
Nathan Sienicki. Returning to his home at 15 Rue de
Vaucouleurs, which he had left on July 16, 1942, he sat at the
table and listened to the silence. In the days that followed he
wandered lost through the three rooms of the apartment,
weeping and thinking of his wife and daughter, without the

will to prepare himself something to eat and not daring to touch anything in the house. Then one day he pulled himself together and opened a drawer. It was empty. Sienicki found some of his things in the concierge's house and even a coat being worn by one of his neighbors. Many people looked after the belongings of the deportees and gave them back when they returned, but many Jewish apartments were plundered. The Linens' sewing machine was taken by the concierge as soon as the police had left. And there was quite a market in the property of the Jews. Mr. Gillouin was moved to write a memo to Pétain, pointing out that the liquidation of the property of the Jews opened the door to corruption all over France. Often, returning deportees found their apartments occupied, and they would be told, "You won't need so many rooms now; there are fewer of you." Which was very true.

Of thirteen thousand people, about thirty adults returned and not one child. July 16, 1942, was not the only black day, however; every one of the fifteen hundred days of the occupation was a black day in which the Nazis and the Vichy men took their toll. As the years passed, their methods improved, and the Paris police gained experience. On November 5, 1942, Roethke noted: "Of 1,460 Greek Jews listed in the census for the Seine region, the French police has just arrested and sent to Drancy 1,060. The results are remarkable, and the police are to be congratulated." Instructions for arrests were perfected after Black Thursday, and on the eve of a large roundup on February 3, 1944, they read as follows:

> Where it is impossible to transport listed individuals without the use of a stretcher or an ambulance, either because they are severely sick or bedridden or weak or women on the point of giving birth or blind (in this case make sure of disability), they are to be left at home for the UGIF to transfer to the Rothschild hospital. The rest of the family of the invalid is, however, to be arrested, without exception. Neighbors or the concierge can be asked to look after the invalid until he is transported to the Rothschild hospital.

> Where there is no reply at the apartment of a person
> to be arrested, the door is to be broken down and the
> apartment searched.

As late as August 17, 1944, five days before the liberation of
Paris and two days before the strike of the Paris police, the last
convoy left Drancy for Germany. In June and July, 1944, only
a few weeks before the Liberation, the Vichy government gave
up all political prisoners in the French prisons and camps to
the Germans. French gendarmes handed them to the Gestapo
in handcuffs. An unprecedented act of treachery. At Drancy the
poet Max Jacob died that year and, at the camp at Gurs, the
Spanish poet Antonio Machado. Though they were hard
pressed, with fronts in Normandy and Provence and the
harassment of the *maquis* to deal with, the Germans were able
to think about feeding their death factories right to the end.

We have already listed the balance of the deportations—
3,000 survivors out of 110,000 Jewish deportees and 29,000 out
of 120,000 political deportees. The survivors will always be
haunted. The inflection of a voice, two words of a conversation
overheard, will bring back Black Thursday and all the other
black days. They can fill their days with activities that will keep
them occupied, but their nights are crowded with memories
and pain for which there can be no compensation.

And the rest of the world is left with one nagging question:
How could all this happen?

Appendix A

The Jews in France

When the Nazis decided to put into effect the Final Solution, they intended the extermination of eleven million European Jews, among whom were 861,000 Jews from France. As it turned out, this figure was incorrect.

It is in fact impossible to make a precise estimate of the number of Jews residing in France at the time of the German invasion. For one thing, any census based on religious or racial criteria was inconceivable in Republican France. Secondly, there had been a large influx of refugees, many of them Jewish, into France during the years immediately before the war when the fear of the Nazis had set in motion a sizable migration.

The most constant and most likely figure, on which both historians and statisticians agree, for the number of persons in France who would be affected by the program elaborated at the Wannsee conference in Berlin is three hundred thousand. This number included a wide diversity of people who came under the same definition. Some were Jews merely because their enemies defined them as such. In other words, for some, being a Jew meant simply that other people had a certain attitude toward them. In Sartre's words: "It is the way one looks at a man at a certain moment that makes, of an anonymous individual, a Jew."

The Germans had worked out a definition of who is a Jew, in their statute number 7 of March 24, 1942, based on the Nuremberg racial laws. Marshal Pétain's government meanwhile had made a somewhat wider definition. There is no need to quote a summary of this definition as published in the official journal *L'Etat Francais*. The French newspapers of the time published, without any sign of embarrassment, small explanatory diagrams alongside the definition, in the manner of Mendel's genealogy of peas. In any case, whether they were only fourth part Jews, or half Jews, or Jews by adoption or partly French, they had no grounds for illusion; sooner or later they would be affected.

Jews of French nationality had no difficulty in proving the authenticity of their nationality when they wanted to. They could easily show that they were more royalist than the king. If nationality is defined by place of birth, they and their ancestors had lived in France longer than many Frenchmen. They could boast family ties going back to the Jewish communities that were settled in Gaul at the time of the Roman occupation. They had settled in the Mediterranean ports, then all over the south of France, and eventually reached Paris, having come from the Roman Empire, where they had either been taken as captives of war or had emigrated voluntarily after the fall of Jerusalem and the destruction of the Temple. Much later, but still five centuries before 1940, Portuguese and Spanish Jews had come to join these Jewish communities, especially in the Bordeaux area.

Over the centuries this stock of Jews from Judea had produced the oriental Jews. There were other Jews, such as the Alsatian Jews, who had been French as long as the Alsatians. They had, like many others, lived in German Alsace for centuries. These were Central European and Eastern European Jews and did not all originate from Judea. Indeed some Jewish colonies on the Tancred peninsula in the Crimea had come from Greece at the time of the Greek domination. They had called their communities "synagogues" from the Greek word meaning "assembly." They had lived there and, without intending to be missionaries, had converted to Judaism a Khazar chief called Kagan (from the Hebrew *Cohen* or from the Khazar *Khan*) together with his tribe, which outnumbered the Jewish colony.

Later these communities dispersed and became the founders of the first Jewish communities in Central Europe, those later to be called "Aschkenazim." Descendants of true Khazars, mixed with Jews as Palestinian as Jesus and also with Greeks, Slavs, and Germans, they constituted what the racists in their aberration called the pure "Jewish type."

Whether they were Alsatian Jews, annexed to France at the same time as Alsace, or Judean Jews who had settled in France when it was Roman Gaul, surely these French Jews were as French as anyone else. They had fought and died for France in both world wars. There had been no distinction then. The Alsatian Jews could furthermore point to their solid support of France when the question of annexing Alsace to Germany was put to the vote.

And yet, while the French Jews in 1940 were regular French citizens and had perfectly integrated themselves socially, politically, and economically, this had not always been the case. The reasons were religious.

On July 31, 1941, the Grand Rabbi Kaplan wrote to Xavier Vallat, informing him that to conform with the new law, he had just officially declared that he was a Jew and was proud of it:

> When a pagan or an atheist tries to disparage Judaism, one is not surprised. Even if it is a mistaken criticism, it is understandable. But when a Christian does the same thing, does it not seem spiritually inconsistent, a mark of ingratitude? Do I have to remind you that Judaism is the mother of Christianity and that Judaism, long before Christianity, proclaimed the existence of the one true God, the brotherhood of man, respect for human life, love of one's neighbor, and the Ten Commandments?

And yet even though Christianity stemmed from the Jewish religion, and Jesus and Mary were Jews (historically as well as by Pétain's definition) , and even though the distinctive tenets of Judaism which differentiated its followers from the barbarians, monotheism and the banning of idolatry, were adopted by the Christians, and the Church was modeled on the

Synagogue, Christians in France and elsewhere have not always
been tolerant of the Jews.

The essential rift between Christianity and Judaism which
separates the Church from the Synagogue dates back not to the
crucifixion but to the end of the fifth century A.D. and rises
primarily from the conflicting interpretations in the scriptures
of the personality of Christ—the Christians, unlike the Jews,
believing him to be the risen Messiah. How can the Jews
believe in the Word made Flesh, the Incarnation, or the
Trinity when their creed is based on: "Chema Israel: Adonai
Elot"—"Hearken, O Israel, God is One"?

But beyond the basic divergences, and as a result of the
teachings of Saint Paul, the Christians rejected the Mosaic
Law. (Ironically enough, it was in the quarter of Paris called
Saint-Paul that most of the Jews lived and the roundup took
the heaviest toll.) In the rejection of the Mosaic Law lay the
real rupture. Until then the Christians could be considered as
schismatic Jews like the members of the Church of Jerusalem
under the bishopric of James the Less.

Why is so much importance attached to events which took
place two thousand years ago? Because the hostility of a
conflict which should long ago have been forgotten survives
to this day, largely as a result of the "doctrine of contempt."
The phrase was that of Jules Isaac, who was always very
attached to his country, France. His grandfather had played
the trumpet in the band of a regiment in the Grande Armée,
his father was a colonel in the artillery and had fought in 1870,
while he himself fought in World War I. Two or three
generations of high school students have been learning French
history from the well-known Mallet and Isaac textbooks.

During the German occupation, Isaac's wife and daughter
were arrested at Clermont-Ferrand and handed to the
Germans. They were then deported to Germany, where they
died. In 1945 Jules Isaac, finding himself alone and
disoriented, tried to discover the reason for the disaster that
had beset him and thousands of others. And so he began his
researches as a historian, a scholar, and a man of letters.

Eventually he found what he was looking for. According to
him, most of the evil lies in the teachings of Christianity and
in particular what he calls the doctrine of contempt.

> A certain traditional Christian teaching which has
> been professed century after century from generation
> to generation by thousands of voices has ended by
> insinuating itself into the Christian mind, modeling and
> shaping it to the depths of the subconscious. . . .
> The responsibility of the Germans for these crimes,
> overwhelming as it is, is really a derived responsibility
> which, like some hideous parasite, attached itself to an
> age-old tradition originating in the Christian teachings.
> Yes, even after Auschwitz, Maidanek, Dubno,
> Treblinka, Christian anti-Semitism continues. Oblivious
> of or unwilling to recognize the hidden bond which links
> it to the Nazi anti-Semitism which has brought about so
> much horror, this unchristian racism of the Christians
> goes on.

And it is indeed true that Christian teachings perpetuated
the ancient and essentially religious conflict, though with the
evolution of ideas and especially after the French Revolution
the violence of Christian anti-Semitism abated.

On March 27, 1790, the rights of man and citizens were
proclaimed in France. There were in France at the time three
categories of citizens who did not have equal rights and would
benefit from the new declaration: Protestants, Jews, and
Negroes.

The cause of the Jews had been taken up by Father
Grégoire at the Constitutional Assembly. On September 27,
1791, the Assembly recognized complete equality of rights and
duties for French citizens who were Jews. In July, 1790, the
Assembly had given equality only to the Portuguese and
Spanish Jews of the South, the "Sefardim," the reason being
that, numbering only ten thousand persons, they were better
integrated into the French community than the forty thousand
Alsatian Jews. Even so, the Jews saw their newly won rights
threatened for at least a period of ten years under Napoleon
(the restrictive measures of March 17, 1808). However, in 1806

at a meeting with the Grand Sanhedrin, Napoleon established
an agreement of sorts with the Jews, recognizing their freedom
to worship in the constitution of the Year Three. Thus having
gained their rights as individuals and citizens at the time of the
French Revolution, the Jews now attained the right to worship
as a community.

This emancipation of the Jews spread throughout Europe in
the wake of the victorious French armies. And from that time
onward, in spite of subsequent restoration of conservative
measures, such as under Louis XVIII (who nonetheless
recognized the freedom of worship) , the fundamental rights
proclaimed at the French Revolution were never questioned
until the Government of Marshal Pétain. On October 1, 1941,
the anniversary of the decree of 1791, General de Gaulle, the
head of Free France, wrote to Rabbi S. Wize, president of the
Jewish World Congress in New York: "The famous decree
emancipating the Jews in France, like the declaration of the
rights of individuals and citizens, cannot be rescinded by the
Vichy laws and shall always remain valid. . . ."

Until their legal emancipation the Jews had not been
integrated as completely and as quickly as other minorities, in
spite of their centuries-long residence in France. The reason
for this had been one of religion, though their standing had
varied with the temper of the times.

After the founding of the Kingdom of the Franks, the Jews
had been suppressed by the Church and the Merovingian
monarchy. Having failed to convert the Jews to Christianity
(like the pagans who were to be found in France still) , the
French, being themselves recent converts to Christianity,
resented the Jewish resistance very strongly. This antagonism
led to the persecution of the Jews, an essentially religious
drive aiming at their conversion and baptism (incident of
Priscus and Chilperic in Paris, Avitus at Clermont, Dagobert's
decree of 629 A.D., etc.) .

In spite of fluctuations in the climate of feelings, friendly
and peaceable coexistence with the Jews proved to be the most
beneficent solution for all concerned. This attitude persisted

throughout the reign of Charlemagne and while France, Italy, and Germany were united under his empire. Not much later, when the French bishops, notably Agabord of Lyon, were found to be returning to the "doctrine of contempt," Louis the Debonair did not fail to reprimand them.

But the most tragic moments in Jewish history, and for which they were in no way to be blamed, came during the Crusades when the Christian armies set out to free the sepulchre of Christ. The knights who formed these legions were full of a zealous faith, greedy for glory, and also searching for fabulous treasures. Serfs were also recruited into the Crusades with the promise of freedom on their return; and, like any other army, this one attracted bandits, plunderers, and adventurers. On the way to the Holy Land and the battles with the Moslems, these soldiers practiced on the Jews. Those who were converted were spared; the rest were shown no mercy.

The upper Rhine was the scene of the worst of these exploits carried out in the name of the Cross. It was there that during the First Crusade the Massacre of Worms took place. Forty years later, during the Third Crusade, a similar massacre took place in York, England. André Schwarz-Bart, in *The Last of the Just*, gives the most up-to-date description of this event.

Only Spain escaped this surge of intolerant and murderous faith that swept Europe, taking its first victims among the Jews. With Jewish and Arab culture flourishing side by side, Spain at the time was in its golden age. But very soon the Spanish Church, with its Inquisition, was to catch up with the rest of Europe.

Forced to live in a community apart from the rest of their society, the Jews reacted by preserving all the more intensely everything that made them Jewish. They not only "persisted in their errors"—in their faith and tradition, that is—but they took up activities and specialized in professions permitted to them by their religion. A kind of ghetto was formed by the attitude of the people among whom they lived and by their own attitude. But apart from extreme episodes, they continued to live in these conditions, developing their own activities and economy. Whenever there was conflict, whether personal or otherwise, usually of an economic nature, the Gentiles could find in the "doctrine of contempt" motives for hostility toward the Jews and, it must be mentioned, reasons for robbing the Jews of their property.

One accusation against them was deicide. However serious the charge, it had weak points. It had happened too long ago; more modern motives were needed. So the profanation of the host and the legend of ritual murder were evoked. Pope Innocent IV proclaimed in a bull:

> We have heard the bitter complaints of the Jews who are being falsely accused of the most abject crimes just as a pretext to attack them and take over their property. . . .
> We forbid the persecution of the Jews whose return [to Christianity] God in His mercy awaits, and order you to treat them with kindness. If the Jews are again illegally oppressed by the Church, the nobles, or officials of government, you must not tolerate it.

In his book *Jesus Christ, Jew by Birth,* Martin Luther wrote:

> These popes, bishops, and monks with their great asses' heads have behaved toward the Jews as they would toward dogs, insulting them and stealing their property. The Jews are the brothers of our Saviour. God has honored them above all the other nations and given them the Holy Scriptures.

Here we must note that during the German occupation and under the Pétain regime, the fugitive Jews very quickly found sympathizers in the central part of France among the descendants of the Huguenots who had been persecuted at the hands of zealous Christians.

In spite of being ostracized, and in spite of the fact that they themselves sometimes isolated their own communities from the rest, little by little, from the sixteenth century onward, the Jews made a place for themselves in France. When the Germans from the first days of the occupation prepared themselves, with the help of the French authorities, to persecute the Jews of France, nearly a third of the Jews in France were aliens or of foreign origin and recent immigrants. The other two thirds were French Jews whose history we have just outlined. Had it not been for the foreign Jews, it might have been difficult to speak of the Jews or even recognize them. The time for Holy Wars had passed, and anyway the Nazis, when they became the champions of anti-Semitism, did not pretend to be defending Christianity. Religion was very rarely used as a justification for Nazi acts. What they accused the Jews of was their origin. As far as the French Jews were concerned, or at least the majority among them, their race was the only reason for their persecution, since by 1940 their links with Judaism had become very tenuous. Already, in 1880, one hundred years after their legal emancipation, Judaism in France had almost disappeared.

There were believers and practicing Jews, but it was of their own free choice. They were citizens of a liberal country belonging to a religious minority. Many had so completely integrated themselves with the French that they had left their traditions and religion and had given up everything that would make them appear different from the French. Though this abandonment of religion, which was contemporary with a certain evolution of ideas, was not peculiar to the Jewish faith, it was more accentuated among the Jews. There were some conversions too, probably prompted more by a wish to be readily accepted by the non-Jewish society than by any religious conviction. Whatever the motives, whenever they had been put under constraint, the Jews had until then refused baptism.

Liberated from their former isolated position, these French citizens of Jewish origin threw themselves energetically into the new and modern activities open to them. They tended to belong to the middle class and in general had firmly republican and leftist political views. They were also profoundly patriotic. They belonged to the liberal professions and became tradesmen, sometimes bankers and industrialists, and sometimes craftsmen and workers.

Things would have continued in this way had it not been for two factors: the immigration and the Dreyfus affair. These were to have the most deeply felt influence on the lives of the Jews in France until the Nazi occupation in 1940.

The immigration of Jews into France, which started in 1880 and continued in stages until 1939, brought Russians and Poles in the beginning, then Jews from Central Europe and Germany as well as a small number of Jews from the "Sefardim" colonies in Greece and Turkey. By 1940 some of these immigrants had spent sixty years in France. Their reasons for coming to France had been above all ideological. They were part of a huge migration involving some three million people, most of whom emigrated to the "new" countries—the United States, South America, and Australia. The movement had begun as a result of events in Russia, where an attempt on the life of the Czar on March 13, 1881, had launched a series of pogroms. There was indeed a Jewess, Guessia Guelfman, among the insurgents, and it was not difficult for people to believe that it was the Jews, these sons of Satan according to the teaching of the Pope, who had assassinated Alexander II.

For sixty years this immigration into France continued, and by the end there were some one hundred thousand immigrant Jews living in France. But the movement had hardly begun (by 1900 only six to ten thousand immigrants had entered France) when the Dreyfus scandal broke. The presence of the new immigrants was used as a valuable anti-Semitic argument by those who were against Dreyfus: "The Jews are all aliens." From the first moments the anti-Dreyfus faction condemned him, not from any evidence against him but because he was Jewish.

On February 5, 1898, *Civita Cattolica* commented on the Dreyfus affair as follows: "The Jews were created by a special decree of Providence so that there should always be traitors to noble causes." The French paper *La Croix* on February 8, 1898, headed the anti-Dreyfus campaign with the words: "Freedom of thought has protected the Jews, the Protestants, and all the enemies of France."

As for Captain Dreyfus himself, the victim of this conspiracy, he was a typical French Jew. Born at Mulhouse in 1859, he was one of eight children. His father owned a spinning factory. Having decided on a career in the army, he went to the Polytechnic Institute and to the War College. He became a captain in 1880. He proclaimed his innocence with great courage but seemed uninterested in the whole Dreyfus affair, even during the humiliating ceremony of degradation. Later Léon Blum was to say, "If Dreyfus had not been Dreyfus, he would not even have been pro-Dreyfus." In the same way, certain French Jews could easily have become supporters of Marshal Pétain if they had not been Jews and Pétain had not been anti-Semitic. Pétain's anti-Semitism, which he was unable to put into practice until the Germans brought him to power sixty years later, was already manifest during the Dreyfus affair.

The French Jews were disturbed by the scandal and watched to see who were the friends and who were the enemies of justice. In spite of the demonstrations of Gobineau and Drumont and a few others, they could not believe that there could be racial or religious discrimination in France. When the scandal had blown over, they regarded it as an unfortunate episode. Poincaré went so far as to declare, "After the Dreyfus affair, there can be no anti-Semitism in France."

But not everyone had that confidence. In the respect of Liberty, Equality, and Fraternity, the people of France were regarded as a standard. If the Dreyfus scandal could happen in France, what could one hope for elsewhere? One of the journalists covering the affair was a brilliant young lawyer and journalist from Austria, Theodore Herzl. He was so worried by the events that in a fever of indignation he wrote his book *The Jewish State* in a few nights. He then became the head of a political movement—Zionism.

A short time before, a Russian Jew, Leo Pinsker, had formulated the same ideas in a book called *Auto-emancipation,* which was successful much later in very different circumstances.

THE JEWS IN FRANCE

The immigrants had settled in certain limited areas, not only because they chose to be near their fellow immigrants but because it was more economical. For example, Rue de Citeaux in the XII Arrondissement very soon was almost entirely inhabited by German Jews. The companies owning the buildings and apartments on that street would send representatives to the Gare de l'Est to wait for the refugees and offer them accommodations on arrival. Of the thirty families or so, with their numerous children, who lived on that street, only two persons were left at the time of the liberation of France. One had been able to remain in hiding throughout the occupation, and the other had survived the concentration camps.

In certain quarters—around the Rue des Rosiers, for example—whole communities of Jews sprang up. On the shopwindows of butchers and booksellers one saw signs in Hebrew letters. On Saturday there would be bearded men in the traditional black caftan. The Germans, in their propaganda against the Jews, did not fail to take suitable pictures of the narrow streets and the quaint clothes.

But aside from these small and picturesque patches of Jewish living, most of the immigrants quickly integrated themselves into the French way of life. The children felt no different from their French playmates except that they had German, Polish, or Russian grandparents while their friends would have Italian or Spanish or Corsican or Breton grandparents.

The latest immigrants and the older French Jews had a similarity in their language and customs. They would both speak their own native tongue and often Yiddish, the archaic Frankfort German laced with Hebrew. The Jews of Turkey and Greece spoke Sefardi (ladino) or fifteenth-century Spanish with just a little mixture of Hebrew and Turkish. These were far fewer than Jews from other countries and were very strongly influenced by the French schools most of them attended. Paradoxically they were more "westernized" than other groups. There were many intellectuals and tradesmen among them, and they were closer to the French Jews.

The two groups of Jews, the immigrants and the French Jews, not only lived apart in separate worlds, but there was a very particular tone to the relationship between them, bordering on hostility at times. The immigrants loved France, which they had chosen as their adopted country, and their loyalty to France was linked to the ideal image they had of it, while the French Jews were not altogether pleased with the presence of these newcomers, who could be indiscreet and could disturb the peace they were enjoying.

The most recent arrivals were Belgian and Dutch Jews fleeing before the German army to the south of France, the area that was to become the free zone. After the armistice they had returned to their countries, where they suffered the common lot—extermination up to 80 per cent—while those who remained were grouped with the marked class of Jews and aliens by the Vichy government. Before them, there had been since 1933 successive waves of German Jews escaping from Nazi Germany and seeking asylum in France. Most of these had not planned to remain in France but were in transit, waiting for a visa and travel arrangements to go to the United States or South America, or sometimes Palestine, which at that time was only a "Jewish national Home."*

In 1940 there were in all some ten to fifteen thousand refugees from Germany. They were Jews, but they also were German to the tips of their fingers, and proud of being German. They had been proud of the decorations they had earned fighting next to their fellow Germans in the First World War. But since 1933 they had been rejected by their own country and persecuted. They had to flee, deprived of their country and their possessions but unable to rid themselves of their feelings, outlook, and even German features.

They were unhappy and felt strange in France, almost

* There are two books which give a vivid impression of the atmosphere of this wait for visas: *Transit* by Anna Seghers (Editeurs Français Réunis) and *La Solution finale,* a novel by Richard Nollier (Flammarion).

ashamed of having been forced to ask for shelter there. They
had hoped to find some understanding among the French Jews
but found the same impenetrable incomprehension they had
found elsewhere, and worse perhaps. Certainly they were
pitied and roused people's sympathy. French Jews were not
unmoved by the news of the persecutions in Germany. They
had seen the photographs of Jewish "mamas" cleaning the
streets of Munich, Stuttgart, and Vienna with toothbrushes
under the hostile gaze of an SA. But now the refugees were in
France, pitiful, miserable, and with no legal status, labor
permit, or identity card, but still having to live and feed their
children.

And they were so very German! In Germany they were
persecuted and hunted. In France they were interned, in the
camps at Gurs and Rivesaltes, whole families together. Then
one day in October, 1940, another 7,500 German Jews from
Bade and the Palatinate were brought from the Oloron
station to join them. They were all eventually handed back
to the Germans.

In 1940, France was occupied territory. At various times
immigrant Jews, then stateless Jews, aliens and naturalized
Jews, and finally the French Jews were to suffer discrimination
and persecution. Both those who were conscious that they were
Jews and those who were almost surprised to discover they
were Jews when the persecution hit them accepted their
condition with a certain valor mixed with humor, and
suffered various fates, for the most part tragic.

The reactions to the discrimination were very different.
Some proudly declared themselves Jews and even inspired
friends and relatives among the non-Jews to do the same, while
others tried to hide their origins. When the Germans had
suggested the enforcement of the distinguishing yellow star in
Denmark, the King of Denmark had been able to oppose the
measure by saying that he himself would wear it. The head of
state in France did no such thing, and it became law in France
for Jews to have to wear the yellow star. As a reaction and in
a way to save the country's honor, a number of non-Jewish

Frenchmen sported the yellow star, mostly young students and workers who wanted to demonstrate their sympathy. They paid a high price for their courage, most of them being arrested and spending several months in the camp at Drancy.

On June 20, 1942, the newspaper *Le National Populaire* printed the following: "The government should cut these undesirable elements out of the community and satisfy their wish to belong to the Jewish community by providing them with an authentic Jewish status, treating them as such. They will thus be fully affected by every measure that we bring against the Jews." There also are a number of reports by policemen who arrested Frenchmen sympathizing with the Jews.

While on a visit to the Rothschild hospital, where the Jewish sick were treated, Dannecker was infuriated by a Swiss patient in the surgery ward, who told him that he did not feel in the least dishonored by sharing a ward with Jews. Before leaving the hospital he demanded that a notice saying "Honorary Jew" be pinned to the Swiss patient's bed.

Then there were husbands and wives or fiancés of Jews who went to prison with them rather than be separated. There were Frenchmen of Jewish origin so totally cut off from Judaism that they could easily pass for non-Jews, but in the tragic circumstances they refused to behave ignobly by hiding their origin.

The philosopher Bergson was among this class of Jew. In his ideas he had moved a long way from Judaism and could almost have been converted to Catholicism. To explain why he never took the step which would have merely formalized the spiritual conversion he had already experienced, he wrote in his will on February 8, 1937, "I wanted to remain among those who will one day be persecuted." And then, after being relieved of all his professional posts, one icy morning in the winter of 1941 Bergson joined the line in front of the Passy police station; an old man suffering from rheumatism, he stood with the Jews from whom he refused to be separated and was registered with them as such. In column B of the Jewish

census he was entered as: Bergson, Henri. Born 1859.
Nationality: French. Profession: Academic, Philosopher,
Nobel Prize Winner. Jewish. He fell ill after this wait in the
cold and died a few weeks later.

In a camp near Toul, Father Rousselot was surprised to be
approached by some Jewish boys and girls asking him for
communion. They had been converted, baptized, and
confirmed, but they wanted to take communion secretly
without their parents' knowledge, because their parents
didn't know of their conversion and they did not want to be
dissociated from their parents. They wanted to stay with them
in their misfortunes. Which they did and were deported.

Then there was the Sefardim business. A journalist called
Sam Levy managed somehow to persuade two Parisian
specialists to write a paper establishing that the blood group
and the facial structure of the Sefardim Jews would include
them among the Aryans. The racial institute at Munich would
have accepted this assessment, but the final decision lay with
Laval, who hesitated. He had scruples about granting the
Sefardim Jews a favor which could be claimed by the Alsatian
Jews. Meanwhile the hope of those who had spent so much
energy trying to spare at least one group of Jews the rigors of
persecution grew as they waited anxiously to hear the decision.

But things were more complicated than that. The leaders of
the Sefardim community met and discussed the whole business.
Taking part were Mr. Arditti, Mr. Rodrigues, Mr. Ezrathi, and
Dr. Modiano. First of all, the specialists in question seemed to
be utterly unknown. Furthermore, they had each demanded
the fabulous sum of one million francs for their paper. The
success of the undertaking seemed very uncertain. Above all,
Dr. Modiano expressed the fear that the whole idea was a trap
and thought that it would be undignified to proceed with it.
This final decision was communicated to Mr. de Monzie, and
the Sefardim retained their classification as Jews.

If the Swiss patient at the Rothschild hospital was called an
honorary Jew, there were also honorary Aryans. There were
Jews who were determined to hide the fact at all costs. Not

only did they change their names to French-sounding names like Durand, Martin, or Lambert and try to pass themselves off as Frenchmen, but they dissociated themselves entirely from the Jews. If changing one's name means saving one's life, it can hardly be called cowardice to do so. But the Germans and the Vichy government demanded more. They wanted proof of absolute loyalty, and that meant serving the Germans. The best known of the so-called honorary Aryans was the wife of Mr. de Brinon, the official representative of the Vichy government in German-occupied territory, who was given the rank of ambassador.

Appendix B

Gearing the Machinery

How could the anti-Jewish measures be enforced in France? How could French policemen, only two years after the German occupation in June, 1940, agree to carry out such hateful orders? In Germany the anti-Jewish movement had been going on for twenty years, and the racist propaganda of the National Socialist Party had at every opportunity spread hate for the Jews among the German people. In his address before the Nuremberg tribunal, Mr. Edgar Faure said on behalf of France:

> Certainly the Nazis found the theories that eventually led them to the extermination of the Jews very useful. First, the anti-Jewish theme had always been a ready topic for rousing the criticism and anger of the public. It also lent itself to a very skillful psychological seduction of even a healthy mind. It gave the least privileged and most miserable members of society the satisfaction of being told that in spite of everything they had superior qualities which gave them the right to despise a whole category of their fellows. Finally the Nazis were able to make fanatics of their followers by awakening and fostering the criminal instincts which to some extent are always latent in the human soul. . . .

After their defeat in 1918 the Germans had lived through extraordinarily tragic circumstances resulting from the intransigence of their vanquishers. Even before seizing power, Hitler had been trying to channel the longing for revenge which was one of the driving forces of Nazism. He had to find a scapegoat, a definite object for his vengeance. So, from 1930 on, the Jews were blamed for the humiliation and the distress of the German people.

For Hitler the Jews were a catalyst of hate. In their propaganda drives in France the Nazis reminded the French that in the seventh century the "good King Dagobert" and Saint Eloi had expelled the Jews from France after dispossessing them, and that in the fourteenth century Philip "the Good" had done the same except that he added the Templars to his legitimate prey. Thus on September 5, 1941, in a report to Von Ribbentrop on the exhibition "The Jews and France," ambassador Otto Abetz was able to say:

> The anti-Jewish exhibition was inaugurated this afternoon in the most frequented quarter of Paris. . . . Entitled "The Jews and France," the exhibition presents a historical summary of the role of Judaism in France from the Middle Ages to the present day. . . .

From 1930 on, Jewish shops in the principal cities of Germany began to be sabotaged. Many shopkeepers were murdered. The German leaders considered such actions necessary to political agitation, and the courts of the Weimar Republic intervened only half-heartedly. No serious legal action was undertaken, not only because of the number of false witnesses that would be provided by the Party, but because a considerable number of magistrates held ideas which coincided with the ideals of the National Socialists.

After Hitler's rise to power in 1933, the anti-Jewish manifestations increased. In less than one year, between March, 1933, and March, 1934, approximately sixty-two thousand German Jews are believed to have fled from the Reich, leaving their possessions behind. The persecution continued for several years, intensifying the troubled atmosphere and the feeling of hate until finally on November 9, 1938, a carefully organized pogrom enveloped the whole of Germany in blood and flames.

The assassination of a diplomat at the German Embassy in Paris, Counsellor von Rath, by a young German-Jewish refugee of seventeen, called Grynspan, was taken as the pretext for the pogrom. Grynspan was imprisoned in France and later handed over to the German authorities by the Vichy government. Meanwhile the Nazis set to work on the "Crystal Night," as they called the night of November 9, 1938 (there had already been a "Night of the Long Knives"). On this night, 101 synagogues were burned, 116 destroyed, 8,000 shops were plundered, 60 Jews were killed, and 20,000 were sent to concentration camps. There was no reaction from the German people. It was the eve of Munich.

Less than a year later, on September 2, 1939, having overrun Czechoslovakia in March, the German army invaded Poland. The campaign lasted three weeks. But two SS divisions, the Totemkopf and the Liebstandarte headed by SS general Sepp Dietrich, a former butcher's boy, accompanied the army to carry out special operations.

Sepp Dietrich was one of Hitler's most trusted officers. He had been the main organizer of the "Night of the Long Knives" in June, 1934, during the course of which Captain Roehm and the leaders of the SA had been assassinated. He then became the head of Hitler's bodyguard and was promoted to SS general, in which capacity, having ravaged Poland, he proceeded to do the same in the Ukraine. Later in June, 1944, he was put in command of the first Panzer corps of the SS in Normandy and was the only SS to be entrusted with important military responsibilities. Sepp Dietrich was directly responsible for the execution of one hundred fifty American pilots. In 1947 he was condemned to twenty-five years' imprisonment but was liberated after ten. His most noteworthy achievement after being set free was to reassemble SS veterans. On October 25, 1965, he presided over a gathering of former Waffen SS at Rendsburg whose main object was to demand an increase in military pensions, which were judged insufficient. He died on April 26, 1966, at the age of seventy-five, and at his funeral at Ludwisburg, near Stuttgart, a monstrous gathering of 5,000 former SS sang the Nazi hymn together.

To return to Poland, the two SS divisions were assigned a

very particular mission. Armed with the most modern equipment, these "élite" divisions carried out a task which the Wehrmacht refused and Himmler suggested would be more suitable for the SS. The orders of SS Totemkopf and Liebstandarte were to carry out large-scale massacres outside the combat zones, killing Poles and Jews indiscriminately. After the surrender of Poland, Colonel Blaskowitz, who had been appointed commander of the Polish territory by Hitler, brought charges against two SS generals for the crimes committed by their troops. One of the men he wanted to bring before the court-martial was Sepp Dietrich. Blaskowitz did not know what he was doing. On Hitler's orders he was relieved of his post immediately, and Hans Frank, a lawyer who had become Obergruppenfuehrer of the SS, was appointed in his place and became the Nazi executioner for Poland. Blaskowitz was taken prisoner by the Americans at the end of the war and was murdered by some SS fellow prisoners to prevent him from disclosing Nazi secrets.

When they occupied France in 1940, the Germans used different methods against the Jews from those they had employed in Poland. Even though they knew that they could count on the newly installed French authorities to carry out the brunt of their work against the Jews, the Germans decided to use more discretion this time. They also knew that there was no active anti-Semitic feeling in France as there had been in Poland and that, apart from the traditional anti-Semitic French movements and the fascists who, subsidized by the German Embassy in Paris, had been developing policies on the lines of the German National Socialism, the French in general were not particularly hostile to the Jews. Only forty years before, the Dreyfus scandal had roused the majority of the French against powerful bodies like the army and the church, demanding the liberation of a man who had been unjustly condemned because of his racial origin. The Germans were wary. They decided against any persecution that would attract attention. Furthermore they had learned their lesson in Poland and were careful not to put a general like Blaskowitz in charge of France; they did not want to risk another indignant exposure of inhuman treatment of the population. They set up the Gestapo under Colonel Knochen to act independently of the military authorities. This did not mean that the German military authorities were any less responsible for the perfectly organized looting that took place.

The first military commander of the Paris region, which included the Seine, the Seine-et-Marne, and the Seine-et-Oise regions, was General Stutzitz, with his office at the Hotel Crillon, assisted by General Briesen, commander of Paris, with offices in the Hotel Meurisse. Within two weeks General Stutzitz was replaced by General von Vollard-Bockelberg, while General Briesen was replaced by von Schaumburg.

It was General von Vollard-Bockelberg who signed the statute of July 15, 1940, which declared all works of art in France to be "blocked." This statute was followed by looting similar to the plunder of Jewish property which had already taken place in Germany, after Marshal Keitel himself had instructed General von Vollard-Bockelberg that Hitler had decided "that as well as works of art belonging to the French state, art objects and historical documents belonging to private individuals, especially Jews, were also to be taken into safekeeping."

For this the army was employed with the help of the embassy, to which Otto Abetz had just been appointed. The duties of the ambassador were defined by the Fuehrer himself and consisted mainly of "the protection and the taking into custody of works of art belonging to the state as well as to individuals, and above all to Jews, according to the special instructions to that effect."

The rounding up of works of art began soon after, and within a few days Hitler appointed Rosenberg head of a special office entrusted with the task of collecting and sending to Germany all art objects of interest. The plunder of the possessions of the Jews was to continue throughout the war, and even when Germany was crushed, it was still unfinished. When the Leclerc division arrived at the Aulnay-sous-Bois station on August 22, 1944, it intercepted a train of thirty-one cars loaded with works of art, ready for shipment to Germany.

The Vichy government looked on without protest. They hoped to receive their share of the property of Jews which had been "abandoned" when the owners had fled. A law of July 23, 1940, permitted the sale of confiscated property after the passage of six months, in aid of the *Secours National*. Finding that their share was long in coming, the Vichy government made timid protests on December 14, 1940, and on February 28 and July 25, 1941. They received the reply they deserved. On November 3, 1941, the Germans replied:

> The French government is unjustified in its invocation of the statute according to which the property of Jews (which for the most part was taken after the retreat of the French) was seized and put at the disposition of the *Secours National*. The French state did not gain the power to dispose of the property of the Jews with its own strength; it was enabled to do so only through the victory of the German armies. Therefore it has no right whatsoever to question the measures which the Reich, as the victorious power, decides to apply against the Jews.

After this stinging response, the Vichy government kept silent.

The Germans looked far ahead. They looked on Europe as their property and considered the possessions of the Jews as theirs by right: the possessions of the Rothschilds as well as those of the smallest craftsmen. But the plunder of hundreds of little shops could not be carried out as discreetly as the looting of an isolated country chateau in the absence of its owner. This needed some careful organization. As early as August 17, the ambassador Otto Abetz suggested to the army the first steps in the persecution, and Dr. Werner Best, a high-ranking member of the Gestapo and head of the administrative service of the Militaersbefehlshaber in France, mentioned the ambassador's suggestions in a note dated August 19 and addressed to the various military authorities.

On August 29, the ambassador officially notified the French

authorities that Jews were forbidden entry into the occupied
zone; that is, they were not allowed to come back like the rest
of the French who had fled the capital in the great exodus. At
the same time Otto Abetz stated that all Jews residing in the
occupied zone were to register with their local police stations
immediately for a census of the Jews, and their shops were to
be distinguished by special yellow signs.

Théo Dannecker, who was to preside over the fate of Jews
in France for nearly two years, moved his office into 31A
Avenue Foch and 11 Rue des Saussaies, where the Gestapo had
already been installed by Knochen, in September, 1940. It was
Dannecker's job to centralize the repression of the Jews in
France. In principle he was to act in conjunction with the
German embassy and the German military authorities. But in
fact he was not even bound to his immediate superior at the
Gestapo, Colonel Knochen. Dannecker's orders came direct
from Berlin, from the head of the service, Adolf Eichmann.

The *Au Pilori* newspaper was one of the collaboration
papers, supporting the French Nationalist Party, most of
whose members were to join the PPF organized by Doriot.
From June, 1940, the French Nationalist Party undertook an
anti-Jewish provocation which the Germans did not wish to
carry out themselves in public. The occupation forces wanted
the anti-Jewish measures they were preparing to appear to be
the necessary result of the French people's hostility toward the
Jews. Within the Nationalist Party two groups were formed:
the Garde Française, to which young men over twenty-one
belonged, and the Jeune Front, which recruited boys of sixteen
to twenty-one. These teams of young delinquents concentrated
on attacking shops owned by Jews, mainly during the months
of July and August, 1940. Some Aryan shopkeepers, not
wanting to be mistaken for Jews, tried various methods to
demonstrate that they were non-Jewish. In its issue of July 26,
1940, *Au Pilori* wrote: "The following notices have appeared
on the windows of certain shops: 'This is a French
establishment, no Jews allowed' and 'No Jews admitted.' "

One leading optician took the opportunity to use the slogan:

"Lissac is not Isaac," which was hailed as typically French wit. Outside the famous "Dupont Latin" cafe there was the notice: "Closed to dogs and Jews." A little later the Germans blew up all the synagogues in Paris, to give the impression that the feelings of the Parisians against the Jews were running high.

The Vichy government was represented in Paris by a general delegation which had been installed in the Ministry of Labor. But only the sentries on duty outside the entrance, in their French uniforms, provided an authentic French touch. The first delegate, Mr. Léon Noël, who had been French Ambassador to Warsaw in 1939, spent only a few days at his post. By the end of July, 1940, he had joined the Free French. Noël was soon succeeded by General de la Laurencie, whose name is unfortunately linked with that of Dannecker as the organizers of the Jewish census. The first census was taken on an order of the Germans issued on September 27, 1940, and completed under General de la Laurencie's instructions on October 20, November 5, and December 15, 1940.

The census was first carried out by the Judiciary Police in the buildings of the local police stations. Then, still under the joint instructions of Dannecker and General de la Laurencie, the Prefect of Police created a special administrative service which was part of the headquarters of the general police, with a certain François in charge of it. This François was to become one of the main personalities in the Jewish persecution and was directly involved in the planning of the tragic roundup of July 16 and 17, 1942. The master cards of the census list, on which the details of individuals were noted, were duplicated, and one set was sent to the Gestapo offices on Avenue Foch. The cards were further duplicated to enable the names to be filed in different categories: alphabetically, by address, by nationality, and by profession. This tedious and meticulous work was carried out by Tulard, who put all his energy into the index and considered it his life's work. He looked after it jealously and kept a close watch on the entrance to the offices he had been given, which were used by inspectors from all police sections to obtain information on the Jews. Tulard's

colleague, Peretti, kept an index with information on the
property of the Jews, mainly the buildings they owned, the
commercial establishments, industrial plants, and other
property.

The sum of information kept in the files of Tulard's office
at the Prefecture of Police was a precious weapon in the hands
of the Germans for the enforcement of their measures against
individual Jews or in large-scale operations, whether they were
directed against people or their property. Théo Dannecker
himself was so pleased with the index that he called it a
"model index" in a report dated February 24 and addressed to
Eichmann in Berlin. Knochen later said:

> I only want to say that the general index of information
> on the Jews was the only means for finding Jews,
> discovering the number of children who had stayed
> behind and all other details, and was used only with the
> agreement of the French police. Other reports and figures
> relating to the Jews reached the *Sipo* through the French
> Service for Jewish Affairs. I don't know, for example,
> whether the Security Police had a similar index or even
> that there was one, but I think that all administrative
> details were dealt with by the French police.

During the month of October, 1940, the census of the Jews
was taken in the French police stations. There were
particularly unpleasant scenes, such as old men standing about
on the pavement for hours before their turn came to go inside
the police office. As we said earlier, Henri Bergson lined up
with the rest to be registered.

While the census of the Jews was going on, a new order was
issued by the Germans on October 18, 1940, "defining the
notion of Jewish economic enterprise exactly." This order
purported to be motivated by the attack on Jewish shops
during the months of July and August, and was connected
with the order that every Jewish shop should bear the notice
"Jewish business" in its window. The plain object of the order
was the Aryanization of Jewish enterprise. Paragraph 5
stipulated that an administrator could be put in charge of

Jewish enterprises. It was for all practical purposes pure and simple theft.

If the German authorities seemed pleased with the total of 21,000 shops and other commercial enterprises listed, they were less satisfied with the total of 160,000 registered in the census. It seemed to them ridiculously low. Misled by reports from the Fascist Leagues, they had come to believe that the Jewish population in France numbered 900,000. This was the figure that was assumed to be true for France at the Wannsee conference in January, 1942.

Adolf Eichmann had been at the head of the Jewish Section in Berlin from the end of 1939, and during that time he had worked out several solutions to the Jewish problem. He had thought of Jewish emigration to Palestine, but after the French defeat in 1940 the island of Madagascar suggested itself as a Jewish Home. The latter was not a new idea. In July, 1940, Eichmann and Heydrich had proposed to Himmler and then to Hitler that all the Jews of Europe should be evacuated to Madagascar. Consequently from August, 1940, on, all Eichmann's emissaries in Europe, like Dannecker in France, were officially acting with a view to applying the Madagascar plan, which the Nazis had already begun to call the Final Solution.

The Madagascar plan became the subject of conferences at the highest level in Berlin until October, 1941, but it was finally abandoned during the winter of 1941–1942. All the evidence suggests that the Madagascar plan served only as a pretext for the setting up of the machinery for the ultimate persecution of the Jews. Solving the Jewish problem by evacuation would not shock public opinion so much as the actual Final Solution.

The military plans for the attack on Russia (Operation Barbarossa) included the destruction of thirty thousand Slavs with a view to making room for future German colonists who would be summoned to settle in the Russian territory. Another decree was added which was to be put into practice from July, 1941, on and would eliminate all Russian Jews by means of special teams called *Einsatz-Gruppen,* as well as political commissars and militant communists, who were considered to harbor Jewish ideology inasmuch as they were Marxists.

To the three million Jews in Poland were now added the five million Jews supposed to be living in Russia. On July 31, 1941, Heydrich, who had been appointed to the post of Commissioner for Jewish Affairs in the whole of Europe, received a letter from Reichsmarschall Goering, President of the Council of Ministers for the Defense of the Reich, asking him to make all the necessary preparations for a total solution of the Jewish problem in the area controlled by the Germans in Europe. On November 21, 1941, just as the first convoys of Jews from western Europe were arriving at Auschwitz, Heydrich summoned his aides to a conference "at which all the central authorities working on the final solution of the Jewish problem would be drawn into one coordinated plan." This conference was finally held in Berlin at 56–58 Grossen Wannsee Strasse on January 20, 1942.

The Nazis had to work methodically and progressively, keeping the true organizers of the operation in the background. The principle was to find agents among the enemy. And many Jews did indeed fall into the trap. The Nazis treacherously began to reassemble the Jewish organizations which had dispersed after the defeat of 1940, and appointed at their head well-known French-Jewish personalities. They went further and even founded a Committee for the Coordination of the Jewish Charities, with French Jews in charge of it. Before the German invasion in 1940 there were in France a large number of Jewish organizations, international organizations, and charitable societies recognized by the *Comité de bienfaisance israélite de Paris,* founded in 1809. The most important were the various Rothschild foundations—a home for convalescents founded in 1850, the Alphonse de Rothschild Foundation; a hospital; an old people's home; an orphanage, and a clinic (founded by Adolphe de Rothschild) .

SS Hauptsturmfuehrer Hagen, who was inquiring into these

organizations for Dannecker, seemed very surprised to find
that their main role was philanthropic. In his report he wrote:
"Strangely enough, the Jewish organizations in France, unlike
the mass organizations in Germany and Poland, were founded
for the help of immigrants only."

Nearly all these societies had vanished after June, 1940; the
directors had fled or they had been closed and sealed by the
Germans. By October, 1940, only four or five of these
associations had been reactivated—the OSE, a Russian
foundation which had opened an office in Paris in 1935; the
Comité de bienfaisance israélite de Paris; the *Colonie scolaire
et les Asiles israélites;* and the ORT.

The absence of these charities was particularly felt as the
persecutions began and the need for help became more urgent
among the suffering Jews, especially as the Vichy government
had deprived them of help from the *Secours National.* In
December, 1940, Dannecker instructed the Jewish section of
the Gestapo to enroll all the Jews in a single organization
(this, like the index, was to facilitate their eventual
deportation to Germany) . The four Jewish organizations
still in existence agreed on January 31, 1941, to form one
*Comité de coordination des oeuvres de bienfaisance du Grand
Paris.* They hoped to be able to help their fellow Jews more
efficiently by this centralization. There were difficulties; many
Jews, sensing the menace of this institution, tried to stop its
functioning. But part of the Jewish community in Paris,
especially after the election of Rabbi Marcel Sachs as head of
the *Comité* on March 27, 1941, decided to join and the
statutes were finally adopted on March 31, 1941. The
Prefecture of Police, knowing that it had been the wish of the
Gestapo, made no objection to registering the new
organization.

But Dannecker did not stop at that. He pressed for the
creation of a Jewish newspaper, the first issue of which
appeared on April 19, 1941, under the title of *Informations
juives* and was censored by Dannecker's staff. Thanks to the
index at the Prefecture of Police, the first three issues of the

paper were sent free of charge to every Jewish home in Paris. In each issue there was an appeal to the Jews to join the *Comité de coordination*. Membership involved a very small monthly subscription. Dannecker's maneuver succeeded, and thousands of Jews rallied to the *Comité de coordination*, much to Dannecker's glee. He would now know through his agents everything that went on in the *Comité*. The first president, Rabbi Marcel Sachs, pleaded sickness and was replaced by Alphonse Weill, whose conduct so offended Dannecker that he had him arrested. After that everything seemed to be working admirably. "The French Jews are collaborating," Dannecker wrote. He must have enjoyed the irony of it.

Later the German authorities, in the form of the anti-Jewish service of the embassy and the Gestapo, planned even further. Not satisfied with the *Comité de coordination*, they envisaged a "Jewish Union of France." Dannecker mentions it by name in a report on February 22, 1942.

> From our experience in Germany and the protectorates of Bohemia and Moravia, it is clear that by excluding the Jews from a number of spheres of daily life, their segregation into a distinct and separate class follows inevitably (see the General Union of Jews in Germany) . . . .
> We have since June, 1941, been advising the Commission for Jewish Affairs of the necessity for such an organization. On our suggestion the Militaer-befehlshaber has, in a letter addressed to the French delegation in Paris, asked for the creation of a compulsory grouping of the Jews into one organization. Finally on November 29, 1941, the French law instituting the *Union générale des israélites de France* was put into effect. Councils for the administration of the organization in the occupied and free zones will be independent of each other.

Ironically enough, the UGIF took part in the organization of the deportation of the Jews arrested on July 16 and 17, being put in charge of medical care by the Nazi authorities.

Father Paul Vergara described the UGIF as "an infamous trap disguised as a pro-Jewish association." Officially it was responsible for helping the Jews and taking care of their social and professional problems, but in fact it ensured an exclusively Jewish representation with the German authorities and, in typical German fashion, was called on to administer the French ghetto that the Germans were planning to create.

With its administrative council of eighteen persons (half for the occupied zone and half for the free zone) the UGIF for a long time appeared to be a kind of last refuge for many of the persecuted Jews, and this helped to hide from them the reality and extent of the danger that threatened them. In fact, by appointing the UGIF as a representative of the Jews and giving it the role of assisting Jews in difficulty, the Germans achieved exactly what they had hoped for— collaboration from the Jews themselves in their plans. But from the beginning the UGIF was unpopular. In May, 1941, the wives of Jews who had been arrested and taken to the camp at Pithiviers staged a demonstration at the UGIF offices (the UGIF threatened to call the police). Later when the directors of the UGIF, Mr. Baur and Mr. Musmik, visited the temporary camp at the Vélodrome d'Hiver with Roethke, they were hissed and booed by the prisoners. In the end these directors paid dearly for their blindness.

But before going on to the founding of the UGIF, Dannecker thought of developing anti-Semitic propaganda in France by giving it a French aspect. The "Institute for the Study of Jewish Affairs" was founded on May 11, 1941, with offices at 21 Rue de la Boétie, and a dependent "Friends of the Institute" service was soon added. In charge of the whole enterprise was an unintelligent but formidable person, Captain Sézille, who was appointed on June 22, 1941, the very day that Hitler attacked Russia. Dannecker very soon had reason to feel satisfied with the new service.

The business of this institute was to organize meetings, invite anti-Jewish speakers, and make sure that the walls of Paris were permanently covered with anti-Semitic posters. Pamphlets were published, and tracts full of an insane hate and violence were regularly distributed to the public.

Soon the Institute was faced with new work requiring the

expansion of its staff. At the beginning of 1942 the
appropriation of Jewish enterprises was at its height. Aryan
administrators were put in charge of Jewish businesses, some of
which were large and invited greed. The Institute for Jewish
Affairs was flooded with mail from informers, and Captain
Sézille worked hard, taking careful note of every accusation.
For the informers there was money. In 1943, Dannecker's
successor Roethke suggested a reward of one hundred francs
for every Jew arrested. Not a very high price for the life of a
Jew—one day's salary of a skilled worker. In Nice an informer
who betrayed five Jewish children was paid 4,700 francs. Not
only private individuals engaged in this treachery; even
ministers in Pétain's government took part. For example, on
the letterhead of the Ministry of Interior, with regular
reference code, etc., the following letter was sent to the
Commissioner for Jewish Affairs, 54 Avenue d'Iéna, Paris, on
October 31, 1942:

> I have the honor of bringing to your attention that an
> apartment at 57A Boulevard Rochechouart, belonging
> to a Jew called Gresalmer, contains very beautiful
> furnishings.

The signature is illegible.

At the same time as the creation of the *Comité de
coordination des oeuvres de bienfaisance du Grand Paris,* the
UGIF, and the Institute for the Study of Jewish Affairs,
Dannecker arranged some meetings with the military
authorities at the end of January, 1941, with a view to
setting up a Central Jewish Bureau, under French control.
Ambassador Otto Abetz was interested in the proposition and
asked his attaché on Jewish Affairs, the Counsellor of the
Legation, Zeitschel, to put pressure on the Vichy government
and obtain their agreement to assemble public figures who
would be suitable representatives.

With Dannecker's backing, Zeitschel insistently repeated
the proposition, and on March 8, 1941, the Council of
Ministers presided over by Marshal Pétain decided to create
a "General Commission for Jewish Affairs." Three weeks later,
on March 29, Xavier Vallat was appointed as its head.

Vallat's task was to prepare and suggest to Pétain the laws
and regulations affecting the Jews, and to supervise the
liquidation of Jewish property and the appointment of
temporary administrators of Jewish property. A special
Financial Inspector was entrusted with the last two duties.

The powers of this Commission were reinforced by a second
piece of legislation in March, 1941, and it became a fully
governmental body. The Commission could intervene in the
activity of every ministry and could make use of the police
force whenever it saw fit.

The use of the police force by the Commission for Jewish
Affairs proved difficult from the administrative point of view,
however, and so the Germans decided to create a special police
service attached to the Commission and for its exclusive use.
Two SS officers, Limpert and Busch, both aides to Dannecker,
were in charge of this police force. These two officers had been
given an office at the Prefecture of Police on January 17, 1941,
in order to ensure a close contact between the Gestapo offices
on Avenue Foch and Commissioner François' service; they
also were able to make use of the index at the Prefecture.

At the beginning, the Prefect of Police had provided two
interpreters for the German officers, who also served as
inspectors. Slowly the number of inspectors rose to twelve, and
the office became too crowded. Dannecker asked the Prefecture
for the transfer of the office to the former offices of the Jewish-
American association "Joint" at 19 Rue de Teheran, and the
two Gestapo officers and the French inspectors were moved on
April 22, 1941. The French inspectors' work did not change
with the change of address; they remained members of the
French police but working for the Germans—a kind of Franco-
German agglomeration. The interpreters and inspectors
continued to be paid by the Prefecture and enjoyed the usual
benefits. This was a remarkable example of French
"collaboration."

When the Minister of the Interior, Pucheu, created the
Police for Jewish Affairs in November, 1941, the office on the
Rue de Teheran was closed. Inspector Grand and eight other

inspectors were transferred from the Prefecture of Police to
the Police for Jewish Affairs, while three inspectors—Jalby,
Jurgens, and Santoni—were directly employed by the Gestapo
on Avenue Foch.

So the Vichy government created in addition a Police for
Jewish Affairs, which had its offices at 8 Rue Greffulhe in
Paris. This was divided into two parts, one centralizing
Jewish questions on a national basis while the other dealt
with local questions in the Paris area. The latter was made up
of the staff of the Financial Inspector of the Commission for
Jewish Affairs and the group of inspectors who had worked
at Rue Teheran. In charge was Commissioner Schweblin, who
was in direct personal contact with Dannecker. The whole
force totaled some forty persons, half on the administration
and half acting as policemen.

The Police for Jewish Affairs was part of a triple force
created by Pucheu and under the general direction of
Commissioner Detmar. It included:

(1) The Anti-Communist Police Service (SPAC) —directed
by Jurgut de la Salle—whose special brigades (BS) were
known for their cruelty in the fight against the Resistance;

(2) The Police for Jewish Affairs (PJQ) , which was first
headed by Colonel Durieux and then by Schweblin;

(3) The Secret Societies' Service (SSS) , headed by Marquès-
Rivière.

One of the principal uses of the Police for Jewish Affairs was
the enforcement of laws and regulations applicable to Jews
only. The head of the municipal police at that time, Emile
Hennequin, declared during a cross-examination in 1948 that
he thought the Police for Jewish Affairs were involved in
sixteen hundred cases which resulted in the arrest of one
thousand persons.

Dannecker was a great admirer of this police force and was
not sparing in his praises. In a report on February 22, 1942, he
wrote:

> The French inspectors who have been instructed and
> trained with our service for Jewish Affairs have become

an élite group and models for future French recruits to
the anti-Jewish police. Our service is completely confident
of its influence on the anti-Jewish police in the occupied
zone. . . .

One of the leaders of the "élite group," Commissioner
Bouquin, and several other inspectors engaged in such
scandalous thefts that even the German authorities were
shocked and brought them before a military tribunal. The
scandal more or less finished the Police for Jewish Affairs,
since Dannecker felt obliged to withdraw his support of
Commissioner Schweblin. At that point Darquier de Pellepoix,
who had replaced Xavier Vallat as head of the Commission for
Jewish Affairs, suggested and was given in place of the Police
for Jewish Affairs an "Investigative Section" (SEC) attached
to the Commission. According to Emile Hennequin, the head
of the municipal police, nine hundred inquiries were carried
out by this section, and seven hundred arrests were made as a
result.

So far we have mentioned essentially the services whose
activity was mainly administrative and which prepared the
way for the coercive measures against the Jews. It was the
Prefecture of Police which was responsible for the active part
in these measures, though it was controlled by the Commission
for Jewish Affairs and its attached police forces, as well as by
the anti-Jewish services of the Gestapo and the German
Embassy.

Three different services at the police prefecture were in
charge of the measures against the Jews: Commissioner
François' service; the service of Commissioner Permilleux, and
two sections (Three and Five) of the General Information
Office.

As we have already seen, from the end of 1940 it was
François' office which collected census information on the
Jews and passed it to the Gestapo. But this office was soon
given other highly important responsibilities which
necessitated the increase of staff to a total of sixty people. In
addition, this office had the power to make use of the services

of the municipal police, the General Information Office, the Judiciary Police, the guard, and the gendarmerie.

Along with the census of Jews and their property and keeping the index up to date, this office supervised the organization of the Jewish prison camps (Pithiviers, Beaune-la-Rolande, Drancy) and especially the camp at Drancy. Another responsibility was the organization of roundups and preparation of deportations. This office was directly responsible for the carrying out of twenty thousand arrests, including the roundup of July 16 and 17, 1942, and was involved in eighty-five thousand deportations.* François' office was in constant touch with the Gestapo and Dannecker and can be looked upon as one of the French services which collaborated most actively in the policy of racial persecution.

Permilleux' service, too, actively supported the Gestapo in its suppression of the Jews. This service replaced the policemen of the Police for Jewish Affairs when it was dissolved. In August, 1943, it absorbed part of the French service (the index and the preparation and checking of repressive measures) and the service of the Square Rapp Associations. The Permilleux service continued to function until the Liberation. Among its duties were the organization of roundups and the placing of checkpoints on public highways in order to pick up individual Jews who might have escaped. According to Hennequin, it was responsible for thirty-five thousand arrests.

Sections Three and Five of the General Information Office, employing about one hundred inspectors, were concerned with the Jews throughout the occupation. Section Three dealt with foreign Jews and was headed by the following succession of commissioners: Lantheaume, Lang, Tissot, and Bizoire with Inspector Sadowsky at the head of the Jewish section.

Section Five dealt with the deportation of foreigners and especially foreign Jews. Inspectors Lang and Dides headed this section. Some ten thousand Jews were arrested through the

* These figures were quoted by Hennequin in his deposition before Judge Zoussmann in July, 1948.

offices of these two sections, according to Hennequin.

There were three camps in the occupied zone: Beaune-la-Rolande, Pithiviers, and Drancy. Created by the anti-Jewish service of the Gestapo, they were run and guarded by the French gendarmerie.

The Drancy camp had been created by the Prefecture of Police. All three camps, and Drancy in particular, became regular collecting centers for Jews waiting to be deported. The first ruling, which gave Drancy the status of a military penitentiary, was dated August 25, 1941, and signed by the Prefect of Police, Admiral Bard, and the General of the Paris Gendarmerie, General Guilbert, while Captain Lombard of the gendarmerie undertook the command of the camp guards. Until the Liberation it was the French gendarmerie which kept watch over Drancy, and the François service of the French police took care of its administration until July, 1943.

The camp was officially inaugurated at a conference held in the prison offices and attended by Counsellor Lippert of the German Military administration; German officers attached to the French police; Mr. François, the director of the administration of the camp; Garnier, of the Prefecture of the Seine; Luce, a divisional commissioner of the General Information Office; Lefebvre, divisional commissioner of the Judiciary Police; Oudart, the principal commissioner at the General Information Office; Dr. Lestire, the camp doctor; Police Commissioner David; Commander Besanger and Captain Chenu of the gendarmerie; Captain Lombard, the commander of the camp; and Lientz, the interpreter.

When it was first created, the Drancy camp was not intended as a center for assembling deportees. In fact, when he was making inquiries about a suitably located prison, Dannecker looked for one near a cemetery rather than one with a convenient railroad station. It was not until the beginning of 1942, after the decisions taken at the Wannsee conference, that Jews began to be deported regularly, starting with small convoys. By the summer of 1942 the number of departures rose to three per week, each convoy carrying an average of one thousand Jews. These were Jews arrested during the Paris raids

of July 16 and 17 and Jews from the free zone betrayed to
Hitler by the Vichy government. The last convoy from Drancy
left Bobigny station on July 31, 1944. On August 13, 1944, yet
another convoy made up of the prisoners who were left in the
camp was fortunately stopped by a strike. On August 17 the
fleeing SS took with them some fifty prisoners, most of whom
were policemen who had resisted and members of the OJC
(*Organisation Juive de Combat,* part of the Resistance
movement) from Fresnes prison.

Until July, 1943, Drancy camp was under the control of the
Prefecture of Police and its administration undertaken by
François. François asked for additional staff, with the title of
commanders, whose job it was to direct the camp with control
over the gendarmerie. The commanders successively in charge
of the camp were: Savart, a commissioner of police; Laurent,
chief of the Central Administration Bureau; and Guilbert, a
retired police commissioner.

The surveillance of the camp was carried out by two
inspectors, Koerperich and Thibaudat. Thibaudat was fired by
the administration for illegal black market traffic involving the
sum of twenty thousand dollars. The accounting of coins and
valuables taken temporarily from the prisoners and confiscated
from the deportees was supervised by the Cashier-Accountant,
Kieffer. As soon as they arrived at Drancy, the Jewish prisoners
would be searched under Kieffer's supervision.

On July 2, 1943, the Germans took over the administration
of the camp, though the French gendarmerie still continued
to guard the camp and to escort the deportees to the trains.
The François and Permilleux services of the police no longer
arranged the convoys, but they continued to supply prisoners
for the camp, adjusting the pace of arrests to the trains
available. It was from July 2, 1943, on that French Jews, many
of whom had spent two years at Drancy, began to be deported.

The following is a list of the principal measures taken
against the Jews, showing the working of the machinery of
persecution.

On May 14, 1941, the François service was ordered to carry

out a preliminary roundup of foreign Jews, after Dannecker
had decided to fill the prisons of Beaune-la-Rolande and
Pithiviers. Dannecker intended only the arrest of foreign Jews,
whose position was irregular, but in an excess of zeal François
imprisoned even Jews with French children whose papers were
in order and who had nothing against them.

On August 13, 1941, all radios belonging to Jews were
confiscated and, a little later, their bicycles. The index of
property owned by Jews in Peretti's office of the François
service listed Jews owning bicycles. The post office was ordered
by the German authorities to disconnect all telephones in the
homes of Jews. Jews were also forbidden the use of public
telephones.

On August 15, 1941, a sizable roundup took place in the XI
Arrondissement. The arrests were made by German gendarmes
accompanied by inspectors from the Prefecture of Police. The
cordon of police surrounding the XI Arrondissement was
supplied by the municipal police and the Paris guard. The
Jews who were arrested (both French and foreign Jews) were
sent to Drancy.

On August 21, 1941, all lawyers were arrested. Jewish
lawyers were no longer allowed to practice in cases involving
French law, and Dannecker decided to have them arrested.
Again the François service proved useful. Inspectors were
summoned to the François office, where they were given the
names of Jewish lawyers taken from the "Lawyers" file of the
index arranged by profession. Some forty members of the bar
were found at home, collected in the Louis Lépine hall at the
Prefecture, and taken to Drancy.

On December 10, 1941, the Prefect of Police made it illegal
for Jews to change their address and imposed some restriction
on their movements.

Also in December, 1941, all the distinguished members of
the Jewish community were rounded up—doctors, academics,
scientists, writers, etc. Preparations for this roundup were
made by François with the help of the index. The list of names
had to be drawn up in one single night, and François had to

ask Schweblin of the Police for Jewish Affairs for help. He was given twenty people, including some typists.

The writers, doctors, and others who were arrested were collected in the Military Academy and from there taken to the Royallieu camp at Compiègne. Both the roundup of lawyers and that of the writers were aimed at the arrest of French Jews.

On February 2, 1942, a German ruling made it illegal for Jews to leave their homes between eight o'clock at night and five o'clock in the morning.

On May 29, 1942, a German decree made it compulsory for Jews to wear a yellow star sewn onto their clothes. The François service organized the provision of stars *in exchange for one coupon of the clothing ration card.* The stars were issued in the local police station by members of the Judiciary Police.

On July 8, 1942, another German decree closed all public places, theatres, shops, etc., to Jews.

In addition, mention must be made of the fine of twenty million dollars which was imposed on the Jews in reprisal for "the attempts on the lives and property of the German army in Paris." This sum was collected and paid through the UGIF.

On December 15, 1941, ninety-five hostages were shot for the same reason. They were chosen from among Jewish and communist prisoners, the Jews from Drancy and the others from the prisons of Romainville, Fresnes, Fontevrault, la Santé, and Chateaubriant camp. Among the ninety-five were Gabriel Péri and Lucien Sampaix.

The roundups of July 16, 1942, and the days that followed marked the triumph of a system carefully built by the Germans with the help of the French for the persecution of the Jews. It continued to demonstrate its efficiency until the last days of the war.

Appendix C

Sources, Documents, and Acknowledgments

In reconstructing the events of July, 1942, we used three main
sources of information:

(1)   Eyewitness accounts. In the introduction we have given
a brief description of how the survivors were traced and how
their evidence was recorded.

(2)   Documents and archives.

(3)   Books and previously published statements.

There is not one event recorded in this book or one word or
passage quoted which is not supported by the evidence of one
or more eyewitnesses or one or more contemporary documents.
We decided against giving the references for every event, for
fear that too many footnotes might detract from the text.

Listed below are the sources and references for the principal
documents used. There is also a list of the principal people
mentioned, and where it seemed necessary a few biographical
notes were added to help the reader relate the witness to the
events.

We would like to express our gratitude to all those who
helped us by giving evidence, answering our questions, and
putting their personal documents at our disposal, and
especially:

Amicale d'Auschwitz

British Broadcasting Corporation

Centre de Documentation du Mouvement Ouvrier

International Committee of the Red Cross at Arolsen

The Society of Friends

Fédération des amputés de France
Centre de Documentation Juive Contemporaine
Yad Vashem. Martyrs' and Heroes' Remembrance Authority
(Jerusalem—Tel Aviv)
Mr. Maurice Schumann, former spokesman for La France
Combattante

The documents consulted can be found at:
Bibliothèque Nationale
Centre de Documentation Juive Contemporaine
BBC Archives
Bibliothèque de Documentation Contemporaine
Shorthand minutes of High Court cases (taken by the
authors)
Report 1982/2 by Superintendent Roland Monroval
addressed to Judge Rousseau, police magistrate at the Seine
court, concerning Xavier Vallat
Report 1982/3, as above, concerning Emile Hennequin
For convenience we list the reference numbers of the principal
documents used.
   (1) Documents from the Nuremberg Trials, numbered
1–79 in the Monneray Collection (see Bibliography) and
occasionally followed by their Nuremberg Trial number:

Document:			Document:		
3	(RF	1 207)	NG	1	968
9	(RF	1 223)	RF	1	207
12	(NG	2 586)	RF	1	200
16			RF	1	217
17			RF	1	218
19			RF	1	219
33	(RF	1 214)	RF	1	221
38	(PS	501)	RF	1	224
40			RF	1	221
45	(RF	1 233)	PS		710
47	(UK	76)			
48	(5	574)			
49	(PS	17 261)			

(2)   Documents from the Centre de Documentation Juive
Contemporaine:

XX-14a	XXVI-51
XXVa-74	XXVI-52
XXVb	XXV-49
XXVC-213	XXXb-92
XXVG-74	XLIXa-14
XXVc-172	XLIXa-90a, 91b
XXVc-174	XLIX-4
XXVb-29	XLIX-13
XXVb-31, 34, 41	XLIXa-14
XXVb-103	XLIX-38
XXVb-45, 53, 59	XLIX-42
XXVb-60	XLVIII-a31
XXVb-55	C11-70
XXVb-64	CC17 3XXX II
XXVb-77	CXIII-137
XXVb-68	CCXVII-10
XXVb-69-75	CIX-98
XXVb-104-110-114	CCXIV
XXVb-115	CXI-57
XXVb-127	CCXVII-32
XXVb-138	CCXXXIII-73
XXV-51a	CCXVII-29
XXVc-174	CCXVII-28
XXVc-206-208-213-219	CIX-98
XXVb-73-74	CCXVIII-28
XXVc-185-240	CCCLXXXIII-II
XXVc-228	CCCLXXIX-33
XXVG-78	CCXXVIII-117
XXVG-74	CCXXX17-7
XXVb-109	CCXXXVIII-87
XXVb-129-135-145	CCXXXIII-73
XXVb-135-145-129	CCXXXIII-50
XXVI-51a	LXXI-89
XXVI-29-31	LXXIXa-22

Evidence of witnesses, some of whom have asked to be
quoted under fictitious names:
(1) Victims of the Roundup
BARBANEL: Evidence recorded in October, 1965. Escaped
arrest on July 16, 1942, though his wife and two of his
children were arrested and deported. They did not return.
ALBERT BAUM: Evidence recorded in April, 1966. Arrested
with his family, he escaped from the train. Recaptured and
deported, he returned from Auschwitz. His father, mother,
and sister were killed.
Mrs. BECKMAN: Arrested with her children on July 16, she
managed to get out of Drancy. Her twelve-year-old son was
deported and killed.
Mrs. DORAG: Evidence recorded in January, 1967. Arrested
with all her family, she got out of the Vel d'Hiv. Later
recaptured and deported.
BERNARD EPSTEIN: Evidence recorded in 1965. Arrested with
his father, mother, and sister. His family died at Auschwitz,
and he alone returned.
Mrs. GUEN (née FRIEDMAN) : Evidence recorded in April,
1965. Arrested with her father, mother, and brother Jean, at
the age of eight. The children were evacuated to the
Rothschild hospital and survived. Both parents were
deported and did not return.
GOLDENZWAG: Evidence recorded in October, 1965. Arrested
with his wife, daughter, and two sons (aged 19, 16, and 15) .
The whole family was deported to Birkenau. Only the father
returned.
ROMAIN KLEINBERGER: Evidence recorded in September, 1966.
Hid with his family during roundup.
Mrs. MARIANNE LICHTEIN: Evidence collected in September,
1965. Arrested with her daughter, she escaped from the Vel
d'Hiv. Arrested one year later and deported to Auschwitz,
they both returned. Mr. Lichtein was deported and did not
return.
NAT LINEN: Evidence recorded in June, 1965. Arrested with

his mother, escaped from Vel d'Hiv. Mrs. Linen was deported and did not return.

Mrs. IDA NUSSBAUM: Evidence recorded in July, 1965. Arrested with her four-year-old son, she escaped from the Vel d'Hiv. Mr. Nussbaum was deported and did not return.

LOUIS PITKOWICZ (called Picot) : Evidence recorded in June, 1965. Escaped from Vel d'Hiv. His father, mother, and sister, who were arrested at the same time, were deported and did not return.

Mrs. PECHNER: Arrested with her child, survived Auschwitz.

Miss HÉLÈNE ROZEN: Evidence recorded in September, 1965. Arrested with her mother and young brother, she and her brother were saved by a French family. The mother was deported and did not return.

Mrs. PAULETTE ROTBLIT: Evidence recorded in September, 1966. Was not arrested on July 16. Joined the Resistance. Arrested by the militia in June, 1944, was saved by the Liberation.

Mr. and Mrs. RIMMLER: Evidence recorded in January, 1966. Escaped the roundup.

Mrs. RADO: Evidence collected in July, 1965. Arrested with three children, got out of the Vel d'Hiv. Joined the Resistance. Her husband was deported and killed.

ROSENBERG: Evidence collected in November, 1965. Arrested with his wife, his daughter was saved by neighbors. Deported and survived. Mrs. Rosenberg was deported and did not return.

SIENICKI: Evidence collected in October, 1965. Arrested with wife and ten-year-old daughter. All three were deported. He alone returned.

SORAL: Evidence recorded in September, 1966. Arrested with his mother and sister. Escaped from the police station. His mother was deported and did not return.

WALLACH: Evidence recorded in November, 1966. Member of the Resistance. Escaped on July 16. Wife was deported and did not return. Son was executed on July 27, 1942.

(2) Other Witnesses

ALEX (Dr.) (pseudonym) : Evidence recorded in May, 1966. Member of the Resistance. Sent messengers into Vel d'Hiv.

ROGER BOUSSINOT: Evidence recorded in June, 1965. Member of the Resistance. Writer.

PIERRE BLOCH: Member of the Resistance. Evidence recorded in June, 1965.

CAPDEVIELLE (General) : Pseudonym Ursus. Resistant gendarme. Commander of the gendarmerie in the Paris Region, August 20, 1944.

ALFRED CUKIER: Member of the Resistance. Evidence recorded in July, 1965.

DIDIER-HESSE (Dr.) : Member of the Resistance. Was sent to Vel d'Hiv as a doctor. Evidence recorded in March, 1966.

DUBOURG: Policeman: Evidence recorded in September, 1965.

DUMAIL: Member of the Resistance. Evidence recorded in February, 1966.

DUPONT: Pharmacist at the Rothschild hospital. Evidence recorded in June, 1965.

EDINGER: Head of UGIF. Evidence recorded in June, 1966.

FALKENSTEIN: Deported. Evidence recorded in 1966.

SIMON GOTLAND: Deported. Evidence recorded in August, 1966.

Mrs. GOLDBERG: Friend of one of the persons arrested. Evidence recorded in October, 1966.

HALFON: Member of the Resistance. Former head of the Rothschild hospital. Evidence recorded in 1965.

Mrs. LOEWE-LYON (Dr.) : Evidence recorded in June, 1966. Entered Vel d'Hiv as a doctor.

MODIANO (Dr.) : Evidence recorded in April, 1966. Jewish leader.

ANDRÉ MONTAGNE: Deported. Evidence recorded in April, 1965.

Mrs. JONAIS MATHEY: Nurse and member of the Resistance. Deported. Evidence recorded in July, 1965.

FRANÇOIS MAURIAC (Académie Française) : Evidence recorded in August, 1965.

Mrs. ANNETTE MONOD: Red Cross assistant. Evidence recorded in October, 1966.

Mrs. MYRIAM NOVITCH: Member of the Resistance. Evidence recorded in April, 1966.

VAISMAN (Dr.) : Member of the Resistance. Doctor at the Rothschild hospital. Evidence recorded in June, 1965.

Mrs. VIDAL: Evidence recorded in May, 1964.

VILENSKI (Dr.) : Sent into the Vel d'Hiv as doctor. Evidence recorded in November, 1965.

WELLERS: Deported. Evidence recorded in July, 1965.

WORMS (Dr.) : Member of Resistance (FFL) . Formerly of Rothschild hospital. Evidence recorded in June, 1965.

Bibliography

Activité des organisations juives en France sous l'occupation.
Editions du Centre.

AIMÉ, DENISE, *Relais des Errants.* Editions Desclée de Brouwer.

ALGASI, L., *Jean XIII.* Editeurs P. Lethielleux.

AMORETTI, HENRI, *Lyon Capitale 1940–1944.* Editions France-
Empire.

AMOUROUX, HENRI, *La vie des Français sous l'occupation.*
Editions Arthème Fayard.

ARON ROBERT, *Histoire de Vichy 1940–1944.* Editions Fayard.

AUDIAT, PIERRE, *Paris pendant la guerre.* Editions Hachette.

BAUDOT, MARCEL, *L'opinion publique sous l'occupation.* Paris,
Presses Universitaires de France, 1960.

DE BEAUVOIR, SIMONE, *La Force de l'Age.* N.R.F. Gallimard.

BELLANGER, CLAUDE, *Presse clandestine 1940–1944.* Editions
Armand Colin.

BERNFELD, MICHEL, *16 juillet 1942. Dans Complicité des temps
de l'homme.* Editions André Silvaire.

BILLIG, JOSEPH, *L'Allemagne et le génocide* (Nazi plans and
actions) . Editions du Centre.

BORWICZ, MICHEL, *Ecrits des condamnés à mort sous
l'occupation.* Presses Universitaires de France.

BOURGET, PIERRE, and CHARLES LACRETELLE, *Sur les murs de
Paris.* Editions Hachette.

Les Bourreaux SS et leurs victimes. Vienna, Fédération
Internationale des Résistants, 1965.

BOUSSINOT, ROGER, *Les Guichets du Louvre.* Editions
Denoël.

BURGESS, ALAN, *Seven Men at Daybreak*. London, Evans Bros., 1960.

Les Cahiers d'Auschwitz. Panstowe Museum, Auschwitz.

Le Cahier Noir. Editions de Minuit.

Camps de concentration (Documents for a history of the war). Office français d'Edition.

Les camps d'extermination allemands Auschwitz et Birkenau. Office français d'Edition.

CASSOU, JEAN, *Le pillage par les Allemands des oeuvres d'art et des bibliothèques appartenant à des juifs en France*. Editions du Centre.

Catalogue des périodiques clandestins. Bibliothèque nationale.

"La Confession d'un policier de la Grande Rafle," *Le Nouveau Candide*, May 22, 1967.

COTTA, MICHÈLE, *La collaboration*. Editions Armand Colin.

COUROUBLE, ALICE, *Amie des juifs*. Bloyd et Gay.

DELARUE, JACQUES, *Histoire de la Gestapo*. Fayard.

DIAMANT, DAVID, *Héros juifs de la Résistance française*. Editions Renouveau.

DIMONT, MAX I., *Les juifs, Dieu et l'Histoire*. Robert Laffont.

DUQUESNE, JACQUES, *Les catholiques français sous l'occupation*. Editions Grasset.

Les Evasions. Le prix de la liberté. Editions Denoël.

FALCONI, CARLO, *Le silence de Pie XII*. Editions du Rocher.

FIDELKIEWICZ, ALFRED, *Bzezinka Birkenau*. Warsaw, Editions Czytelnik, 1965.

FRIEDLANDER, SAUL, *Pie XII et le IIIième Reich. Documents*. Editions du Seuil.

GILLOUIN, RENÉ, *J'étais l'ami du maréchal Pétain*. Editions Plon.

GOURA, HAIM, *La cage de verre*. Albin Michel.

GOURFINKEL, NINA, *L'autre Patrie*. Editions du Seuil.

GRANT, ALFRED, *Paris, ville du front* (in Yiddish). Editions Oïfsai, UJRE, 14, rue de Paradis.

GROULT, BENOITE and FLORA, *Journal à quatre mains*. Editions Denoël.

GUITTON, JEAN, *le cardinal Saliège*. Editions Grasset.

Hommage à Pierre Massé. Calmann-Lévy.

HOREAU, GEORGES, *Drancy*. Pouzet Editeur.

ISSAC, JULES, *L'enseignement du mépris*. Fasquelle.

———, *Jésus et Israel*. Albin Michel.

Les journées tragiques des 16 et 17 juillet 1942 à Paris. Editions du Centre.

"Judenlager Drancy," *La Revue Internationale,* May, 1946.

Les juifs sous l'occupation. Recueil de textes français et allemands (1940–1944). Editions du Centre.

JÜNGER, ERNST, *Journal de guerre et d'occupation 1939–1948*. Editions Julliard.

KENT, GEORGES, *Les bergers de la Résistance*.

KNOUT, DAVID, *Contribution à l'histoire de la résistance juive en France* (1940–1944).

LATREILLE, ANDRÉ, "Le silence de Pie XII," *Le Monde,* December 28, 1965.

LAZARUS, JACQUES, *Juifs au combat*. Editions du Centre.

Lettres de Fusillés. Editions France d'Abord.

LUBETZKI, *La condition des juifs en France sous l'occupation allemande*. CDJC.

MADAULE, J., *Les juifs et le Monde actuel*. Flammarion.

MAZOR, M., "Le procès d'Auschwitz," *Le Monde juif,* June, 1965.

MESNIL, AMAR, *Ceux qui ne dormaient pas*. Editions de Minuit.

———, *Pages de gloire des vingt-trois*. CFDI.

MONNERAY, HENRI, ed., *La persécution des juifs dans les pays de l'Est présentée à Nuremberg* (collection of documents). Editions du Centre.

———, ed., *La persécution des juifs en France et dans les autres pays de l'Ouest, présentée par la France à Nuremberg* (collection of documents). Editions du Centre.

NOLLIER, RICHARD, *La Solution finale* (novel). Editions Flammarion.

OUZOULIAS, ALBERT, *Les Bataillons de la Jeunesse*. Editions Sociales.

PETITFRÈRE, RAY, *La mystique de la Croix Gammée*. Editions France-Empire.

"La plus belle réussite de la Résistance," *le Courrier graphique,* September–October, 1946.

POLIAKOV, L., *Le procès de Jérusalem.* Editions Calmann-Lévy and Editions du Centre.

———, *Auschwitz* (archives) . Julliard.

———, *L'étoile jaune.* Editions du Centre.

———, *Bréviaire de la haine* (the Third Reich and the Jews) .

———, and JACQUES SABILLE, *La Condition des juifs en France sous l'occupation italienne.* Editions du Centre.

POLONSKI, JACQUES, *La presse, la propagande et l'opinion sous l'occupation.* CDJC.

RABI, *Anatomie du judaisme français. Documents.* Editions de Minuit.

RAISKY, A., *La presse antiraciste sous l'occupation hitlerienne Paris 1944* (collection of newspapers, tracts, and proclamations edited by Jewish organizations in the years 1940–1944) .

ROUSSET, DAVID, *Le pitre ne rit pas.* Editions du Pavois.

SEGHERS, ANNA, *Transit.* Boston, Little, Brown, 1944.

SEHN, JAN, *Le camp de concentration d'Oswiecim Bzezinka.* Warsaw, Wydawnictwo prawnicze, 1961.

STEINBERG, LUCIEN, *Les autorités allemandes de France occupée.* Editions du Centre.

TILLON, CHARLES, *Les F.T.P.* Julliard.

TOULAT, JEAN, *Juifs mes frères.* Editions Guy Victor.

Tragédie de la déportation, 1940–1945. Editions Hachette.

VERCORS, *La marche à l'étoile.* Albin Michel.

VERGARA, PAUL, *Une assistante sociale: Marcelle Guillemot.*

La vie de la France sous l'occupation. Hoover Institute.

WALTER, GÉRARD, *La vie à Paris sous l'occupation 1940–1944. Collection Kiosque: les faits, la presse, l'opinion.* Editions A. Colin.

WEILL, J., *Contribution à l'histoire des camps d'internement dans l'anti-France.* Editions du Centre.

WELLERS, GEORGES, *De Drancy à Auschwitz.* Editions du Centre.

Biographical Notes

Short list of some of the persons mentioned in the text with brief biographical notes:

OTTO ABETZ: German ambassador in Paris 1940–1944. Condemned to twenty years' imprisonment in 1949 by the military tribunal in Paris. Released in 1954. Accidental death in 1958.

AHNERT: SS Lieutenant. Commander of SIPO and of SD in Paris.

ALIBERT: Minister of Justice in the Pétain government. Drew up the "Statute of the Jews," also called "Alibert's Law."

ANDRÉ BAUR: Director of UGIF. Deported with his family, did not return.

BARD (Admiral) : French Prefect of Police.

BENOIST-MÉCHIN: Secretary of State in Pétain's government in charge of the *Légion tricolore contre le bolchevisme,* which later became the LVF (*Légion des Volontaires Français*) and fought on the Russian front against the Red Army. M. Benoist-Méchin is a great authority on and admirer of the German army.

WERNER BEST (Dr.) : Theorist of Nazism. One of the founders of the Gestapo and of the RNSA. Officer in the military administration in France until 1943, then German plenipotentiary in Denmark. Condemned to death but was freed in 1954. Judicial advisor to important firms in the Ruhr (1966) .

PIERRE BLOCH: Member of the Resistance. Former deputy and former minister. (See evidence of witnesses.)

SUZANNE BODIN: Member of the Red Cross. Deported to Ravensbruck, where she died.

BOUQUIN: Commissioner of Police for Jewish Affairs.

JACQUES BOURREAU: Journalist collaborating with the Germans.

ROGER BOUSSINOT: Member of the Resistance, witness. (See evidence of witnesses.)

RENÉ BOUSQUET: Assistant Director of the Police in France in April 1942. In this capacity he directed the national police, the economic control, the GMR, the mobile guard, the passive defense, and the supplementary police forces (that is, anti-Jewish, anti-Masonic, and anti-communist). Was replaced in December, 1943, by Darnand. Arrested in June, 1944, by the Germans, Bousquet was brought before the High Court of Justice after the Liberation and was acquitted. He later became Director, then Joint General Director (1960), of the Bank of Indochina. He is at the same time the President and General Director of the Indochina Cinema Society, Administrator of the Rubber Company of Indochina, Administrator of the Franco-Chinese Bank for Commerce and Industry, Administrator of the Water and Electricity Company in Indochina, Administrator of the Phosphate Company of Oceania, Administrator of the Association of Finance for France and Foreign Countries, Chevalier of the Legion of Honor, and winner of the Gold Medal for Rescue.

BRIESSEN (General): German. Commander in Paris.

BUSSIÈRES: Prefect of Police.

BUSCH: German aide to Dannecker.

CHEYNEAU DE LEYRITZ: Regional Prefect at Toulouse under the Vichy government.

COURRÈGES (Msgr.): Auxiliary bishop at Toulouse.

THÉO DANNECKER (Dr.): Lawyer SS *Ostuf*. Aide to Eichmann, specialist in anti-Jewish activities first in Austria, then in Bohemia and Moravia, then in France, finally in the

Balkans, Rome, and Hungary. Disappeared in 1945
(suicide?) .

DARQUIER (called DARQUIER DE PELLEPOIX) : Born at Cahors
on December 19, 1897. Municipal Counsellor in Paris in
1935, active militant in the fascist leagues, already showing
violent anti-Semitic feelings. Replaced Xavier Vallat at the
head of the Commission for Jewish Affairs in 1942. Fled at
the time of the Liberation and was condemned to death by
the High Court of Justice on June 19, 1947.

FRANÇOIS DAVID: Commissioner of Police.

DEVAUX (Rev. Father) : Organizer of rescue of Jewish children.

DIDES: French policeman attached to Section Five in charge of
foreign Jews. Deputy under the IV Republic, became well
known for introducing the promotion of policemen for work
in the Resistance.

DILLARD (Rev.) : Saved Jewish children, for which he had to
leave St. Louis de Vichy. The first of the working priests, he
went to Germany to bring religious comfort to the workers
recruited by the STO (*Service du Travail Obligatoire*) .
Arrested by the Gestapo, he died at Dachau on January 12,
1945.

JACQUES DORIOT: French Communist Party member but later
became head of the extreme-right *Parti Populaire Français*
(PPF) . One of the founders of the *Légion des Volontaires
Français* (LVF) against Bolshevism. Fought on the Russian
front in German uniform. Returned to France but fled to
Germany at the time of the Liberation. Was killed by
bullets from an American airplane on February 22, 1945.

DURIEUX (Colonel) : First director of the Police for Jewish
Affairs.

ADOLF EICHMANN: SS *Ostubaf*. Head of IV B4 Service of the
RSHA; organized the massacre of Jews in Europe. Born in
Solingen on March 9, 1906, he joined the National Socialist
Party and the SS in 1932. He devoted himself to the
suppression of the Jews, receiving his training in 1934 at
Dachau. Became a specialist in the persecution of the Jews.
Was arrested by the Americans in 1945 but managed to

escape. Lived in Germany from 1945 to 1950. On May 11, 1960, after fifteen years' search, he was found by the Israeli Secret Service in Argentina, where he lived under the name of Ricardo Clemens. Was tried in Israel in 1961, condemned to death, and executed.

FRANÇOIS: French policeman. Commissioner and head of a service at the Prefecture of Police specializing in anti-Jewish activities.

HANS FRANCK: SS Obergruppenfuehrer. Governor of occupied Poland. Condemned to death at Nuremberg and executed.

GARNIER: French policeman at the prefecture.

RENÉ GILLOUIN: Former member of the Municipal Council in Paris. Member of Pétain cabinet. After the Liberation he lived five years in exile in Switzerland. Published an article called "Résistance et résistantialisme." Returned to France. In 1966 published a book called *J'étais l'ami du maréchal Pétain,* in which he asserts that he defended the Jews and used his influence on their behalf with Pétain.

GRAND: French inspector of the Police for Jewish Affairs.

GUIBERT: Commander of the concentration camp at Drancy.

GUILBERT: General of the gendarmerie in Paris at the time of the occupation.

HERBERT HAGEN: SS *Ostuf.* Aide to Eichmann. Member of the SD.

EMILE HENNEQUIN: Chief of the municipal police in Paris.

REINHARDT HEYDRICH: Head of the Security Police and the SD. Put in charge of the Final Solution by Goering. "Protector" of Bohemia and Moravia. Killed by members of the Czech resistance in Prague on May 28, 1942.

HEINRICH HIMMLER: SS Reichsfuehrer and head of the German police. Later Minister of the Interior. Captured by the British, he committed suicide on May 23, 1945.

RUDOLF HOESS: Lieutenant colonel of SS, commander of the camp at Auschwitz. Condemned to death at Warsaw, he was executed at Auschwitz in 1947. Wrote an autobiography *Commandant at Auschwitz,* which inspired the writer Merle to write *La mort est mon métier.*

JULES ISAAC: Inspector of schools. French historian. Wife and
    daughter deported and did not return.
JURGUT DE LA SALLE: Director of the special anti-communist
    police force.
KATZ: Director of the UGIF.
HELMUTH KNOCHEN (Dr.) : SS Colonel. Head of the security
    police and the SD in France from 1940 to 1944. Condemned
    to death in 1954 by the military tribunal in Paris; was
    reprieved in 1958. Freed in 1962.
HÉLÈNE KRO: Member of the Resistance. Entered the Vel
    d'Hiv. Later committed suicide when arrested.
GEORGES LAMIRAND: Secretary of State for Youth of the Vichy
    Government. Later rendered many services to the
    Resistance.
LAURENCIE (General DE LA) : Representative of Marshal
    Pétain in the occupied territories. Countersigned the first
    anti-Jewish measures. Later took an active part in the
    Resistance.
LAURENT: Commander of the camp at Drancy.
LEGUAY: Delegate in Paris of the General Secretary for the
    national police.
MAGLIONE (Msgr.) : Secretary of State at the Vatican.
MARTIN: Prefect of the Tarn.
MARTIN: General of the Gendarmerie. Considered his having
    arranged for the playing of the *Marseillaise* in July, 1942,
    by his band as an act of resistance. In 1943 he complained
    when the newspapers published the information (which was
    exact) that twenty-five terrorists captured by the
    gendarmerie were handed over to the Germans, who shot
    them. Suspended on September 25, 1944, he was condemned
    to one year's imprisonment on February 21, 1947, but was
    freed and pardoned after five months.
GEORGES ALEXIS MONTANDON: Born in Switzerland on April
    9, 1879; took French nationality on July 27, 1941. Member
    of PPF and professor of ethnology, attached to the
    Commission for Jewish Affairs. At the same time he
    became scientific editor of the journal *l'Ethnie Française,*

created in October, 1940. Built an impressive fortune through selling "certificates of Aryanization" to Jews threatened with deportation at an average price of two hundred dollars each. Died in Germany at the end of 1944, having fled there after the liberation of France.

MORANE: Prefect of the Loiret during the occupation.

MOREAU: Inspector of the French police. Organized a search for escaped Jews.

HEINRICH MULLER: General SS. Head of Service N of the RSHA (Gestapo). Took part in the Wannsee conference. Disappeared in 1945.

LÉON NOËL: Delegate of the Vichy government in Paris. Very soon joined the Free French.

FRANZ NOWAK: Aide to Eichmann. Responsible for the transportation of deportees. Arrested in Vienna in 1961, was condemned to eight years' imprisonment in 1964. Appealed and was acquitted.

KARL ALBRECHT OBERG: Army general. Prefect of Police in Saxony, then Chief of Police at Radom, Poland, then in France (June, 1942, to December, 1944). Commander of Waffen SS on the Eastern Front. Arrested in 1945. Condemned to death in 1954. Reprieved in 1958. Freed in 1962. Now at Flensburg in Federal Germany.

PERETTI: French policeman who worked in the office of the Jewish index.

GABRIEL PÉRI: Communist deputy. Shot by the Germans.

PERMILLEUX: French policeman, commissioner at the prefecture.

PEYROUTON: High-ranking member of Pétain regime. Minister of the Interior until 1940, when he was eliminated by Laval. Ambassador in Buenos Aires. Went to North Africa at the end of 1942 and took part in Admiral Darlan's and then General Giraud's attempts to govern Algeria.

RAHN: Advisor at the German Embassy in Paris.

RATH: German diplomat killed in 1938 by a young German-Jewish refugee called Grynspan.

LUCIEN REBATET: Born in 1903. Pseudonym François Vinneuil. Journalist for *l'Action Française*. During the

occupation collaborated on the *Petit Parisien* newspaper
and *Je suis partout*. In 1942 published *Les décombres*. Fled
to Sigmaringen in August, 1944. Now works on publications
of the extreme right.

JOACHIM VON RIBBENTROP: Minister for Foreign Affairs in the
III Reich. Condemned to death by the international
military tribunal at Nuremberg, was executed in 1946.

Mrs. ROBINEAU: Showed notes taken by Dr. Robineau when he
visited the Vel d'Hiv.

ROETHKE: Lawyer, then officer in German Army. Captain in
the military administration in France. Disappeared in 1945.
According to recent sources is again practicing law in West
Berlin under a false name.

ALFRED ROSENBERG: Born in 1893. Nazi theorist on race,
though of Jewish descent. Architect (studied in Moscow).
Director of the "anti-Jewish Institute" at Frankfort.
Minister of the Reich for Eastern occupied territories.
Condemned to death at Nuremberg and executed.

SADOWSKI: French policeman. Director of the Jewish section
of Section Three of the General Information Office.

SALIÈGE (Msgr.): Bishop of Toulouse. Launched a celebrated
appeal in favor of the Jews.

LUCIEN SAMPAIX: Communist deputy. Shot by the Germans.

SAUCKEL: *Gauleiter* of the III Reich. Condemned to death at
Nuremberg and executed.

SAUTS (Commander): Aide to Leguay.

VON SCHOMBURG (General): German commander in Paris.

SCHWEBLIN: French Director of Police for Jewish Affairs.

SÉZILLE (Captain): French Director of the Anti-Jewish
Institute.

STUTITZ (General): German. First military commander of the
Paris region.

EDITH TAVERNIER: Social worker.

THÉAS (Msgr.): Bishop of Montauban. Protested against the
arrests.

EDITH THOMAS: Member of the Resistance. Wrote *Les Lettres
Françaises*.

TISNE: Doctor at the prefecture.

TROCME: Protestant pastor, appealed for help for the Jews.

ANDRÉ TULARD: Born in 1899. Director of the Jewish index at the prefecture. Died on February 3, 1967, having kept the titles of Honorary Director of the Prefecture of Police and Chevalier of the Legion of Honor.

XAVIER VALLAT: Born on October 24, 1891, at Villedieu (Vaucluse). Fought in the First World War and became a deputy on November 16, 1919. In October, 1936, became president of the Republican Federation. After the Liberation, Vallat was brought before the High Court of Justice and condemned to twenty years' imprisonment. Pardoned in 1950. In 1966 he was on the staff of the weekly *Aspect de la France*.

PAUL VERGARA (Rev.) : Protestant minister; saved Jewish children.

VOLLARD-BOCKELBERG (General) : German commander of the Paris Region.

WEILL-HALLÉ (Dr.) : Doctor sent by the UGIF to the Vel d'Hiv. One of the promoters of BCG TB vaccine in France.

ZEITSCHEL (Dr. CARL THÉO) : Advisor to the German legation in Paris. Disappeared in 1943.

Translations of Documents

See facsimiles of the original documents on pages 104–105, 110, and 114.

Paris, July 13, 1942
Head Office of the
Municipal Police   SECRET
General Staff   Circular No. 173–42

         For the attention of:

                    . . .

The occupation forces have decided to arrest and muster
a number of alien Jews.
         I. Principles
   A. To whom does this measure apply?
   a. categories
The above measure applies only to Jews of the following
nationalities:
   —German
   —Austrian
   —Polish
   —Czechoslovakian
   —Russian (both refugees and Soviet citizens, that is both
      "white" and "red" Russians)
   —Stateless Jews; that is, whose nationality cannot be
      determined.
   b. age and sex
The above measure applies to all Jews of the above
nationalities, regardless of sex, between the ages of 16 and 60
(or 16 and 55 for the women) .
   Children below the age of 16 will be taken away at the
same time as their parents.
   Exceptions:
The measure does not apply to the following:
   —pregnant women near to giving birth
   —nursing mothers
   —mothers with children under the age of 2, that is, born
      after July 1, 1940
   —wives of prisoners of war
   —widows or widowers who had been married to non-Jews

                                             279

—Jewish men and women married to non-Jews who can
   prove that their marriage is legal and that wives or
   husbands are non-Jewish
—Jews carrying the beige or yellow UGIF card
—Jews legally married to persons of nationalities other
   than those mentioned in (a)
—parents who have one or more non-Jewish children. In
   cases where the measure does not apply to one member
   of a family, the children need not be taken away unless
   they are Jewish and over 16 years old.

B. Execution:

Every Jew (male and female) to be arrested is listed in an
index. The index cards are classified by arrondissement and in
alphabetical order.

Teams for arresting the Jews will have to be organized.
Each arrest team should be made up of one guard in uniform
and one plain-clothes policeman or an inspector from the
General Information Bureau or from the Judiciary Police.

Each arrest team should be given several index cards. The
total index cards for arrests in each arrondissement will be
issued by my office today at 2100 hours.

Arrest teams are to carry out their assignment as quickly
as possible, avoiding any superfluous conversation or comment.
Furthermore, during an arrest the justice or injustice of the
arrest is not to be discussed. You are responsible for the arrests
and it is up to you to review doubtful cases that are brought
to your attention.

In every arrondissement or district one or more gathering
places are to be set up, protected by a guard. It is at these
centers that doubtful cases will be reviewed. Should it be
impossible to make a decision, the family in question is to be
taken with the rest for the moment.

Buses, whose numbers will be indicated below, will be put
at your disposal.

As soon as enough people are gathered to fill one bus, they
are to be taken to the following places:

a. Single Jews or families with no children below the age of 16 to the camp at Drancy.

b. The rest to the Vélodrome d'Hiver.

The maximum capacity at Drancy being 6,000 people, the number of people in each busload directed to Drancy should be recorded and reported to this office. You will be informed when the camp at Drancy has been filled so that all the remaining Jews may be sent to the Vélodrome d'Hiver.

STORY OF THE TREATMENT INFLICTED
ON JEWISH FAMILIES IN THE PARIS REGION
BEGINNING JULY 16, 1942

This story is far from complete. Little by little, one
succeeds in learning what is happening, through the
testimony of survivors, of nurses, even of police who
guard the camps.

ARRESTS

On Thursday, July 16, French detectives and police,
generally accompanied by young Doriotists, began to knock
on the doors of Jews whose names appeared on their lists.

The news spread through the city like a trail of gunpowder,
and a general panic followed. All those who were able to flee
ran out, scarcely dressed, seeking shelter with their French
neighbors—with concierges, in cellars or attics. Some simply
refused to open their doors. In cases where the doors were
opened, or sometimes broken open, one saw heartbreaking
scenes taking place. Women fainted, children wailed, and
many of the persecuted took refuge in suicide. One mother
threw her four children out the window on the fifth floor and
then, as the door was being forced, leaped after them. A little
ten-year-old girl, crazed with fear, jumped from the sixth
floor. In one apartment they had broken into, the police found
a man, half asphyxiated, with his mouth over the gas outlet. A
young woman, twenty-four years old, did the same thing. At
Montreuil, a doctor killed himself and his family with
hypodermic injections. Similar events took place during the
following days.

As soon as they entered an apartment, the police arrested the
Jews found there. These people were told to pack up quickly,
taking along a few necessities and enough food for two days.
Some of them did not have any food, or very little. They were
forced to fast for the first two days.

The police, having been ordered not to take into
consideration the state of health of persons named on their
lists, rounded up not only the very sick but also the dead. A
child who had died the night before was carried out in a sheet.

282

Women were taken, and children over the age of two, pregnant
women in the seventh, eighth, and even ninth month, sick
people dragged from their beds and carried on chairs or
stretchers; a paralyzed woman was taken away in a wheelchair.
Old people of sixty and seventy were not spared.

But it is the roundup of children that must be especially
stressed. Children over two years old were considered fit for
concentration camps. Theoretically, French children were to
be spared; actually, the majority of children arrested are
French. In several cases where the parents were absent, children
of six, ten, and twelve were seized; the proof of this is that
several French children arrested while alone were released after
three days of detention. One young woman went to the Vel
d'Hiv to find what had happened to her sister, who was ten
years old. Children were rounded up with fevers of 102 and
103 degrees, with measles, whooping cough, chickenpox, scarlet
fever, and even typhoid. Some of them were sent to the Claude
Bernard Hospital. Desperate mothers tried in vain to stand
between the police and their sick children. In a number of
cases the mothers were separated from the children by force;
they were taken away sometimes by force, sometimes by ruse.
Cries and sobs filled the streets. Neighbors and passersby could
not help weeping.

September 26, 1942

From the Subprefect of the
Director of Police in the
Occupied Zone

to Obersturmfuehrer Roethke
31A Avenue Foch
Paris

To confirm our telephone conversation earlier today:
A convoy of about 80 to 90 alien Jews coming from the free
zone will be crossing the demarcation line at Vierzon on
9/29/42 at 2241 hours.
Departure from Vierzon on 9/29/42 at 2324 hours.
Arrival at Bourget-Drancy on 9/30/42 at 0449 hours.
Please take the necessary steps for informing the
Feldgendarmerie of this arrival.